CW00350696

Music, Witchcraft And The Paranormal

Dr Melvyn J. Willin

Published by

**MELROSE
BOOKS**

An Imprint of Melrose Press Limited
St Thomas Place, Ely
Cambridgeshire
CB7 4GG, UK
www.melrosebooks.com

FIRST EDITION

Copyright © Dr. Melvyn J. Willin 2005

The Author asserts his moral right to
be identified as the author of this work

Cover designed by Bryan Carpenter

ISBN 1 905226 18 7

All rights reserved. No part of this publication may be reproduced,
stored in a retrieval system, or transmitted, in any form or by any means
electronic, mechanical , photocopying, recording or otherwise,
without the prior permission of the publishers.

This book is sold subject to the condition that it shall not,
by way of trade or otherwise, be lent, re-sold, hired out or
otherwise circulated without the publisher's prior consent
in any form of binding or cover other than that in which
it is published and without a similar condition including this
condition being imposed on the subsequent purchaser.

Printed and bound in Great Britain by:
Bath Press Limited, Lower Bristol Road,
Bath, BA2 3BL, UK

Acknowledgements

The author is confident that his list of acknowledgements is guarenteed to omit people that really should have been mentioned (like my parents) but were not because of any number of reasons ranging from memory loss to sheer vindictiveness. However, that aside I am really sorry if you think you should have been here and were not. Perhaps further editions will rectify this intolerable state of affairs!

The originator of my love affair with music was Donald Riddell when he was the Head of Music at Francis Bacon Grammar School and he must have pride of place accordingly. I also received a great deal of help in more recent years from Professor Eric Clarke at Sheffield University. My parapsychological and witchcraft studies would not have emerged without the guidance and friendship of Professor Bob Morris at the Koestler Unit, Edinburgh University and Professor Ronald Hutton at Bristol University.

On a purely personal front the list could become endless so I must limit my thanks to people who were directly involved in this recent venture including Tracy, Jackie, Karen, Steve, Serena, Jeff and Anthea. There were also many members of the witchcraft fra/maternity who helped me in my studies, notably Carol.

As to organisations, the Society for Psychical Research has been very supportive throughout my recent academic life.

A series of essays on
parapsychology & psychical research
with special reference to paganism & witchcraft,
from the perspective of MUSIC

Introduction

This collection of six essays and two prologues has been taken from the research I undertook as part of two doctoral theses. The first was entitled *Paramusicology: An Investigation of Music and Paranormal Phenomena*. It was successfully completed in the Music Department of the University of Sheffield (UK) in 1999 under the supervision of Professor Eric Clarke and Professor Robert Morris from the Koestler Unit of Parapsychology in Edinburgh. The second thesis, *Music in Pagan and Witchcraft Ritual and Culture*, was likewise completed in the Historical Studies Department of the University of Bristol (UK) in 2004 under the supervision of Professor Ronald Hutton. Neither of these subjects has previously been researched in any detail and this is therefore the first time that scrutiny of the subjects concerned has been made available to the public. I have had to leave out a great deal of detail through lack of space.

The first prologue introduces parapsychology and psychical research to both the general and more knowledgeable reader. The first three essays investigate the place of music in what might be called paranormal situations. The first recounts an experiment of over one hundred trials where music was used in an attempt to make telepathic contact between two individuals in a controlled environment. How the experiment (referred to as the ganzfeld) was set up, the people involved and the results are scrutinised. The second essay analyses the claims of spiritualists, psychics and mediums to be in contact with dead composers and performers. Comparisons are made between the allegedly channelled music and the original composers' works. The third essay studies the many claims of people to have witnessed 'ghostly' music, i.e. music being heard when there was no obvious sound source. Details of investigations in haunted castles, public houses, etc., are related as well as interviews with people who have witnessed this phenomenon.

The second prologue introduces the place of witchcraft in early modern and contemporary society. The remaining three essays consist of the research undertaken concerning the place of music in pagan and witchcraft culture and ritual. The first provides an overview of the place of music in witchcraft before and at the start of its modern revival. A number of stage works and examples from literature are cited. The second essay, the most musicological of the series, traces the history of witchcraft as it has been personified in classical music throughout the centuries. This includes references to a large repertoire of music from the fields of opera, vocal/choral, and instrumental/orchestral sources. The third essay brings the place of music in paganism generally right up to the present century. The results of questionnaires sent to over a hundred practitioners of different forms of paganism are presented to provide an account of what pagans use in their rituals and why they use it. This final essay crosses over into the world of the paranormal since the magickal [sic] effects sometimes spoken of are outside normal human experience.

The book's conclusion attempts to bind together many of the issues raised and provides further speculation concerning the future of music's role in these fields. The references/bibliography provide a wealth of information for readers and scholars wishing to pursue the subject further.

Melvyn J. Willin 2004

Prologue One

The paranormal continues to intrigue people throughout many sections of society and it might be argued that mankind's belief system requires a striving for matters beyond human comprehension. Surveys concerning people's beliefs in various aspects of the subject frequently provide evidence for the acceptance of mind to mind communication (telepathy) and other psychic or extrasensory powers (cited in Marks and Kammann, 1980 and West, 1995). Further selective exposure can lead to self-perpetuating beliefs and self-fulfilling prophecies. Each new experience is interpreted as to where it can fit with past experiences and this process of assimilation within existing schemata builds up a 'life picture'. Phenomena that are viewed as anomalous to current bounds of time, space and matter can be defined as paranormal but these conditions are relative to historical times and cultures.

This craving for the miraculous may have been satisfied in the past by the supernatural activities contained in some religious texts, but these have become increasingly less acceptable in the twenty-first century and even in 1750 the philosopher David Hume wrote about miracles as being "violations of the laws of nature" (cited in Inglis, 1985). Marks and Kammann express a modern psychological viewpoint, which is widely accepted in some circles, (1980, p.156): "We seem to have a profound yearning for a magic formula that will free us from our ponderous and fragile bodies."

The focus on the millennium may have provided another reason why people believe that a move away from materialism and a more spiritual viewpoint might solve ecologically-based problems. However, in the present day the paranormal is often misrepresented through media sensationalism, superstition or ignorance. Historically,

9

different individuals, groups and cultures have produced their own definitions and explanations of supposedly paranormal events, based upon prevailing belief systems, assumptions and experiences (Clarke, 1995). For example, a Spiritualist might well accept as 'normal' a conversation with departed souls whereas the non-Spiritualist might describe this as delusion or 'paranormal' activity. Contrary to most Western beliefs, some Eastern cultures accept reincarnation as part of 'life's plan' and ancient descriptions of demonic possession are now more usually ascribed to mental illness. Thus, for the purposes of this research it is necessary to decide upon a working definition, which might encompass two types of paranormal experience. The first contains those experiences which involve a means of perception beyond that of the accepted senses, e.g. clairvoyance and clairaudience. The second involves events which may well be perceived using taste, touch, sight, smell or hearing but appear to have an origin which lies beyond the scope of generally accepted reality in time and space. The use of the term 'paranormal' is preferred to 'supernatural' since it is not wished to imply that the phenomena studied are necessarily outside or beyond nature. As to whether 'science' eventually accepts the paranormal within its definitions or whether it (the paranormal) will always remain outside has implications as to how proof can be sought. The predominant scientific perspective is one based on the reality of evidence achieved through replication and control. These may not be the correct laws to apply to such forces or powers.

Even in the earliest known examples of pictorial and linguistic representation, e.g. cave paintings, one can find possible evidence of belief in, or experience of, paranormal events (Bessy, 1963). Perhaps this reflected a need to explore and understand matters that were initially beyond comprehension. For example, the representation of magic being used by an apparently 'witchdoctor-like' character can be found in cave paintings in the vicinity of Lake Onega in Russia dating back some twenty thousand years (ibid.). However, one must take care in not providing modern interpretations to material that may have had a very different purpose at the time of production. One cannot assume that these reflect genuinely magical occurrences but if this is the case it may be possible that, with exceptions, present day 'civilised' humans have lost some of the powers of their ancestors (Eysenck and Sargent, 1982). It is not possible to justify such speculation but the aborigines of Australasia, the bushmen of the Kalahari and many tribes of American Indians have maintained their ancestral links through traditions that include paranormal beliefs. American Indians are often cited as spirit guides in Spiritualistic gatherings and if genuine this may reflect their spiritual survival. A sceptical approach might claim this to be a form of cultural stereotyping making itself felt. (There exist interpretational difficulties in using the term 'sceptic' since its original meaning is one of doubting the evidence but it has increasingly in colloquial terms taken on a harsher meaning of denying belief [Truzzi, 1987.]) The continuation of these abilities in the present day may also be demonstrated by the well-documented powers of Indian yogi to perform paranormal acts in trance states (Broughton, 1991). Other apparently paranormal activities, such as the ancient Chinese practice of acupuncture, are increasingly being accepted into medical practice but opinions differ as to their explanation as physical or otherwise.

Western civilisation would seem to have less to offer the student of the paranormal in the twenty-first century than the East but this has not always been the case. Ancient Western civilisations accepted many paranormal events which may not all be ascribed to fraud or ignorance. The 'gift' of prophecy or communication with spirits was executed by seers and prophets in similar circumstances to shamans and witchdoctors in other cultures. The many oracles of ancient Greece were notoriously ambiguous but seven of them were evidently investigated in approximately 550 BC by King Croesus of Lydia (Herodotus, cited in Broughton, 1991). It is hard to believe that a civilisation as advanced as the Greeks, and later the Romans, should have been duped by many oracles for hundreds of years if there was no substance to their utterances. However, as part of their belief system it is possible that they accepted the declarations of such oracles without the need to question their validity. Jaynes (1993) has argued that the nature of primitive consciousness was very different to that of modern 'problem-solving' humans.

The legitimacy of the paranormal was undoubtedly hotly debated in these times with opposing viewpoints concerning the gods' powers and existence and similarly it might be felt that the idea of the Bible, as a source book on such phenomena, would encourage widely divergent opinions. The prophets of the Old Testament could be viewed as the shamans of their times and especially Moses with his apparent propensity for what could be described as magic, including his magic staff and the parting of the Red Sea. In the New Testament, Jesus might be identified as being representative of the most powerful shamans, sharing their powers of prophecy and levitation but surpassing them with his ability to also turn water into wine, raising the dead and even returning from the dead himself.

The Roman Catholic Church in particular has promulgated the paranormal activities of its believers notably in the feats of saints (including levitation, divine healing capabilities and lack of corruption after death) and stigmatists (people displaying the physical signs of crucifixion through contemplation). It is tempting to believe that a superstitious medieval population would be easily deceived by trickery or hallucination concerning the abilities of some of their divine figures. However, the closer to the present one comes, the more the Church has scrutinised its saints, even to the extent of removing and demoting some of them from the official Roman Catholic Calendar in 1969, e.g. St Christopher, St George and St Nicholas. To confirm the legitimacy of a person's sanctity the Catholic Church created the 'Promoter Fidei' or 'Devil's Advocate'. His task was to ensure a divine source for all manifestations rather than the Devil, a misunderstanding of nature or fraud. The Church has been particularly wary of beatification because of the possibilities of bringing the faith into widespread ill repute if mistakes were made. Saints displaying paranormal powers have been mentally and physically pained by their experiences and risked, in the past, investigation by the notorious Inquisition (Inglis, 1985). It seems unlikely, therefore, that they were always producing their alleged phenomena through fraudulent means. In the process the Catholic Church acquired more expertise in a form of psychical research than any other organisation until secular institutions started serious investigation. Missionaries preaching in distant lands would have increased their own knowledge through exposure to tribal witchcraft and exorcism. One such 'psychical researcher', Prospero Lambertini, was ordained as Pope Benedict XIV in 1740 and he also wrote about apparitions of the living and the dead (cited in Grattan-Guinness, 1982).

Nevertheless, the Church did not hold a monopoly on the investigation of psychic matters and alchemists also devoted considerable amounts of time to the paranormal. It could be argued that their experiments formed the basis of modern science. John Dee (1527-1608) was one such person who experimented with trying to contact the spirits of the dead and since he claimed to have no talent of his own he employed scryers (crystal gazers) and astrologers to help him. He held positions of some importance in the court of Queen Elizabeth I, acting as an astronomer and adviser. He studied magical works before writing his own treatise the *Monas Hieroglyphica* and received several royal appointments despite the Papal Nuncio accusing him of necromancy (Suster, 1986).

In the seventeenth century, as witchcraft mania erupted throughout Europe, investigation of the paranormal was treated with extreme caution. Involvement with abnormal activity could easily lead to an accusation and torture usually secured an 'appropriate' confession. The claims made of supernatural powers by adherents to, or accusants of, witchcraft might well have emanated from hallucinogenic plants and herbs, extreme torture or simply repeated accusations and suggestions of dalliance with evil forces, which were finally accepted by the victim as being true.

Fortunately, the more enlightened eighteenth century encouraged the further development of psychical research and considerable interest was aroused by the work of a doctor from Vienna, Franz Anton Mesmer (1734-1815). In the 1760s he developed a theory that the universe contained a: "Fluid, which pervades the universes and associates all things together in mutual intercourse and harmony" (cited in Broughton, 1991, p.55). His theory combined astrology and alchemy with the use of magnets to channel treatment to patients. Later on, the 'animal magnetism' of the healer was used to direct the energy and relaxing music was provided. (Mesmer was friendly with the Mozart family.) His methods were publicly successful and some of his supporters extended his techniques and dispensed with the magnets. Two reports were prepared by the Paris Faculty of Medicine and the Royal Academy of Sciences, and the Royal Society of Medicine in August 1784 which were hostile to Mesmer's work but a number of favourable pamphlets were distributed which gave him even more publicity (Gauld, 1992). In 1826 a further inquiry found favourable evidence for the healing capabilities of Mesmer's methods and throughout Europe the seeds had been sown for what eventually became medically accepted as hypnotism (Broughton, 1991).

The eighteenth century was also important in preparing Western society for the creation of Spiritualism in the next century. There had long been a belief that 'gifted' people could converse with the dead but the teachings of Emmanuel Swedenbourg (1688-1772) focused attention on this idea. He was a highly qualified scientist but after a vision he believed that he was in communication with spirits and he devoted himself thereafter to writing about his experiences, which included precognition and prophecy (Gordon, 1992). It is unlikely that his works had been read by the originators of Spiritualism in its present day form, Margaret and Catherine Fox, since they were both in their early teens and lived in a relatively poor area (Hydesville) in New York State in 1848 when their alleged contact with spirits first occurred. However, prior to their spirit contact, other examples had been written about and clairvoyant powers and the receipt of teachings from the spirit world were publicly acknowledged (Gordon, 1992).

One of the far-reaching effects of the spread of Spiritualism was the formation of the Society for Psychical Research (SPR) in London in 1882 with the Cambridge University Professor Henry Sidgwick as its first president. The SPR's aim was to:

> "...investigate that large body of debatable phenomena designated by such terms as mesmeric, psychical and spiritualistic" and to approach these varied problems "without prejudice or prepossession of any kind, and in the same spirit of exact and unimpassioned inquiry which has enabled Science to solve so many problems, once not less obscure nor less hotly debated."

> (Society for Psychical Research, 1882-3, pp.3-6)

The first council appointed six committees to investigate thought reading, Mesmerism, Reichenbach lights (alleged electro-magnetic auras), apparitions and haunted houses, physical phenomena and literary matters. The investigations were very thorough and many Spiritualists were alienated by their exacting standards. The poet and SPR member William Butler Yeats complained: "It's my belief that if you psychical researchers had been about when God Almighty was creating the world, He couldn't have done the job." (cited in Grattan-Guinness, 1982, p.23).

Their investigations of Madame Blavatsky, the founder of the Theosophical Society, led to a report claiming her to be "one of the most accomplished, ingenious, and interesting impostors in history" (ibid.). The fame of the SPR spread abroad and the American psychologist William James wrote in 1897: "Were I asked to point to a scientific

14

journal where hard headedness and never sleeping suspicion of sources of error might be seen in their full bloom, I think I should have to fall back on the proceedings of the Society for Psychical Research." (ibid.). The SPR attracted men of the calibre of F. W. H. Myers who quoted Gladstone as speaking of psychical research as "the most important work which is being done in the world" (cited in Tyrrell, 1954, p.231). Not everybody held such positive views even concerning the technological inventions of the day as can be read from reports by Professor Tait, University of Edinburgh, who believed the invention of the telephone to be physically impossible and the Paris Academy of Sciences attributing fraudulent ventriloquism to the sound production from Edison's phonograph (ibid.).

The American Society for Psychical Research was founded in 1885 in imitation of the British SPR and work was undertaken in France by Charles Richet, the Professor of Physiology at the University of Paris. However, it was in America that funds were made available for the study of psychical research at Stanford, Harvard and Clark Universities. After the appointment of the British psychologist William McDougal to Duke University in 1927, the study of parapsychology, as it had become known, received a considerable impetus with the appointment of the botanist J. B. Rhine to the department. He started research in 1930 with card guessing experiments, which involved the reading of cards telepathically. He was aided by a colleague who devised a set of cards with symbols on them that were easily distinguished (the so-called Zener cards). Rhine was joined by his wife and two full time graduates (Charles E. Stuart and J. Gaither Pratt) and in 1934 they published their results in a monograph entitled *Extra Sensory Perception*. Public and press interest focused further attention on the subject and the *Journal of Parapsychology* was inaugurated in 1937, though World War II caused a major setback as funds were diverted to the war effort (Grattan-Guinness, 1982). After the war the first university chair in parapsychology was given in 1953 to the researcher W. H. C. Tenhaeff at the University of Utrecht, Holland and the chair for border areas of psychology at Freiburg University, Germany was taken by Hans Bender the following year. These indicated a greater recognition of the desire to study the subject seriously. Since then the credibility of parapsychologists has at times undergone setbacks with admissions of falsified figures and the alteration of results. Nonetheless, research of a scientific nature into parapsychological phenomena is still being undertaken at such institutions as the University of Edinburgh where the Koestler Chair of Parapsychology was founded in 1985 and was held by Professor Robert Morris until his untimely death in 2004.

Music and Extra Sensory Perception

This essay explores the idea that musical experience might be communicated by means of the presence of an additional method of information transference known as ESP. It starts with a definition of ESP and its development with particular reference to ESP in altered states and 'ganzfeld' studies where subjects attempt to receive information from a psychic source. Details of the background to, and arrangements for, my own experiments using music as a possible source of extrasensory contact are presented. Despite evidence for ESP in non-human organisms (e.g. Bardens, 1987; Sheldrake and Smart, 1997), for the purpose of this research experiments were solely conducted using human subjects.

The term 'Extra Sensory Perception' was popularised by J. B. Rhine in the 1930s to denote general clairvoyant and telepathic abilities and it became the title of his first monograph published by the Boston Society for Psychical Research in 1934 (Rhine, 1934). ESP can be defined as a belief that knowledge is acquired by a mode of perception that is currently independent of the known laws of physics (Braude, 1979). It has subdivisions that would include telepathy, clairvoyance and precognition.

Much of the early experimentation carried out in the Rhine tradition lacked an interest in what was happening in the minds of the subjects, although some of Louisa Rhine's studies attempted to redress this (e.g. Rhine, 1961). However, an important article by Rhea A. White (1964) helped to change this situation. In particular, she argued that the subject's impressions should be recorded during or shortly after the experiment, since signs of ESP might be demonstrated there, and a study of the mental states of successful subjects might give clues as to the conditions which favour ESP. More generally, the widespread 'drug culture' of the 1960s fostered an interest in 'inner states' of consciousness which fed into and influenced both psychology and parapsychology (Tart, 1969).

Many people who claim psychic gifts or awareness seem to enter into altered or trance states during their psychic experiences (Eysenck and Sargent, 1982). Some mediums and Spiritualists allegedly demonstrate psychic perception when in full or partial trance (Tart, 1969). Other percipients report clairvoyant insights while dreaming. Related to this are the hypnagogic and hypnopompic states of mind which occur at the points of going to sleep and waking up respectively and which seem to be particularly conducive to ESP (Mavromatis, 1987). Altered conditions of consciousness can be self induced or achieved through drugs as was apparently the case with the famous oracle at Delphi (Berger, 1991). What seems to happen during these times is that the subject relaxes his critical faculties and allows a dream-like state to pervade his mind. Depending on the strength of the ability to relax, the subject achieves different levels of entrancement. One of the biggest problems encountered is sensory distraction. If the brain is constantly being stimulated by its physical surroundings, then the survival-related instinct to stay alert may overcome possible psychic experiences. If the imagination is curtailed in this way, what lies below the surface may be suppressed (Watson, 1998). The hypnotherapist uses a form of sensory relaxation to achieve an altered state of mind that combines awareness with a fully relaxed situation.

Over the last twenty-five years, parapsychologists have tried out various devices for promoting the flow of imagery in their subjects by means of sensory deprivation. These have included a flotation tank (used by P. Kubzansky and S. Freedman) which consisted of a tank filled with salt water heated to blood temperature. The sound-and sight-proofed subjects floated in it and reported their thoughts and sensations (cited in Panati, 1975). The so called 'witches cradle' which was used by Krippner and Honorton at the Maimonides Hospital in New York (Honorton, Drucker and Hermon, 1973) consisted of a cradle that subjects were strapped into. It could be moved in any direction and subjects wore eye shields and ear mufflers whilst it was kept in constant motion for thirty minutes. The aim of both techniques was to mask the physical senses, facilitating psychic manifestations. The sensory deprivation effects of these techniques seemed ethically rather dubious and were anxiety arousing for some subjects. Furthermore, the machinery was expensive to maintain. However, at the same institution a series of experiments published between 1966 and 1972 provided evidence for dream-mediated psi (e.g. Ullman, Krippner and Vaughan, 1973, cited in Bem and Honorton, 1994).

Probably the most notable parapsychologist to bring attention to the importance of internal attention states was Charles Honorton. He argued persuasively that "Psi functioning is enhanced when the receiver is in a state of sensory relaxation and is minimally influenced by ordinary perception and proprioception" (Honorton, 1977, p.466). To test this proposition he conducted many experiments, including a study which required subjects undergoing sensory deprivation to identify by psychic means pictures which a 'sender' was attempting to transmit. In one example (Honorton, Drucker and Hermon, 1973) thirty volunteers each contributed a thirty-minute session whilst suspended in a sensory isolation cradle - blindfolded and wearing headphones. The results showed that the subjects who had relaxed into a semi-hypnotic state scored significantly above chance, whereas those who had resisted this state only scored at chance level. (For an overview of further literature see, for instance, Roney-Dougal, 1986.)

Of the available methods of sensory deprivation, the ganzfeld (whole field) technique is often accepted as being the most conducive to the manifestation of ESP (Honorton et al., 1990) having previously been used in non-ESP experiments (Honorton, 1977). For the purpose of the experiments reported in this research it was adapted using music as the target. The ganzfeld technique consists of sensory masking caused by diffused red light and white noise played to a subject through headphones, while he sits or lies comfortably. The idea is that this causes the brain to have fewer sensory cues to interpret and therefore allows subconscious thoughts and feelings to be manifested. These are recorded for further discussion. This is sometimes enhanced by the use of additional relaxation techniques. Psychologists have indicated that the optimum amount of time for this altered state to be achieved is about fifteen to twenty minutes and then a similar period before distractions return. The conditions most commonly sought in ganzfeld experiments in parapsychology have been:

- The reduction of external sensory noise.
- Directing the attention internally.
- Encouraging the link with a remote target.
- Recording information conveyed by the receiver.
- Confirmation of receiver/sender interaction.

The first study to adopt this procedure was reported by Honorton and Harper (1974) who used thirty receivers in single thirty-five minute sessions. Senders were either friends of the receivers or laboratory staff and the targets were taken from a pool of photographic slide reels. The ganzfeld procedure was adopted and afterwards the receiver was shown four different slides and asked to choose the one that best fitted his report and to place the others in order. A significant number of hits were obtained. Braud, Wood and Braud (1975) reported twenty sessions where only half the receivers underwent ganzfeld stimulation whereas the others received none. The ganzfeld teams produced significantly better results than the non-ganzfeld teams who produced chance results. Habel (1976) reported on thirty trials where the auditory masking was varied, consisting of either white noise, the playing of Ravel's Bolero or a simple regular drum beat. Overall results were not significant in terms of showing any one of these to be more effective than the others, but results from those researchers using an auditory masking agent as opposed to none produced significantly higher scores. Habel did notice that her earlier experiments were conducted in a more relaxed manner with fewer trials per day and with no deadlines to meet, and these presented a significantly higher hit rate. This may indicate that when external pressures are brought to bear on experiments, the degree of ESP achieved is lessened.

In the last twenty years the ganzfeld has continued to be used as a method for investigating ESP. Schlitz and Honorton conducted a series of ganzfeld experiments at the Mind Science Foundation, San Antonio, Texas in 1992 using an artistically gifted group of students from the Juilliard School in New York. Overall, the results were superior to that of the general population with the musicians scoring a seventy-five per cent hit rate where chance indicated twenty-five per cent (Schlitz and Honorton, 1992). Dalton (1997) drew further links between creativity and psi in ganzfeld sessions using musicians, artists, creative writers and actors. The musicians in particular scored significantly above chance. Further ganzfeld sessions in Europe and the USA have been conducted including those at the University of Amsterdam by Bierman and Houtkooper (1981); at St John's University (USA) by Stanford (1986); and at Edinburgh University by Delanoy (1987) and Milton (1988/89). Honorton used an 'autoganzfeld' consisting of video clips and procedures whereby the experimenter did not know the target being sent until after the trial was concluded. His results suggest that dynamic targets might produce more evidence of psi (Honorton et al, 1990) and Bierman's results (1995; 1997) suggest that emotional targets might be similarly productive.

The most significant conclusion to emerge from examining the prior studies would seem to be the enhancement of psi receptivity by sensory relaxation. Henri Bergson had previously attempted to explain this using his 'filter' theory, which states that the brain and the nervous system function primarily as filters to protect one from the mass of mainly useless information that surrounds one leaving behind only that which is necessary to the homeostatic condition (Broad, 1953). As a result, alleged psychic tendencies remain latent within the unconscious, only emerging when sensory demands are minimised. Aldous Huxley (1963, pp.23-24) wrote:

> "According to such a theory ('filter'), each one of us is potentially Mind at Large. But in so far as we are animals, our business is at all costs to survive. To make biological survival possible, Mind at Large has to be funnelled through the reducing valve of the brain and nervous system...Certain persons, however, seem to be born with a kind of bypass that circumvents the reducing valve. In others temporary bypasses may be acquired either spontaneously or as a result of deliberate 'spiritual exercises'."

It might be possible that ESP interactions occur more frequently than is generally believed on an unconscious level but that the 'filter' system prevents them from becoming consciously experienced (Kreitler and Kreitler, 1972). (See Stokes (1987) for a summary of other theories.)

Experiments using music as the sending target have not been conducted very often. Brief reports appeared in the *Journal of Parapsychology* (Shulman, 1938) and in the *Parapsychology Bulletin* (George, 1948). The ganzfeld procedure was not used and only simple melodies played on a variety of instruments were listened to. This precluded the possibility of an emotional response from the sender and the results were only those expected by chance. H. H. Keil (1965) conducted tests at Duke University using music as the sending agent but the ganzfeld procedure was not used and the music was chosen by the subjects themselves. Further to this, an exploratory study was designed by Altom and Braud (1976) to "determine whether there might be any unique difficulties with the use of musical targets...". They believed that the overall results suggested that musical targets might be "useful" in this type of research.

The purpose of the experiment undertaken in my research was to investigate whether it is possible for a person in the ganzfeld condition to be contacted telepathically using music as the target. Unfortunately there is not space here to give an account of a second, smaller scale experiment that aimed to replicate the high scores that were achieved by some of the participants in the first experiment. (See Willin, 1999 for details.)

It has already been stated that many difficulties are encountered when attempting to explore a subject as elusive as ESP whilst still applying scientific rigour to the test situation. In setting up a ganzfeld experiment it is vital that the choice of people, locations and experimental procedures should not allow later accusations of bias or fraud to be made. To this end the procedures used in the following research were devised in consultation with Professor R. L. Morris, who held the Koestler Chair of Parapsychology at the University of Edinburgh and had extensive knowledge of this field. To find sufficient participants for the one hundred trials of the first experiment, hundreds of circulars were sent to adults around the country who responded by letter or telephone. There were no formal selection criteria other than availability at suitable times and a willingness to participate. Several pieces of personal data were recorded about each receiver at the beginning of each trial in order to contribute to later analysis of characteristics with reference to the trials' outcomes. These included gender, age, receiver/sender relationships, extra/introversion, profession, hobbies and experience of paranormal activity.

The trials took place in several different locations where safeguards were in place to prevent sensory leakage and external auditory sounds and vibrations were generally minimal. For the trials in Essex at my house, two buildings separated by twenty-five yards were used for the receiver and sender respectively. Nobody was present for the ganzfeld trials except participants and only the front door of the main building could be partially seen via a side window (with blinds) of the other building and vice-versa. During night-time sessions, security lighting would light up automatically should anyone leave or approach either building.

For the sessions in Sheffield, one trial took place in the Music Department of the University. The receiver and helper were situated in a fairly well sound-proofed room on the first floor at one end of the building and the sender and experimenter were situated on the second floor at the other end of the building. The remaining three Sheffield trials took place in different houses separated by approximately half a mile and with absolutely no visual or audible contact. For the sessions in Edinburgh, all the trials took place in the Koestler Parapsychology Unit of the University. The receiver used the unit's own sound-shielded room designed for ganzfeld experiments and the helper remained in an adjacent room. The sender and experimenter were situated in another room along a corridor quite some distance away and with no possible sound or visual leakage. In York, two sessions took place in residential blocks belonging to the University College of Ripon St John in separate rooms on the same floor and three trials took place in private detached houses in York - two in separate rooms on the same floor and one in separate rooms on different floors. For the sessions at the Arthur Findlay College in Stansted, Essex, different rooms on different floors were used separated by stairs and long corridors, allowing no possibility of sound or visual leakage.

To allow for reliable randomisation it was decided to create a 'pool' of twenty packages of music with four pieces within each, making a total of eighty different pieces of music available. For ease of identification, each package was numbered one to twenty and each track within each package was identified by letter (*a, b, c* or *d*). Each lettered track was chosen intentionally to be as different as possible from the others and of approximately five minutes' duration. This was to minimise any confusion between each track and to allow repeated hearings of the same music during each trial.

- The *a* tracks consisted of orchestral music from the Baroque to the twentieth century.
- The *b* tracks consisted of vocal/ choral music from the Medieval period to the twentieth century.

- The *c* tracks consisted of solo instrumental music from the Medieval period to the twentieth century.
- The *d* tracks consisted of percussion or electronic music exclusively from the twentieth century.

The target sets, which were concealed in thick paper envelopes, were compiled by myself and nobody else had knowledge of the music recorded. Great care was taken to ensure that not only the musical genre of each track (within a package) was very different from its neighbours but also that the imagery that it was felt might be produced was as distinct as possible, e.g. package no.1 presented:

   a. The opening to Mozart's *Eine kleine Nachtmusik.*
   b. A Christmas mass using Gregorian chant.
   c. The opening to Beethoven's 'Moonlight' sonata.
   d. Traditional drumming by the Burundi Drummers.
The other packages had similarly diverse contents.

	A	B	C	D
1	Eine kleine nachtmusik (opening). Mozart.	Xmas Mass Gregorian Chant.	Moonlight sonata (opening). Beethoven.	Trad. drumming from the drummers of Burundi.
2	Symphony no.5. (opening) Beethoven.	Serenade to Music (choral entry). V. Williams	Lute suite in Em.(gtr) (opening). J .S. Bach.	Galan Kangin (opening) gamelan music of Bali.
3	Symphony no.3.'Eroica' (funeral mch). Beethovn.	Madrigal: Too much I once lamented. Tomkins.	Toccata & Fugue in Dm (opening). J.S. Bach.	Kontakte 1. Stockhausen.
4	Symphony no.5 (opening). Shostakovich	Kyrie eleison :Mass for 5 Voices. Byrd.	Piano sonata no.2 (opening). Tippett.	Kontakte 2. Stockhausen.
5	Adagio for Strings (opening). Barber.	Worthy is the Lamb. from Messiah. Handel.	Medieval songs for pipes flutes, jew's harp & tabor.	18 Bricks left on Apr.21. Bedford.
6	Alle vittime di Hiroshima (opening). Penderecki.	St.Matthew Passion. (opening). J.S. Bach.	Serenade for tenor, horn & strs (solo horn). Britten.	We are the Robots. Kraftwerk.
7	Symphony no.40.in Gm (opening). Mozart.	Lux Aeterna. Ligeti.	Raga Hamer. Sitar solo.	2nd Construction for 4 Players. Cage.

8	Mars from the Planets. Holst.	Now the drenched land awakes. Bedford.	Pathetique piano sonata (opening). Beethoven.	Pulse 1939. H. Cowell.
9	Sinfonie Fantastique (4th.movt). Berlioz.	The Self Banished. Blow.	Medieval & tradn. music for bagpipes & bladders.	Sisu 1976. T.l. Lundquist.
10	Night on a bald Mtn. Mussorgsky.	Missa solemnis (Credo). Beethoven.	Concierto Aranjuez (slow movt.cadenza). Rodrigo.	Hierophonie 1974. Y. Taira.
11	Symphony no.6.(Past.) (opening). Beethoven.	This is the record of John (anthem). Gibbons	San Dan. Solo koto music.	Apache. The Shadows.
12	Ride of the Valkyrie (overture). Wagner.	Golden Rain. Balinese Monkey chant.	McAllistrum's March & Mss. Hamilton. Harp.	Ionisation. Varese.
13	1812 Overture (opening). Tchaikovsky.	The Wllow Song. Anon.	Sonata in G minor. (h.psichord). C.P.E. Bach	Warizie field recording: marimbas, xylophones.
14	Symphony no.9. (opening). Beethoven.	Xmas Carol: First Noel. Tradn.	Gymnopedies for piano. Satie.	Electronic plant music.
15	Arrival of the Queen of Sheba. Handel.	Towards the Unknown Region. Vn. Williams.	Density for flute. Varese.	Intro. to Funeral for a Friend. Elton John.
16	Brandenburg Conc.no.2. J.S. Bach.	The Miserere. Allegri.	Sokaku Reibo. Solo shakuhachi.	Oxygene. Jarre.
17	Swan Lake Suite (concln.). Tchaikovsky.	Hymn to St.Cecilia. Britten.	Farewell: A fancy.(lute). Dowland.	Final movt. Brand.Conc. no.3. on Moog synthesr
18	Rodeo Suite. (opening). Copland.	Spem in alium. Tallis.	Trad.kora solo from the Gambia.	Concln. Variations. Lloyd Webber.
19	Rite of Spring (opening). Stravinsky.	'Tis you tis I : Carmen Bizet.	Trad.alphorn solos from Switzerland.	Highlife from Trinidad. Steel band music.
20	Water Music (opening). Handel.	Alleluia Nativitas. Perotin.	Rondena for flamenco guitar.	Tubular Bells (opening). Oldfield.

Typically, a group of three people (receiver, sender and helper) arrived at the place of the experiment and were made comfortable. Then, after approximately ten minutes, the experimental procedure was explained to everyone present. The participants knew in advance via the circulars sent to them what was involved in the roles within the trial and had usually already decided who would take on each of these. I allocated the roles if the group was undecided and expressed no preferences. The choice was then based on such criteria as the roles chosen in any previous participation and the feeling that husband and wife receiver/sender partnerships could be effective.

The receiver was informed that he would sit in a very comfortable armchair and have translucent table tennis ball halves secured over his eyes with medical tape. Headphones would then be placed over his ears by the helper. He was told that a red light would be directed towards his covered eyes and that at the start of the trial a cassette tape would be played through the headphones. This would allow him to hear a few seconds of white noise to acclimatise to the sound. He was told that what followed would be a fifteen-minute relaxation tape during which time he would be spoken to as an aid to relaxation. After this the ganzfeld trial was to begin with the return of the white noise and he was asked to say out loud in a normal speaking voice any sensations which might come to mind. These would be tape-recorded. It was stressed that he did not have to speak the whole time and that the decision was always his as to whether to speak or not. It was further stressed that complete confidentiality would be maintained and that should he wish to stop the experiment at anytime he was at liberty to do so. The receiver and sender were told that whilst the receiver was listening to the white noise, the sender would be listening to one piece of music repeatedly in the other building and trying to communicate the target telepathically to the receiver. He would try to do this via any visual, auditory, emotional or other sensations that were experienced as a result of hearing it. The receiver, having heard the white noise stop, would attract the attention of the helper who would remove the table tennis ball halves and headphones. The helper would then open the large brown envelope selected earlier. Inside it, one package would be specified which corresponded to a cassette tape which the helper then played to the receiver. Each tape contained four tracks to be scored by the receiver from one to a hundred according to how closely each piece fitted the receiver's experiences in the ganzfeld. He was asked to give a different score to each piece and to be careful not to choose the music according to prior musical preferences. This procedure lasted anything from twenty minutes to forty-five minutes. Once the receiver had given four scores on the form he was told that he could re-join the experimenter and sender in the other building. Before departing to the music studio the experimenter invited the receiver to respond to a range of questions about themselves and notes were subsequently made on the scoring form. These included details of age, sex, occupation, interests and experience of the paranormal. This information was important for the eventual analysis of the results.

The receiver and helper were not invited to inspect the second building - where the sender and experimenter would be situated during the experiment - to enhance security precautions. A randomisation procedure was carried out to select the potential target music. After final confirmation of the arrangements, the experimenter and the sender departed to the other building where they had a period of about twenty minutes before needing to begin the formal part of the session. This period of time corresponded to the receiver being made comfortable in the ganzfeld and hearing a fifteen-minute relaxation tape. The experimenter set up the playback machine to allow just the one extract to be played and explained to the sender that he would be asked to repeat his thoughts after each playback into a separate tape recorder.

Immediately before the receiver's thirty minutes of white noise, the sender would open the two previously-selected envelopes, one containing details of the tape to be listened to and the other specifying the precise track. The sender would then listen to the track repeatedly and attempt to convey his perception of the piece to the receiver. During rewinds of the track by the experimenter, the sender would be encouraged to briefly speak into a tape recorder to give an indication of what his thoughts were concerning the music. All participants would then return to the house to discuss the result, which would be known as soon as the experimenter was sure that the scoring form had been completed.

Four sets of twenty large, thick, brown envelopes were used for the receivers' choices; four sets of twenty white envelopes were used for the senders' choices; and four sets of twenty small brown envelopes were used for the senders' track choices. Each of the large brown and white envelopes contained a folded card bearing a number from one to twenty and each of the small brown envelopes contained a card bearing a track letter of *a-d*. This had been sealed and placed into the white envelopes only. The large brown and white envelopes had been sealed and stapled together in pairs by the experimenter, thus producing a target pool of eighty possible pieces and an identical set of empty envelopes were available to allow re-insertion of pieces after each trial. It was not possible to identify which pieces were enclosed in the envelopes after this procedure had been carried out. All present were invited to shuffle the pile of eighty identical pairs of envelopes. The receiver was asked to choose either his own date of birth or the date of the experiment. The digits were then added together e.g. 04 02 1951 = 22. The sender was then asked whether the appropriate envelope (in the previous example the twenty-second pair) should be chosen from the left or the right. The stapled pair of envelopes were removed from the pool and separated. The helper was given the large brown envelope containing the package number and the sender was given the white envelope containing the same package number as well as a further small brown envelope containing a track letter *a-d*. All numbers were written on the inside of a folded card to avoid recognition from the outside.

For the first experiment it was decided to use a panel of 'blind judges' to give an objective opinion regarding the correlation between the receivers' verbal responses and their subsequent choice of music. This was to be achieved by providing them with a full transcript of the spoken comments and the tape of the music associated with a particular trial. They would then be able to make their own selection of the track which most closely matched the responses by scoring each piece in the same way as the receiver, i.e. by using their own numerical scoring system up to one hundred as a maximum score. I decided to approach three people who had not participated in the trials in any way. Further criteria for their choice was that they should be of different age groups, at least one of each sex, have musical expertise in different ways and be responsible in their attitude to the task. Suitable people were found and none had any specific interest in parapsychological matters.

Those procedures were applied within each of the separate trials to ensure the validity of the results and to minimise the influence of uncontrolled factors. It was further hoped that rigorous security and procedures would counter any future possible claims of fraud and lessen the subjectivity of interpretation of the results. The hundred trials took place over a period of fifteen months before the results were subsequently analysed.

Of those who responded to the circulars sent out agreeing to participate, the sources were twenty-three amateur music students of my own; fifteen members of the Society for Psychical Research; thirteen members of the Ghost Club Society; twenty friends; six musical colleagues; and forty-three complete strangers. Altogether, one hundred and twenty different people took part in the trials: seventy-six different receivers, sixty-nine different senders, and thirty-eight different helpers. Ages ranged from eighteen to seventy-five years, with a mean age of forty years. Seventy-two women participated and forty-eight men. A wide range of different personalities and backgrounds were involved in the research.

The professions of the receivers reflected the broad range of sources from which they were drawn. It would not be relevant to list every one but where several receivers were involved in similar types of work, it was felt worthwhile to investigate any links between professions and apparent telepathic ability. These included teachers, students, administrative workers, self-styled housewives, etc. The receivers were involved in a similarly broad range of hobbies including music, the paranormal, books and sport.

Fifty-six people (seventy-four per cent of the total) claimed previous paranormal experiences, which included seeing ghosts and alleged contact with spirits. Twenty people (twenty-six per cent of the total) claimed not to have witnessed anything paranormal. The large number of those claiming prior experience may have been due to the fact that such people are more likely to have an interest in the subject and therefore offer to be involved in research. This larger number could also be significant to the results of the trials as it is often felt that belief in the existence of paranormal activity is conducive to experiencing it.

On their conclusion, an extensive analysis was made of the results looking at both the number of 'hits' and 'misses' achieved as well as possible contributory or explanatory factors. The outcome of a single trial was classed as a hit when the receiver gave the highest score to the piece of music that the sender was actually listening to. The purpose of the session was for the receiver to identify the target correctly despite the same/different interpretations of the music by the sender. A score of one hundred points indicated that the receiver was absolutely sure of their choice and zero points meant they were equally sure that the piece was not being sent. Scores between these two extremes indicated varying degrees of conviction. The final hit rate did not take into account the actual score value that subjects used as some subjects used high scores throughout and others used low scores. Neither did it differentiate between weak hits (only a few points between each score) and dramatic hits with a large difference between the hit score and the other scores. The overall receiver hit rate was twenty-four per cent where chance would have indicated twenty-five per cent, a result not demonstrating in itself any evidence for the existence of ESP. However, during the course of the trials and after scrutiny of the results, some data seemed to indicate favourable conditions that might indicate evidence for ESP in a musical context.

A study of the receivers' transcripts provides data of recurring visual, auditory, tactile, olfactory and emotional material which may have had a telepathic origin and comparisons of receivers' personal details, e.g. age, sex, professions, hobbies, etc., with their results provides information as to whether certain personality traits may be more conducive to the experience of ESP. The dates and places of the trials were also investigated to ascertain any significance in geographical locations, times of the year and times of day. A study of the music chosen by receivers in the different categories also provides information concerning possible personal preferences and music which may have prompted a stronger emotional signal from the sender for the receiver to pick up.

In an attempt to find links between the receivers' spoken thoughts and the music that was being sent to them, written transcripts of the tapes of everything that was spoken, sung or tapped out by the receivers were made by the experimenter and the results were presented under the headings of visual images, auditory sensations, olfactory sensations, tactile sensations and emotional experiences.

By far the largest number of references fell within the visual category. Most of the personal visual imagery that probably originated from the receivers' natural preoccupation with daily activities was eliminated from the list by excluding single references, e.g. shopping lists, the video watched the night before, etc. The results at least provide quite an interesting insight into what comes into the human mind in a relaxed state - regardless of the attempts of a hidden sender to communicate with them. For example, pastoral landscapes and people were among the most common images. These lists provide a partial description of what ran through the receivers' minds whilst acknowledging that it is impossible to relate these accounts directly to the thoughts of the senders. It is clear that the white noise was probably the cause of a large number of people referring to water and water-related subjects. Twenty-eight per cent mentioned it by name and a further twenty-four per cent spoke of waterfalls. However, it was stressed that the receivers should only dwell on this imagery if it continued to be relevant to their thoughts. Similarly, the red light may have been responsible for twenty-eight per cent mentioning the sun and nineteen per cent speaking of brightness but not all the common images can be accounted for in this way. The ten most frequently occurring visual images also included children, birds, black, green and at the top of the list 'blue' with twenty-nine per cent.

Association of ideas seemed to play a part in some of the receivers' dialogues. For example, having started with a comment on the white noise, the receiver would move on to waterfalls and suitably pastoral surroundings, perhaps containing a reference to the sea or cliffs. Above the cliffs in the blue sky, birds would be seen and on this bright sunny day people and children would be out walking. This rather stereotyped British coastal scene contains twelve of the most frequently occurring visual images. The transcript of one receiver's spoken dialogue below provides an example of some of these visualisations:

"Blue skies; birds; trees; walking; green and blue; children playing; stream; very slow; female voices; happy; travel; moving; grass; hills and blue sky; up in the sky but not birds; outside; very green; coaches and horses by a lake; female laughter; water; no children; boat on water; roads, tracks very straight leading towards horizon; lake; no boat nor people; lake beside road; guitar music...no; fish in water; blue sky; church; dark; people in field; very happy; Salisbury Plain - Stonehenge; sunshine; hill looking down; black snakes; not calm; spiders; snakes; black; orange; inside and can't get outside; hiding; cathedral roof; grey; patterned ceiling; austere; way up; stain glass; plain glass; carriages back; lake; trees; shady leading towards water; rowing boat tied up on bank; long dresses and hats; very elegant; running children; the sky; clocks; fireplace; painting; people in trees; reflection."

The sender was listening to the peaceful opening of the '1812' Overture by Tchaikovsky and the receiver correctly chose this piece with a high score. The receiver wrote that the mood felt wrong for the other pieces despite intellectual connections. The least musically knowledgeable of the three blind judges also scored this trial a hit. This could therefore be an example of a coincidence between the mood of the piece and the naturally common images in the human mind when in a relaxed state. However, why is it then that not every receiver chose the music with the calmest mood?

In some trials common visual elements (cliffs, sun, sea, etc.) were juxtaposed with contradictory images. Nevertheless, hits were achieved because of the 'feel' of the music received:

"Got to get out; a shore; panic; all is OK; waterfall; people and children all happy; sky blue; hot sun; peaceful; lots of violins playing dramatically like a thunderstorm; one big drum; always water; drowning people screaming; I'm tense because I can't help because I'm not really there; it has gone; death; coffins; dead people; looking for goodness but can't find it; everyone's bad; castle on cliff; peaceful because no-one's there; calm sea and gulls; peaceful; ocean; bloody white noise could drive you mad; happy and energetic; want to run and say 'Yes'; ocean and water; I'd like to dive in and swim; looks nice."

The receiver scored a hit by choosing correctly the powerful opening to Beethoven's Ninth Symphony, giving it full marks despite obvious contradictions with some of the images in the transcription. Two out of the three blind judges also scored this a hit.

Receivers did not always move along these traditional lines. On fifty-six occasions, non-pastoral visualisations were produced with twenty-eight per cent achieving direct hits. The following is an example of a case that cannot be so readily explained in terms of coincidence or frequently occurring images when in a relaxed state:

"Mood is serious but not sad; heavy orchestral music; perhaps it's Beethoven or something like it; tension; I see an orchestra; music connected with a serious event; solemn not emotional; grey buildings; monument; grey; orchestral strings; people standing together; solemn; in a square or something; grey; Russian Revolution perhaps?; powerful music; strong; people walking in grey; crowds."

The sender was listening to the *March to the Scaffold* from Berlioz' *Symphonie Fantastique*. The music conveys the journey of a condemned man to the guillotine during a period approximating to the French Revolution. It is a serious piece of music for full orchestra with the main texture provided by the string section. The receiver identified the piece correctly and the three blind judges were unanimous in scoring this a hit. This provides a good example of the possibility of telepathy being used to convey the feelings inspired by a particular piece of music. Neither person had heard the piece before and as far as one knows they had not recently been exposed to images of such an event or had by coincidence been reading about nineteenth century revolutions.

Further analysis of the receivers' visual imagery reveals a preponderance of outdoor scenes despite the fact that the trials all took place indoors. A possible explanation for this might be the attempt to dispel the slightly claustrophobic feel of the sensory deprivation by conjuring up bright, open images. Perhaps instead it may be a matter of an individual's present prevailing environment exerting the strongest effect on predominant imagery. One wonders whether people from completely different climates and cultures would have produced similar visual material.

In some cases, it has been difficult to differentiate between visual and auditory commentary. For instance, when the receiver mentioned Mozart, they may have seen his face as they imagined it to be from a painting or a film rather than hearing his music and recognising its composer. However, it was decided to include such examples if they contained references that occurred in more than one transcript. Obviously when they either sang themselves or specified that they could <u>hear</u> sounds this problem did not arise.

The influence of the human voice on the nature of the auditory images is very apparent here since vocal manifestations were reported by the largest number of receivers. The drums may well have been chosen in response to the receivers' awareness of their own heartbeats or due to the fact that low frequency external sounds may have penetrated the white noise. The musical tastes of many of the receivers (middle class and classically orientated) might explain the fairly frequent occurrence of the violin. However, it is also possible that genuine ESP was taking place when the sound of the instrument was being sent telepathically on the occasions when the violin featured in the music listened to by the sender.

Although many receivers heard music - they knew the nature of the experiment in advance so this was to be expected - few were willing to communicate it in song. This was almost certainly due to personal inhibitions or a lack of willingness to disrupt their relaxation through conscious singing or whistling. One trial, which was a miss, showed an interesting feature. The music being sent was the opening of the fourth movement of Berlioz' *Symphonie Fantastique* (also previously mentioned in the section on visual imagery but with a different receiver and sender). It bore quite a strong resemblance to the French tune 'Frère Jacques' that the receiver sang during the experiment. There was only a semitone difference between the key of the Berlioz and the receiver's voice. Not being a musician she did not realise the connection and neither did she know that Berlioz was French. In conversation after the trial, the receiver spoke of the tune "just coming into her head from out of the blue". In another trial the receiver heard a recurring rhythm which he tapped out which bore some resemblance to the music that was being sent (*Mars* from the 'Planets' Suite). The receiver did not like the sensations he was receiving - the sender was thinking of death and the holocaust - and he rejected that particular track. The trial was therefore a miss, although the blind judges were later unanimous in awarding it a hit.

Despite music being 'heard' by the receivers, there was not a single instance where the precise title of a piece of music was given and proved to be correct. Success was encountered in terms of general information, e.g. "I can hear string music", "I can hear drums beating", etc., and pitch and timbre were spoken of in similarly general terms. Where receivers scored most highly was in their recognition of the 'feel' of the music rather than in specific terms. They often spoke of this in conversation after the trials. It would seem that the limited number of auditory references could have any of the following possible causes that are similar to those discussed with the visual images. Firstly, cultural influences could be finding expression in common mental imagery. Secondly, there could be physical explanations based on association with recently heard sounds and thirdly genuine telepathic communication may be occurring. There is not enough evidence to support any of these explanations individually, especially bearing in mind the relative dearth of specific musical references.

It is, of course, difficult to separate normal bodily functions and reactions from those that may have been brought about specifically by communication within the ganzfeld experiment. A further difficulty arises from the fact that physical movements would not be recorded on the tape unless they were of an extreme nature or referred to verbally by the receiver. There were a limited number of these sensations mentioned. Sixteen receivers spoke of being cold but eight mentioned they were heavy or warm. Five receivers used words such as 'floating', 'heart faster', 'speeding' or 'shivering' and four spoke of flying or needing the toilet. Three spoke of feeling their own heart beat and the same number felt 'lightness', 'spinning', or 'tingling'. There were two examples each of 'jumping', 'numb', 'slow movement' or 'swinging'.

It should be stated that many of the trials took place in the summer and during cold periods rooms were heated with either central heating or (in the case of the Essex trials) a log fire. A blanket was usually available in case of further warmth being necessary. Some receivers may have felt the cold more because of a lack of physical activity whilst immobile in the ganzfeld trial and this relaxed immobility could easily account for the feelings of heaviness described. Of the remaining sensations, some may be said to be similar in nature, e.g. flying, lightness and swaying, but the numbers are not sufficient to be useful even when they were used in the receivers' judgements.

There were very few olfactory sensations mentioned: Three mentioned 'flowers' or 'perfume' and two spoke of 'candles' or 'incense'. There is a possibility that one reference to perfume was caused by the helper wearing strong perfume and one mention of candles could have been caused by candles being in evidence in the room. The mention of 'flowers' may have been brought about by their presence outside the building but as each occurs only very infrequently there are insufficient data to warrant further analysis.

The trials led to the expression of many different emotions by the receivers which may have already arisen prior to the experiment, have been caused by the experimental situation or have been conveyed via the sender. These include only those emotions named and not those that might be inferred from the images expressed. Some of these could also appear to be tactile sensations, e.g. spinning and stillness, but they have been interpreted in the context of the receivers' full statements.

The highest numbers of emotions expressed were 'happy' (eight) and 'relaxed' (seven). 'Peaceful' and 'unrelaxed' were mentioned five times and 'alone', 'calm', 'sadness', and 'tense' four times respectively. There were three statements each of 'anger', 'apprehension', 'laughter', 'feeling nervous', and 'tranquil'. As can be seen, quite a wide range of emotions were felt by the receivers and there is a fairly even distribution of happy, peaceful and relaxed feelings and tense, stressed sensations. If one selects only those emotions expressed by the receivers who scored direct hits, supported by the blind judgements, there is similar variety. However, it may be stated that out of ten examples, on three occasions feelings of speed and movement through space were felt and a sinister mood prevailed on four others. Each time the mood of the music was appropriate to this.

The one hundred trials did not produce a significant hit rate overall but nevertheless a number of potentially interesting observations can be made when analysing the personal characteristics of the participants and their relationship to the results of the trials. Statistical analysis did not produce significant results but some z scores were calculated to clarify certain findings of possible further interest. In calculating the standard deviation used in the z scores, N rather than $N-1$ has been used since the results apply only to the population of the individuals taking part in the experiment.

Statistical analysis was not applied to data where the numbers involved were too small. For instance, the times and places of the trials; the months of the year when they took place; and the ages of the receivers. Their degree of extra-introversion was similarly discarded since it relied on the experimenter's informal observations.

The following details the roles taken in the trials by females and males respectively and the relative numbers of hits achieved.

Sex	Role In Experiment	No. of different individuals	% of 1 or more hits scored
Female	Receiver	43	24.00%
Male	Receiver	33	16.00%
Female	Sender	45	24.00%
Male	Sender	24	38.00%

These results indicate that women were more likely to score hits in the role of receiver than men were. However, men achieved a higher hit rate when participating as senders. It might be argued that these tendencies reflect what some consider to be traditional roles within human society where the male adopts a more assertive manner than the female, but this would be a subjective generalisation. Information regarding the sex of participants was then scrutinised from the point of view of the pairs of receivers and senders. In cases where there was more than one sender there was always at least one of each sex.

Receiver	Sender/s	% of 1 or more hits scored
Female	Female	24% (z = + 0.18)
Male	Male	13% (z = -0.73)
Female	Male	26% (z = +0.34)
Male	Female	35% (z = +1.09)
Female	Both male & female	33% (z = +0.92)
Male	Both male & female	0% (z = -1.81)

The greatest number of positive results were achieved when males and females participated together but the z scores were not significant. The male/female figures' apparent swapping was caused by one pair scoring particularly in a reversed capacity. Whilst women seem to have still managed to communicate, though less successfully with their own sex, men displayed little ability in this direction. Dalton (1994) has argued that men may be unwilling to disclose their imagery when partnered with another man and it is further possible that they may even block communication in some way, especially if intimate imagery is produced. On both occasions when men were paired and hits were scored, they were close personal friends with shared interests and similar backgrounds. When the men were strangers, the results were all misses. Women were similar in this respect but not to such a marked degree. Recent ganzfeld trials (ibid.) using visual targets also produced a similar correlation between the sexes, with pairs of men scoring the lowest.

There is generally believed to be a tradition of psi ability in women. It has often been stated that child rearing and changes at the time of puberty seem to allow women access to insights that men are apparently denied. Greater numbers of women than men have been reported as involved in witchcraft and as the focus of poltergeist activity. The latter has been linked to heightened emotional states and incidents often involve pubescent girls (Picknett, 1990; McBeath, 1985). Female 'intuition' is colloquially understood to signify access to knowledge apparently beyond the normal senses. Philosophically, intuition is defined as the ability of the mind to see concealed truths and perhaps the present research indicates some evidence of its existence in females as a possible aspect of ESP.

Eighty different partnerships were used during the ganzfeld sessions. These broke down into the categories in the following table. Where partnerships scored more than one hit only one was taken into account reported in the column headed 'hit rate'. The multiple hit rate column shows the corresponding percentages if all the hits for each pairing are taken into account.

Relationship	No. of Trials	No. of Hits	Hit Rate	Multiple Hit Rate
Family / Living together	16	3	19.00%	30.00%
Friends	28	7	25.00%	46.00%
Acquaintances	22	2	9.00%	13.00%
Strangers	14	2	14.00%	13.00%

This indicates that family pairings and especially friendships could be viewed as a strong factor in ESP enhancement where extra sensory communication may be important. This may be due to the fact that in a non-psychical scenario such pairings are more accustomed to communication with each other.

The professions of the receivers reflected the variety of their backgrounds and included teachers, students, administrative workers and self-styled housewives.

Teachers scored higher than other professions although administrative officers also gained positive results. It could be argued that the authoritative roles quite often required in these professions may have an effect on psi ability and may also relate to a tendency for extraversion which was previously noted. These professions also benefit from quite a high degree of interpersonal skills and self-esteem which could be conducive to success in experiments involving communication whether telepathic or not.

The receivers' hobbies included music, the 'paranormal', book-reading and sport. Often more than one was indicated. The book readers and those interested in the paranormal scored higher than the others. There may have been further confusion concerning music being specified as a hobby since this might be categorised further into playing/ singing in addition to only listening to music. Furthermore, professional musicians may not have listed music as a hobby having already quoted it as their job. Most participants claimed to enjoy a wide range of music. Fifty-six different receivers claimed previous paranormal experience, of whom twenty-one per cent achieved hits.

Twenty different people claimed no previous paranormal experience of which twenty per cent achieved hits as receivers. From this group of different people, seventy-four per cent claimed previous paranormal experience. It could be inferred that this high percentage could be expected because, as a result of self-selection for the experiments, people already interested/experienced in the paranormal would have responded favourably to the invitation to participate. However, it must not be forgotten that many of the participants became involved via a musical connection rather than an interest in the paranormal (forty-one per cent).

People were keen to achieve hits and disappointment was often expressed when misses were forthcoming. One lady who informed the experimenter at the start of the session that she was a medium and very psychic, having scored a miss, accused the experimenter and sender of having been listening to the wrong piece! A gentleman of a very sceptical nature having been a sender on a hit trial and having helped on another hit session exclaimed that his credibility as a sceptic was being lost ...to his chagrin!

I wanted to see whether a falling-off effect had occurred in this experiment.

In purely numerical terms, taking the trials in groups of ten the hit rate was as follows:

Trials	z scores	Percentage
1-10	1.92	50.00%
11-20	-1.03	10.00%
21-30	0.44	30.00%
31-40	0.44	30.00%
41-50	1.18	40.00%
51-60	0.44	30.00%
61-70	-1.03	10.00%
71-80	-1.03	10.00%
81-90	-0.29	20.00%
91-100	-1.03	20.00%

It is very clear from these results that from the first fifty trials a hit rate of thirty-two per cent was achieved (chance of twenty-five per cent) whilst the last fifty trials scored only sixteen per cent. This, rather than the particular months in which the trials took place, would seem to be the important factor, though none of the z scores reached significance. It perhaps indicates that after the initial novelty of undertaking ganzfeld trials a considerable lessening of enthusiasm may be reflected in the results. The experimenter tried not to convey this feeling but psychically it may have been sensed and receivers and senders returning for second or third trials often scored misses. The actual scores given by receivers to their first choice of music were scrutinised to see if there was any difference between the pattern of scores given to the four choices when the receiver achieved a hit or miss respectively. The majority of hits were obtained with targets which subjects had rated between ninety-one and one hundred on the scoring system. It would seem to indicate that subjects who correctly identified the music were more convinced of its identity than persons who chose incorrectly. This could have been because they received information telepathically. The results were analysed using a t test but although the difference was suggestive it failed to reach significance (two-tailed t test; $t = 1.827$, $df = 98$).

In each of the trials conducted there was a possibility of any one of four pieces of music lettered a, b, c or d being the target piece once the tape had been randomly selected, the letters corresponding to categories containing similar types of music:

- In 100 trials track a randomly appeared 25 times.
  It was chosen by the receiver 35 times and produced 10 hits (29%).

- In 100 trials track b randomly appeared 27 times.
  It was chosen by the receiver 25 times and produced 5 hits (20%).

- In 100 trials track c randomly appeared 28 times.

  It was chosen by the receiver 15 times and produced 3 hits (20%).

- In 100 trials track d randomly appeared 20 times.
  It was chosen by the receiver 25 times and produced 6 hits (24%).

A number of conclusions can be drawn from these results. Firstly, the comparatively even number of appearances of each group indicates that the randomisation procedure was successful. Secondly, the fact that the track *a* music was the target in a higher number of hits than the other tracks might suggest that it could be more conducive to telepathic communication but it is possible that the track *a* music was more popular with receivers regardless of any telepathic connection, especially with receivers who found it difficult not to let personal preferences influence their choice. The Romantic content (in musical terms) of many of the track *a* pieces and its relative familiarity to a group of subjects with classical music knowledge certainly encouraged the sender to think in visual terms more easily, e.g. *Swan Lake*, '1812' Overture, *Ride of the Valkyries, Mars,* etc. It was discussed earlier that certain moods and pastoral images tended to recur frequently in the receivers' transcripts and it may not be totally coincidental that music reflecting similar moods would be more likely to appear as track *a*. Furthermore, track *a* was inevitably the first track listened to. Rotation of the types of music in future trials is strongly recommended since it would ensure that track *a* was not being chosen simply because it appeared as the first on the list.

Track *c* was chosen considerably less often and tended to be of a more abstract nature which could mean that it did not attune readily with the mood of sender or receiver and was considerably more difficult to convey. Some of the lowest scores and greatest numbers of misses were achieved when the *c* track was the target piece. The choice of tracks *b* and *d* were in line with chance expectations.

Within the twenty-four trials where hits were scored, a range of choices were made across four categories, *a, b, c* and *d,* but despite track *a* being by far the most frequently selected, the *z* score failed to reach significance.

- Track *a* was chosen 10 times as the successful hit music ($z = 1.57$)   42%.
- Track *b* was chosen 5 times as the successful hit music ($z = -0.39$)   21%.
- Track *c* was chosen 3 times as the successful hit music ($z = -1.17$)   13%.
- Track *d* was chosen 6 times as the successful hit music ($z = 0.00$)   25%.

Possible reasons for the selection of at least some of the *a* tracks have been discussed in the previous section as have explanations for the lack of *c* tracks chosen. The *b* and *d* tracks chosen seem to lead to no particular conclusion regarding reasons for their selection and the number of times they were chosen accords with chance. The two tracks that were chosen more often (four times each) than the other pieces were the 'Pastoral' Symphony by Beethoven and Shostakovich's Fifth Symphony. Beethoven's symphony is a rather obvious choice bearing in mind the white noise/waterfall connections but the popularity of the Shostakovich is less accountable except perhaps for its obviously dramatic nature compared to the other items in its package. ('Kyrie eleison' from Byrd's Mass for 5 voices; the opening of Tippett's Piano sonata no. 2.; *Kontakte 2* by Stockhausen.)

The most successful piece of music in terms of receiver hits was the *Ode to St Cecilia* by Britten since it only appeared in the target pool twice and was chosen as a hit on both occasions. The *Night on a bare mountain* by Mussorgsky was also chosen correctly twice but was a miss on a third occasion. Both pieces prompted strong visual imagery, but this was also true of several other pieces that were not selected.

Two tracks scored particularly few hits: The Lute suite in E minor by J. S. Bach scored misses on each of the six times it appeared and *Lux aeterna* by Ligeti scored four misses. Senders had great difficulty with the abstract nature of the Bach item and with hindsight it was probably not a good choice for the target pool. The Ligeti item caused some confusion for senders since the ethereal quality of the music led some senders towards 'ghostly' images, while others who were aware of its use in the film *2001 Space Odyssey* chose a more science fiction interpretation.

The experimenter (myself) was in the physical presence of the sender for ninety-two per cent of the trials and acted as the actual sender for the remaining eight per cent. It would therefore not seem unreasonable to expect some sort of influence to have been exerted by me. When I was acting as sole sender I achieved one hit and seven misses. When I was acting as sole sender, my relationship with the receivers varied. The single hit was with a close friend but on two subsequent visits misses were scored. A stranger, acquaintances and another close friend all fared no better. This might seem to suggest that the experimenter in other trials could again influence results towards negative outcomes. The evidence base here is small but there is other literature that documents the tendency of experimenters' expectations or personalities affecting results. (For instance, Roney Dougal, 1991.)

Prior to this research my participation in ganzfeld experiments was limited to acting as the receiver in two sessions using video clips as the targets at the University of Edinburgh. The first session was a hit and the second was a miss. The trials using music as the target under investigation were the first that I had undertaken in this capacity.

I started the sessions with an open mind about the possibility of telepathic communication using music in ganzfeld conditions. After the early high success rate, this attitude changed towards the positive but then altered as the results tended increasingly towards a chance outcome. It was hoped to minimise any possible experimenter effect but this is always difficult to achieve. The possible influence might be eliminated or at least diluted by undertaking two sets of experiments: One where the experimenter truly expected the subjects to score hits and another where the expected results were misses. A pilot study was undertaken to explore this by Parker in 1974 which produced a significant result that experimenter expectations influenced results (Parker, 1975).

One couple achieved above chance scores and I decided to investigate them more fully. Colin and Alison (husband and wife) participated in ganzfeld trials on six different occasions. Colin was the receiver for five of these trials and Alison once. Colin scored four out of five hits and Alison scored one out of one hits. During the trials that he undertook, Colin often wrote brief notes about his experiences which indicated that he 'felt' certain pieces of music were the right choice because of their overall mood and not because he could literally hear them. Trial 59 provides one such example. Colin wrote: "I felt a lot of restless movement and a feeling of nature in the raw." His correct choice of music being sent was tribal drum music played by the Burundi Drummers. These results could indicate that a high level of psi was generated between the partnership of Colin and Alison, though it remains only an isolated case and a greater number of trials would be needed to claim significance.

It was felt that a hundred trials constituted a reasonable number to allow the possible demonstration of ESP through the agent of music. The overall hit rate of twenty-four per cent where chance would have indicated twenty-five per cent is not statistically significant. However, during the course of the trials and further scrutiny, some data would seem to indicate favourable conditions for ESP in a musical context.

From the results achieved no specific conclusion could be drawn as to the relative merits of the places of the trials but night-time seemed to be more conducive to psi than day-time. The latter third of the year produced a high number of hits and the first few trials produced a seventy-one per cent hit rate! As the trials continued there was a marked deterioration in hits scored which may have been caused by a lessening of interest on the part of the receivers and senders, particularly those who participated in several trials, or by an unintentional sceptical effect being induced by the experimenter.

Receivers aged forty-one to sixty years scored higher than other age ranges, especially if they were teachers/lecturers or worked in administratively responsible careers. The preferred hobbies were books and an interest in the paranormal. Friends scored the greatest number of hits, particularly when females were receivers. Dramatic music that provided strong visual imagery and stirred the emotions produced a far better hit rate than purely intellectually stimulating music.

Overall, it would seem that randomly chosen music with a wide range of people does not lead to the demonstration of ESP. However, it would appear to be possible that some people with certain characteristics and presented with appropriate music might be able to make telepathic contact to a degree. (As previously stated, the results of a further experiment using selected participants who had been involved in the initial experiment and had achieved noteworthy scores can be found in Willin, 1999.)

It is recognised that the procedures used in my experiments may have been improved by adopting the following suggestions. Blind trials where a sender was not used were not undertaken because within the procedures used the experimenter would know which track was being played as he was responsible for playing and rewinding it. He therefore might have inadvertently acted as an unconscious sender. A method of overcoming this might be to create separate tapes each containing one of the four tracks played continuously. The auto-ganzfeld procedures used in laboratories such as the Parapsychology Unit at the University of Edinburgh avoid such problems.

Carrying out ganzfeld experiments and reporting the results are extremely time-consuming. Should further researchers wish to explore the use of music as a target pool in ESP experiments they should consider the following points:

The music used needs to be very contrasting in mood and style and it should also produce strong reactions from the receivers and senders. When the music is unknown to the participants it might be useful to provide information about it.

It would seem that what might be described as intellectually stimulating music should be avoided since this type of music achieved comparatively poor results in terms of hit rate. This may have been because an analytical frame of mind on the part of the sender could militate against an 'intuitive' psychic response. Some would claim that this is an inevitable characteristic of psychic experience.

The role of the helper might be explored further as to their possible influence on the proceedings and outcomes as their presence and/ or actions in some cases had a definite effect on the mood of the receiver.

It might also be advisable for the sender to hear a relaxation tape prior to attempting to send the target music and for him to maintain this state whilst the receiver is scoring the musical items. This would ensure that the sender was not distracting the receiver telepathically during the scoring period. Both receiver and sender might also be monitored by machines to measure their bodily responses during the trials to explore any changes that occurred without cognition. An alternative to white noise needs to be found. Too many people started from a water-based situation before moving into other domains in their meditations. Perhaps a continuous 'OM' chant as used in some Buddhist meditations might be more suitable despite it similarly producing fairly strong imagery.

Musical Mediumship

Mediums have existed throughout history in most societies, albeit under different names - shamans, witchdoctors, prophets, etc. Their roles have been similar in contacting the spirits to provide help to their believers but in the process they have brought upon themselves condemnation from the Church in some societies and ridicule from secular authorities. However, the modern Spiritualist movement is generally believed to have begun with the alleged spirit communications surrounding the Fox sisters in America in 1848. In the context of a considerable amount of other spiritualist activity that is documented as taking place at this time (see Gauld, 1968) one might ask why the general tenor of the period during which the Fox sisters were active was seemingly so conducive to a belief in spiritual matters. One possible explanation could have been the forbidding of the teaching of religion in American public schools that may have contributed to the emergence of many sects and self-announced prophets. New York State was a focus for this type of activity in the mid nineteenth century, producing Adventism and the first Shaker settlements of the early 1800s, Joseph Smith, the founder of the Mormons in 1827, and Mary Baker Eddy, the founder of the Christian Scientists, in 1892. The blurring of the boundaries between life and death, and fact and fiction were enthusiastically received by readers of the works of Edgar Allan Poe in the 1840s and 1850s. The period also produced faith healers and clairvoyants such as Andrew Jackson Davis - the 'Poughkeepsie Seer' - who after having been mesmerised in 1843 decided he was a clairvoyant and started to have mystic dreams. New religions of the time required more than just evidence of strange physical phenomena to convey the reality and significance of spirit contact, and in time more complex theological and philosophical dogmas were incorporated in, for instance, Madame Blavatsky's Theosophical Society founded in 1881.

Within Spiritualist circles, the format for spirit communication remained constant and often made use of an entity referred to as a spirit guide for contact between the living and the dead. There were similarities with the Shaker movement, many of whom became Spiritualists, who often danced and sang in communication with native Indians and indulged in glossolalia (speaking in tongues). Men and women claimed direct access to their own personal spirits and even physical proof to accompany their beliefs via raps, manifestations and other phenomena. The mediums tended to be categorised in two ways - mental and physical. The former either used clairvoyant powers or went into trance under the control of the spirits. In this altered state they might speak, paint, write or play/compose music at the spirit's direction. The latter produced physical manifestations often by use of a supposed 'spirit substance', later known as 'ectoplasm'. The conversion of spirit into physical matter allowed rappings and the movement of physically present objects, including musical instruments. A comprehensive list of most séance phenomena both past and present was published in the January 1874 issue of the *Quarterly Journal of Science*. It included:

- Movement of heavy bodies with contact, but without mechanical exertion.
- Percussive and other allied sounds.
- Rising of tables and chairs off the ground, without contact with any person.
- Levitation of human beings.
- Movement of various small articles without contact with any person.
- Appearances of hands, either self-luminous or visible by ordinary light.
- Direct writing.
- Phantom forms and faces.
- Special instances which seem to point to the agency of an exterior intelligence.

(cited in Brandon, 1984, p.82)

The spirit rappings of the Fox sisters were expanded by others and subsequently connected with the mesmeric movement which, one might say in accordance with the rationale of the times, postulated a 'scientific' theory for its findings in the form of the quasi-electrical fluid referred to as 'animal magnetism'. It was supposed by some Spiritualists to be instrumental in producing raps, table tilting, etc., and to be the means by which spirits controlled the medium's physical actions. This can be paralleled to the idea that fluid was transmitted by a mesmerist to a patient, who then came under the will of the operator and in more general terms it can be thought of as the intermediary between mind/will and nervous system. Music played a part in these proceedings as an accompaniment to the treatments.

Music plays a role in many aspects of life and in most religions. The singing of popular songs and well-known hymns has long been thought conducive to binding a group of people together and, in the case of Spiritualism, to encourage the communication of spirits. Sceptics could argue that in the dark conditions, which often provide the context for a séance, the singing might be used to obliterate the sounds of mediums' confederates entering a room or trap doors opening, etc., to allow the perpetration of fraudulent activities. Musical instruments have quite often been used to prove the alleged presence of spirits. Examples include the sound of shaking tambourines or the ringing of bells without physical contact. The Davenport brothers - Ira and William - became widely known in Spiritual circles for their staging of feats involving musical instruments.

> "The musical instruments were placed near them on a table, and the sitters joined hands. The moment the light was extinguished, the instruments while playing, flew about the room, circling near the ceiling and floor and close to the sitters, who were touched by them and felt the strong currents of wind they made, for they moved with great velocity...After a minute or so the light was turned up, when the mediums were found bound as before, and the musical instruments on the sitters' knees."

> (Campbell Holms, 1925, p.331)

A number of companies around the turn of the century (such as Sylvestre's in Chicago, Gamage's and Hamley Brothers) issued catalogues and lists of trick instruments and other devices for sale (Sylvestre, 1901). These included a trick guitar that served a double purpose - a false panel allowed access to the inside where masks and muslin for drapes could be stowed for the purposes of fraudulent spirit manifestations. Further to this the attachment of a one-tune spring music box would allow the instrument to play by itself when activated (Dingwall and Price, 1922).

Some mediums have played instruments without direct access to them or have produced them as apports allegedly from the spirit world. Outstanding musical feats have been achieved using instruments on which mediums have claimed to have little technical ability. Other mediums have spoken of direct contact with the spirits of departed composers and performers. They have played their music, written it down under dictation from these discarnates and provided information about composers and their works conveyed from an allegedly spiritual source. Musical practices have varied in their importance amongst mediums. For some it has been very much a minor aspect of their mediumship but for others it has been the most important focus of their powers.

One of the most famous mediums of the nineteenth century to be producing allegedly spiritual music phenomena was D. D. Home. One of his best-documented activities was his playing of an accordion in conditions that were apparently foolproof against conjuring skills. In addition to this, music was said to be heard from unknown sources in his presence (Shepard, 1984). A report by Sir William Crookes spoke of a large, well-lit room with a new accordion, bought by him personally to allay suspicions of trickery, enclosed in a wire cage. Home allegedly caused the instrument to play by itself:

> "...it (the accordion) was held suspended in the cage by one of Home's hands extended over and resting upon the upper wire of the cage. This was under the table, but in such a position that the company could witness all the proceedings; Professor Crookes' assistant being permitted even to go under the table and give an accurate report of what was going on. In this position there was first the regular accordion movements and sounds with the instrument suspended from Home's hand; then it was taken out and put in the hand of the next sitter, still continuing

to play; and finally, after being returned to the cage it was clearly seen by the company generally, moving about with no one touching it."

(cited in Britten, 1883, p.147)

Spirit music was reported on the eve of Easter 1867 when, in front of several witnesses, Home produced:

> "...sweet, soft, simple music, like a lullaby, for a few minutes, then it became intensely sad for some time, and then we distinctly heard through the music the regular tramp of a body of men marching...it was followed by the most triumphal music we any of us had ever heard...The accordion was carried round the circle, played on Mr Hall's head (a sitter) then played in the air round the circle, Mr Home's hand not being near the instrument, 'The Last Rose of Summer' and several other airs."

(Britten, 1883, pp.143-144)

'Home Sweet Home', another of Home's favourite songs, was performed on the piano by a little-known medium, Miss Catherine Mettler in a séance where the spirit of Mozart was said to have been present (Britten, 1870). From a sceptical viewpoint it could be argued that the relative melodic and rhythmic simplicity of these songs would allow their performance by any amateur musician and perhaps the Sylvestre Company had produced self-playing instruments which performed these very pieces.

However, Home's musical demonstrations were not limited to phenomena involving accordions. In a New York Conference, held for the distinguished Judge Edmunds, a guitar played by itself in Home's presence. According to the report:

> "...A guitar in the corner of the room was seen to move. Daniel placed it on the table before them. In this position, the conference report said, the guitar was played upon repeatedly. No hands were seen near it. The report continued: There was no chance for trick. The room was sufficiently lighted for all to see the exact position of every person and thing in the room. The writer went on to say

that the playing was adequate but not the highest grade of the art."

(cited in Edmunds, 1978, p.46)

Home's acquaintances amongst the nobility were common knowledge and a few peers put into print their experiences with him. Lord Adare published his *Experiences in Spiritualism with Mr D. D. Home* in 1870 and 1924. He wrote of an event in Northwood, London:

> "We had not been in bed more than three minutes, when both Home and myself simultaneously heard the music: it sounded like a harmonium; sometimes, as if played loudly at a great distance, as if very gently, close by."

(cited in Shepard, 1984, p.915)

Apart from the possibility of trick instruments being used, which was virtually impossible in some of the séances mentioned, various explanations have been proposed as to how Home could have achieved these demonstrations. James Randi has suggested the use of a small harmonica concealed in the mouth (Randi, 1995, p.159). However, it is unlikely that Home's moustache could have concealed such an instrument when brought to the lips for blowing. Randi claims that a collection of such instruments were found among Home's belongings when he died (Randi, 1995) but he has not been able to substantiate this statement. Further explanations include 'skilful suggestions' (Brandon, 1984, pp.268-269) but it stretches credibility to believe that Home could induce an audio hallucination in every person that encountered his performance. It was even suggested, by some sceptics, that he was using his feet to play the instrument (Metternich, 1921) but it must be remembered that the instrument was sometimes contained within a wire cage and that reports also describe deliberate restrictions to Home's movements. The controversy concerning the origin of Home's gifts as spiritual or feats of conjuring continues unabated (see *JSPR*, Volume 61, no. 843, April 1996. Correspondence) and in the absence of more definite evidence of fraud, a spiritual source must remain a possibility.

Miss Catherine Mettle, the sixteen-year-old daughter of a Hartford, Connecticut doctor, perhaps deserves a further mention since she claimed that the spirits of Mozart, Beethoven, Weber and others "compelled her to commence the most astonishing improvisation, evidencing an extraordinary mastery over the instrument and a thorough knowledge of the science of harmony" (Britten, 1870, p.203). This was despite having only taken a few lessons on the piano and having little musical interest or talent. However, she was not subjected to laboratory testing as was the case with the French musical medium George Aubert. During his teenage years he was allegedly called by the spirits to play the piano and to everyone's astonishment he "executed a long piece so scientifically that we saw plainly that he was 'possessed'" (*Annals of Psychic Science*, Volume 3, 1906, p.130). The spirit composer gave his name as Mehul. Aubert claimed to have only a very basic ability on the piano when not entranced but despite this he later played works supposedly dictated by Chopin, Schumann, Rubinstein, Mozart, Glinka, Liszt, Schubert, and especially Beethoven and Mendelssohn. He further claimed no real interest in music and readily agreed to experiments being conducted on him at the Institut General Psychologique:

"Two experiments have been tried with M. George Aubert at the Institut General Psychologique: the first consisted in bandaging his eyes and introducing into his right ear the tube of a phonograph which played the March from Verdi's 'Aida', and into his left ear the tube of a second phonograph which performed the 'Marche Indienne' by Sellenick. In spite of this cacophony, wounding to the ears of a musician, the medium rendered in a faultless manner a sonata inspired by Mozart. The second experiment was not less conclusive. M. Aubert's eyes were free, but he had to fix them on a philosophical work placed on the music desk of the piano and to read aloud, slowly and very attentively, a whole page of this book, while his hands were quite unconsciously playing a delicious melody.

Lastly, to prove the insensibility of his hands, M. Yourievitch informed M. Aubert that he would prick his right hand while he was playing; and in the midst of a brilliant piece he thrust a needle into the left hand without causing M. Aubert to wink or to slacken by a comma the tempo of the symphony which he finished up with a masterly chord."

(*Annals of Psychic Science* Volume 3. 1906, p.131)

There was no evidence of autism, a condition that can give rise to the extraordinary skills of so-called 'savants'. Therefore comparison with the feats of such people as Pepito Ariola (a three-year-old Spanish child whose musical abilities were presented by Charles Richet at the International Psychological Congress on August 21st 1900) or Blind Tom (a five-year-old South Georgian child who could play two tunes at the same time with different hands and sing simultaneously in different keys) is not felt to be appropriate (Shepard, 1984).

Other musical mediums have provided clear documentary evidence of their own experiences. Emma Hardinge Britten (1823-1899) wrote several books about her experiences. She trained in Paris for an operatic career but extreme bouts of somnambulism affected her training adversely. Emma turned to the piano after Pierre Erard, the founder of the French piano-making firm, loaned her a piano on the condition that she practised at his warehouse to attract prospective buyers. Her mother terminated this arrangement since she was frightened by Emma's ability to predict telepathically which music would be requested. The daughter therefore returned to England and became an actress. It was in New York that she became involved with the Spiritual movement and befriended Leah Underhill (the sister of Margaret and Kate Fox). She formed a choir but her involvement with Spiritualism became deeper: "At times the piano on which my choir rehearsed to my playing was lifted bodily up in the air, obliging me to request the good invisibles to let us proceed with our practice." (Britten, 1900, p.53). She wrote a cantata called *The Song of the Stars* for her choir while she was in an inspired state and it was performed at the Academy Hall, New York, on April 24th 1857 to press acclaim (Britten, 1900, p.67). Although there were other occasions when musical manifestations such as voices and drums occurred while she played the piano it was through her talks and writings about Spiritualism and music that her influence was mainly disseminated.

Jesse Shepard (1849-1927) was believed to be the finest musical medium of the late nineteenth century and early twentieth century. His full name was Benjamin Henry Jesse Francis Grierson Shepard and though born of Scottish / Irish descent he was taken to the USA at a very early age and grew up there. He started to play the piano at the age of twelve and little else is known of his early childhood. In 1869 whilst attending the theatre in St Louis, a spirit called 'Rachel' came to him with advice to develop his singing. He visited a music professor who was astonished at the power of his voice but he warned that it was "too wonderful to be permanent" (Shepard, 1870). The professor, whose name is not known, arranged for him to sing an 'Ave Maria' and an ode to St Felicia by Haydn in St Xavier's Church after only two weeks of tuition. All present were amazed including his sister. At the age of twenty-one he made his way to Paris earning his living by demonstrating various psychic skills but in particular by displaying musical gifts. After consulting various French authorities including Wertel, the Director of the Paris Conservatoire, Shepard renounced the idea of tuition and started to become well known as a musical medium (Wisniewski, 1894). Despite some initial scepticism as to his own powers, he travelled to London, St Petersburg, Berlin and even Australia to give performances. He was invited by nobility to perform for them and his patrons included the Queens of Denmark and Hanover, Prince Phillip of Bourbon and Braganza, Princess Marie of Hanover and many others (Wisniewski, 1894). One of his greatest artistic achievements was to sing in the basilica of the Sacre Coeur at Montmartre in Paris in May 1889 at the clergy's request.

Shepard possessed many gifts. He was said to be able to give addresses in trance in English, French, German, Latin, Greek, Chaldean and Arabic and during a sèance at the Hague, Holland in 1907 it was reported that direct voices were heard speaking through him in Dutch, Sundanese (a Javanese dialect) and Mandarin Chinese (Shepard, 1984). However, it was in musical matters where he truly excelled, claiming to be possessed by the spirits of Mozart, Beethoven, Meyerbeer, Rossini, Sontag, Persiani, Malibran, Lablache, Liszt, Berlioz and Chopin. It was alleged that he played the piano and organ with the piano lid closed sometimes and that he could sing through the whole range from bass to soprano. A report documenting his piano playing at a séance in Paris on September 3rd 1893 was written by Prince Adam Wisniewski:

> "After having secured the most complete obscurity we placed ourselves in a circle around the medium, seated before the piano. Hardly were the first chords struck

when we saw lights appearing at every corner of the room...The first piece played through Shepard was a fantasia of Thalberg's on the air from 'Semiramide'. This is unpublished, as is all of the music which is played by the spirits through Shepard. The second was a Rhapsody for four hands, played by Liszt and Thalberg with astounding fire, a sonority truly grand, and a masterly interpretation. Notwithstanding this extraordinarily complex technique, the harmony was admirable, and such as no one present had ever known paralleled, even by Liszt himself, whom I personally knew, and in whom passion and delicacy were united. In the circle were musicians who, like me, had heard the greatest pianists in Europe; but we can say that we never heard such truly super-natural executions."

(Wisniewski, 1894, p.86)

Professor J. Niclassen, the organist and music critic of the *Fremdenblatt* of Hamburg, spoke of his singing and playing in darkness:

"Soft, mysterious, spherelike tones, coming and going, fall on our ear...tone-pictures full of poetic charm. Most remarkable is the unfailing surety of touch, in spite of the darkness, especially in octave and wide jumps. Between short pauses, four or five selections followed one another, all completely different in character, giving the widest play to the imagination of the listeners. Suddenly one hears a basso of colossal register, the singer at the same time playing an accompaniment that makes the grand piano quiver; as, of old, the trumpet sounded before the gates of Jericho, so thundered certain passages of the piano music, while the mighty basso penetrated to bone and marrow...the accompaniment becomes more subdued, and to a melodious theme rises a soprano voice of sympathetic quality, which to about the second 'G' has a youthful boyish character, but in the highest notes it becomes a decided soprano. A duet is now carried on alternately between a powerful basso and a beautiful soprano, which decidedly belongs to the most extraordinary manifestations in the realm of music."

(cited in Campbell Holms, 1925, p.239)

Professor M. Bernardin Rahn, a distinguished music theorist, also spoke highly of Shepard's music but he [Shepard] was not without his critics. In 1875 Madame Blavatsky wrote an article condemning him as a fraud after he made some derogatory remarks about Russia in the *Religio-Philosophical Journal*. She did not mention his musical attributes and one can only speculate that she either felt that they were beyond criticism or that she was not in a position to comment (Blavatsky, 1875).

Most of his performances were to private audiences and it was said of his music that it was "not intended to amuse the masses or to beguile the leisure hours of the superficial" but rather to "uplift and to inspire those (who) are ready to listen" (Wisniewski, 1894). In 1907 after his great successes and further visits to the USA, he settled in London, changing his name to Francis Grierson, and discontinued his musical medium exhibitions, devoting himself to writing essays and books on philosophy and mysticism. He died in total poverty (Shepard, 1984).

Mediums have received a wide variety of different types of information from composers and performers. For instance, the medium Mrs Leonora Piper, to whom the psychologist William James referred as his "one white crow", i.e. the exception to the rule (cited in Smyth and Stemman, 1981), claimed J. S. Bach to be one of her spirit guides. Another nineteenth-century medium, William Stainton Moses, who received spirit messages through automatic writing, was given one such script from Mendelssohn, complete with an 'authentic' signature (ibid.). In a number of cases more substantial literature is available detailing alleged communications of a musical nature from the dead.

Florizel von Reuter was born in the USA but moved to Europe at the age of seven and having started violin lessons at the age of three, passed his diploma at nine years of age and began touring as a child prodigy. It is claimed (von Reuter, 1928, p.7) that he wrote three operas and orchestral music and that he was nicknamed 'Paganini redivivus' because of his exceptional talent on the violin. Up to the age of thirty he was not interested in psychic matters until, whilst attending a séance at a friend's instigation, the spirit of Paganini manifested itself to him and later made physical contact by directing his violin bow. Through a different medium the spirit of Sarasate, the famous Spanish violinist and composer, made contact and von Reuter's mother also started to receive messages. Further European tours did not allow time to study psychic matters but in Germany he purchased a type of ouija board, similar to a planchette - a mechanical device used for the alleged contacting of spirits - which was referred to as an 'Additor'. Von Reuter's mother found very many messages were spelt out through it in a number of different languages, some of which either she didn't know or in which she was not fluent. For reasons unknown, the messages were often inverted with the words spelt out backwards and Mrs Reuter would have her eyes bound to avoid accusations of fraud or unconsciously choosing letters to clarify statements made. The main communicator at these séances was Paganini. However, spirits of less well known musicians also made contact, including Professor Heinrich Barth of the Berlin High School of Music, who gave details of his life which von Reuter later found to be true. His other spirit contacts included Tartini, Locatelli, the Polish violinist K. Lipinski, the French violinist F. Baillot, Charles de Beriot, H. Vieuxtemps, Joachim, Herold, Lalo, Reger, Korsakov and Grieg. The seventeenth century Italian composer A. Stradella communicated a dubious poem:

"Music is the soul of the world.
Music is joy.
Jazz is the voice of the Devil on earth.
Music is the speech of God,
The voice of nature,
Pure as mountain snow..."

(von Reuter, 1928, p.92)

Aphorisms flowed from Zola and even Dickens was said to have communicated.

Hans von Bulow, the famous conductor, when asked about his opinion of Schoenberg's music replied "He deserves what he occasionally gets", a possible allusion to when his music was hissed at in a Berlin concert. Bulow was more kindly towards Reger whom he referred to as being "holy" and to Bach whom he described as "God" (von Reuter, 1931, pp.155-6).

Infuriatingly, the spirits mainly passed on philosophical statements and abstract comments about the afterlife, which could not be verified.

However, on a few occasions more substantial contact was provided by Paganini. It is alleged that he gave von Reuter advice on how to finger his composition *La Campanella*:

> "Suddenly, without any premeditation, while playing a difficult passage my fingers seemed to be impelled to abandon suddenly the fingering I had used for years, the substitution of a perfectly different fingering taking place as naturally as if it had been a simple passage instead of a very complicated one...in the course of the ensuing hour I received at least a dozen new ideas in nuancing, fingering, and bowing, the effect being as though the suggestions were given me through telepathy, or that my bow and fingers were being controlled by another Intelligence than my own."

(von Reuter, 1928, pp.76-77)

The interpretation of *I Palpiti* (Paganini) was conveyed to von Reuter's mother as he played the violin and Paganini also suggested that von Reuter should learn his *Variations on God Save the Queen* since it would benefit him technically. He gave autobiographical details about himself that von Reuter claimed to have not read before:

> "I was lonely. Always I searched continually for true affection. I never found it. Lies have been told about me. I was not a miser. I always gave much money to the poor and to the badly treated children, but always secretly. It was a caprice of mine to hoodwink the public..."

(von Reuter, 1928, pp.150-1)

It could be argued that a musician of von Reuter's calibre might well believe himself to be guided by violinists of Paganini's fame, but such guidance could take the form of conscious or unconscious influence rather than psychical contact from the spirit world. He also did not request information that would have been entirely outside his own knowledge even if apparently forgotten, such as the whereabouts of lost works or hidden documents pertaining to the lives of his spirit communicators.

Now let us turn to the Yorkshire vicar Charles Tweedale. Contact was allegedly made with him by the great violin maker Stradivarius via the planchette. Tweedale's life ambition since the age of nineteen had been to find the substances used to make the varnish Stradivarius applied to his violins. Tweedale had been told by a medium that the spirit of an old Italian man was with him and the planchette revealed the name Stradivarius. A photographic session revealed ghostly images on the prints and spirit music was heard at Weston Vicarage where Tweedale lived with his wife and family who were also aware of Stradivarius' presence (Tweedale, 1940). Similarly to von Reuter's communications, much of what was provided took the form of non-verifiable philosophical discourses. A poem of extremely dubious merit was reported to have come from Stradivarius:

"Mendelssohn beams all over his face
And say we all, 'Who can take his place?'
Chopin walks around with glee
For he sees some fun in me.
Handel, dear soul, fills us all with awe,
We never heard such melodies before."

(Tweedale, 1940, p.83)

Stradivarius provided details of his life which it is unlikely that Tweedale would have known, even accepting that he would have read extensively about him. For instance, Stradivarius told him that he was born outside Cremona and not baptised there. Concerning his violins he said they were "practically as good in a month as ten years after" (Tweedale, 1940, p.101) and he spoke of their construction: "My slot is too long, hence the wedge inside the fiddle...Where you cut into the fiddle. You know a Strad by that cut, and hence the wedge" (Tweedale, 1940, p.205). Tweedale only once asked Stradivarius for help with the varnish and he declined to answer, saying that it would detract from the merit of Tweedale's discovery if he told him (Tweedale, 1940, p.309). However, the solution to the varnish's content suddenly came to him soon after and he labelled his instrument with the words: "The original varnish of Antonius Stradivarius has been applied."

Tweedale's wife seemed to warrant regular attention from Stradivarius and he spoke to her of his love of the colour violet and even signed his signature through her. She alleged that she was also visited whilst she slept at night by the spirit of A. Patti, the famous soprano, who caused her to sing in Italian beyond her normal capacity.

59

Stradivarius introduced the spirit of Chopin into the family circle in 1930 who seemed particularly attracted to Tweedale's daughter whose hands he would take over when she was playing the piano. Scripts written in trance and supposedly dictated by Stradivarius and Chopin showed markedly different styles according to which composer was communicating. Sceptics could argue that Tweedale's unconscious contained a wealth of information about Stradivarius and that his daughter's predilection for Chopin's music prompted his alleged appearance. Once again no tangible evidence was given that could not have been acquired through normal means and his violin is no longer traceable.

Another example was the case of Jelly d'Aranyi 1895-1966 who was born in Budapest, Hungary, and was the great niece of Joachim. She became known as a leading violinist of her day and in one source (Palmstierna, 1937) it is claimed that she received advice from the spirit world concerning her performance of Bach's Sonata in E minor which contradicted the David edition of the work which she was using. Concerning the tempo (I presume of the first movement) David indicated 'allegro', but this was changed by the spirit contact to "very slowly" and further details were given concerning how the tremolo should be played and the harmony. She was also told to look at Bach's original but she had not been able to find it in the past (Palmstierna, 1937). Jelly was therefore surprised when a colleague at the Royal College of Music (RCM) eventually provided her with a small volume of Bach's works built on Vivaldi's themes that contained the sonata where she had been informed it would be found. It is claimed that the work differed from the David edition in the ways of which the alleged spirit had spoken (Palmstierna, 1937). The music in question is a transcription for one violin of a passage from the first movement of Vivaldi's Concerto for 2 violins in D minor (Op.3 no.11) transposed up a tone. Changing the given tempo of *allegro* to 'very slowly' would not be appropriate to the style of the work. There is confusion concerning the exact identity of the work since modern editions (including the *Neue Bach Ausgabe*) do not make reference to a RCM source. On contacting the Royal College of Music to enquire about editions of the music which might confirm these claims, the archivist Oliver Davies informed me that the library copies they possessed had been stolen and that the whereabouts of Jelly's own library of music was unknown. However, he made further searches and came to the conclusion that she probably used the *Bach Gesellschaft* edition, band 43, dated 1894. He further mentioned that an earlier *Peters* edition of the work had been lost.

In March 1933 she was contacted by the spirit of Robert Schumann via a ouija board and informed that she should find and play a posthumous work for "violin and piano and probably in D major" (Palmstierna, 1937, p.351). Few people in London would have known of such a work but subsequently another message was given: "Tell Tovey. Museum Weimar" (Palmstierna, 1937). It was alleged that Tovey knew of the concerto but did not know where to find it. On another occasion the spirit of Joachim suggested the manuscript might be in the Hochschule Museum in Berlin and he spoke of Schumann having shown him the work in Weimar. A friend of Jelly, Baron Palmstierna, the Swedish Minister in London, travelled to Berlin and eventually found the Violin Concerto in D minor - not D major as previously stated - in the archives of the Preussische Staatsbibliothek. He was told that Schumann's daughter had forbidden the publication of the work and that it was unfinished. A spirit communication contradicted the latter statement and enquiries were made about publication but the Preussische Staatsbibliothek declared it to be unobtainable for another twenty-two years. The spirits, however, were evidently very optimistic and gave further advice on how ultimately to acquire the music. The depositor of the concerto, Johannes Joachim (Joseph Joachim's son), wanted the concerto to remain unseen until the hundredth anniversary of Schumann's death, because his father had spoken of it in derogatory terms: "...it is not worthy to rank with his many magnificent creations...For it must be regretfully admitted that there are unmistakable signs of a certain weakness" (cited Gal, 1979, p.59). He eventually agreed to Jelly having a copy but forbade its public performance. Various scores were found which related to the lost concerto and these confirmed what Jelly had been told concerning the work's completion. Tovey was convinced of spiritual intervention in this matter and wrote to *The Times*: "I assert my positive conviction that the spirit of Schumann is inspiring Jelly d'Aranyi's production of Schumann's posthumous violin concerto" (cited in *Psychic News*, 5 April 1969). Jelly is not known to have ever referred to herself as a musical medium.

It would seem that to a considerable extent the same well-known musicians were alleged to have made contact - mainly Chopin,

Beethoven and Liszt with the piano playing mediums and Paganini and Stradivarius (as a maker) with the violinists. The sceptic could argue that the music and attributes of these famous people would be better known by the mediums and might therefore have entered their sub-conscious minds, whereas the Spiritualist might emphasise the lofty nature of these geniuses and stress their greater ability to make contact from the spirit realm. One rarely reads of obscure musicians influencing musical mediums and when this does occur, there is usually a personal connection involved.

Since the spirit-inspired music was not notated by these mediums, it is not possible to state which period of the composers' compositional style was being communicated and one therefore has to assume that the composers produced something that was typical of their work, as opposed to anything less characteristic. For example, the medium would be less likely to recognise communications in the style of very early works or those reflecting continuing changes in the composers' styles after death.

The majority of leading mediums within the Spiritualist movement are female but the most acclaimed musical mediums were male, as were all of the alleged spirit contacts. This is perhaps hardly surprising given the almost total exclusivity of men in professional music circles at the time. Women who claimed spirit contact via their piano playing, tended to mix in private 'society' circles rather than appearing on public tours. None of the musical mediums attributed their powers to God directly as they always spoke of the intermediary contact with spirits. The spirits seemed to provide long discourses on philosophy but very little of a factual nature, which is frustrating for those attempting to verify their statements.

If the hypothesis of self-deception is proposed, one must ask the question why these people believed spirit contact was the source of their ability and not just hard work. Various answers can be offered. For instance, an entrenched spiritual belief system might encourage a spiritually-based explanation for events rather than a more rational approach. Furthermore, in much the same way as non-musical mediums of all classes were able to mix in high society circles through their alleged mediumistic abilities, musical mediums received 'special' attention for their 'special' gifts. Fraud and gullibility were almost certainly factors in some situations even if motives were honourable. One wonders, for instance, how often in the Tweedale family the spirit messages via the planchette were given a little 'help' by a loving wife or daughter, even if unconsciously? It is further possible that a surge in musical excitement leading to increased capability may be thought of as spiritual contact.

In conclusion, the available evidence suggests that the alleged powers of the aforementioned mediums were probably derived from a number of different sources that can be explained via their conscious and sub-conscious minds. The hypothesis of spirit contact requires further evidence to support it. It is worth noting that the preceding mediums' musical prowess is not documented or acknowledged in the musical literature of their own era or that of the latter half of the twentieth century. With the exception of Jelly d' Aranyi, none of them is mentioned in the current edition of the *New Grove Dictionary of Music*. However, although not necessarily claiming spirit contact directly as the source of their inspiration, many well-known and respected composers have undergone psychic experiences which have brought them into contact with an external source which has been described as 'divine'.

Professional composers have had experiences and feelings which could have had paranormal origins but which might well have been explained as coincidences. Schumann, for example, wrote of a funereal passage that haunted him and in due course a letter arrived from his sister-in-law stating that her brother had died (cited Prince, 1963). Saint Saens believed he possessed precognitive powers when he foresaw future events concerning his own life (ibid.).

Perhaps of more interest are composers' and performers' thoughts on the source of their musical inspiration. In contrast to the musical mediums, several 'great' composers have reported their inspirations as coming directly from what they have called God. Brahms, for instance, stated: "Straight away the ideas flow in upon me, directly from God...measure by measure, the finished product is revealed to me when I am in those rare, inspired moods" (Brahms, cited in Klimo, 1987, p.314). Puccini spoke of *Madame Butterfly*: "The music of this opera was dictated to me by God; I was merely instrumental in putting it on paper and communicating it to the public" (Puccini, cited in Abell, 1955, p.117). Strauss believed his 'divine gift' to be a "mandate from God" (Strauss, cited in Abell, 1955, p.100).

When God has not actually been named then a suitable pseudonym has been used on other occasions. Puccini revealed: "It is a supernatural influence which qualifies me to receive Divine truths" (Puccini, cited in Abell, 1955, p.116) and Humperdinck quoted Wagner as saying "I am convinced that there are universal currents of Divine Thought vibrating the ether everywhere and that anyone who can feel those vibrations is inspired, provided he is conscious of the process and possesses the knowledge and skill to present them in a convincing manner, be he composer, architect, painter, sculptor, or inventor" (cited in Abell, 1955, p.137). Wagner introduced the necessity of craftsmanship to convey the 'Divine Thought' to the physical world. Strauss and Brahms also stressed this with "A good composer must also be a good craftsman" (Strauss, cited in Abell, 1955, p.84) and "My compositions are not the fruits of inspiration alone, but also of severe, laborious and painstaking toil" (Brahms, cited in Abell, 1955, p.59). On other occasions a 'semi-trance' state has been spoken of. For instance, Wagner believed himself to be lying at the bottom of the Rhine whereupon from his entranced imagination the opening music of *Das Rheingold* came to him (cited in Abell, 1955).

It has been claimed that the nearest states to entrancement are the hypnagogic and hypnopompic sleep states that tend to be more conducive to dreaming. Several composers have spoken of their musical experiences in relation to dreams. Bruch wrote: "My most beautiful melodies have come to me in dreams" (Bruch, cited in Abell, 1955, p.144) and Berlioz was reported to have spoken in similar terms: "I dreamed one night that I was composing a symphony and heard it in my dreams. On waking next morning I could recall nearly the whole of the movement..." (Berlioz, cited in Henson, 1977, pp.241-242). Possibly the most famous story about a dream conveying a piece of music concerns the composition of the *Devil's Trill* Sonata by the famous eighteenth-century violinist/composer Tartini. He was reputed in his dream to have made a Faustian pact with the Devil who played the violin to him:

> "How great was my astonishment when I heard him play with consummate skill a sonata of such exquisite beauty as surpassed the boldest flights of my imagination. I tried to retain the sounds I had heard. But it was in vain. The piece I then composed, however 'The Devil's Sonata' was the

best I ever wrote, but how far below the one I had heard in my dream."

(cited in Into the Unknown, 1971, p.224)

Tchaikovsky spoke of a lack of control when composing and said: "I forget everything and behave like a madman. Everything within me starts pulsating and quivering" (cited in Klimo, 1987, p.314). This could be explained as a heightened emotional state, extreme effort and concentration or spirit intervention. Mahler put the matter most succinctly when he claimed: "I don't choose what I compose: It chooses me" (ibid.) and in similar fashion Rudolf Friml, the operetta composer, described himself as not composing but being used (ibid.). In some examples a visual element has allegedly been projected from an unknown source into the mind of the composer. Gershwin stated that whilst riding on a train he suddenly heard and even "saw on paper the complete construction of the *Rhapsody* [in Blue] from beginning to end" (ibid.).

In order to explore what, if any, influence paranormal activity has on musicians in the present day a group of eleven renowned composers/ performers (ten British and one foreign) were contacted by letter in 1994. They were asked about any views they might hold on the subject of music and the paranormal. The selection was made on the basis of their previous writings, compositions or interviews, which led me to believe they may be favourably disposed towards the subject. Their responses were varied:

- David Bedford: Replied personally.
- Stephen Dodgson: Replied personally.
- David Fanshaw: Wife replied sending literature.
- Henryk Gorecki: Publishers replied with reprimand for not having contacted them!
- Jonathan Harvey: Replied personally.
- John Lill: Replied personally.
- John Paynter: Replied personally.
- Ian Parrott: Replied personally.
- John Tavener: Publishers replied.
- Sir Michael Tippett: Publishers replied.
- Julian Lloyd-Webber: No reply.

Of the composers who replied, only one, John Paynter, expressed amazement that he should be thought of as having an interest in or being influenced by paranormal matters and Sir Michael Tippett's publishers advised the reading of his autobiographical book *Those Twentieth Century Blues* which contains a section on his dreams. This theme was also mentioned by David Bedford who wrote of an interest in ESP and continued: "I often dream of entire performances of my pieces, but after they have been composed not before" (private letter to M. Willin, 1994).

Jonathan Harvey spoke of relying on dreams or meditation for ideas and wrote: "I meditate twice daily" (private communication to M. Willin, 1995) and similarly Stephen Dodgson wrote: "I only know that for myself I have to stop applying logic actively whilst composing, and reserve it for the scrutiny and self-criticism that comes between times and afterwards. I actually believe in inspiration, and that I suppose is paranormality in action" (private letter to M. Willin, 1994).

John Tavener is often referred to as Britain's leading 'spiritual' composer. This has probably come about because of his deeply-held beliefs in the doctrines of the Greek Orthodox Church and his experience of its music. It was therefore disappointing only to receive literature from his publishers and not a direct communication. I therefore approached him directly at a conference on music and the psyche in London on February 24th 1996. I asked him whether his spiritual music came from within or was it from an external source. After a long pause he answered that he thought it was a difficult question but that he thought it came from an external source but worked through himself. He said: "I can't prove it but I think that would be my answer."

The concert pianist John Lill has spoken in the past about his own spiritual beliefs and his regard for the music of Rosemary Brown. Lill has also spoken of his contact with the spirit of Beethoven whom he claims has influenced the performance of his music and his life. (The contemporary American composer Virgil Fox was also helped with the interpretation of music when he believed he saw the spirit of Liszt and received telepathic communication from him as to how the music was to be played (Klimo, 1987). After an exchange of letters, conversations with his London agent and two letters from Lill himself, he telephoned me to arrange a meeting. He initially agreed to a half-hour 'chat' but the conversation flowed smoothly with very little prompting from me for nearly two hours. He agreed to the interview being taped but asked for confidentiality concerning some of the statements made. (See Willin, 1999, for an edited transcript.) He explained that his spiritual awareness started when he was very young and he felt that his fingers were being "taken over" as he played the piano. It was natural for him to play recordings of Beethoven symphonies despite other boys in his native East End of London all playing football. He won a scholarship to the Royal College of Music but rebelled against the tutors. He knew he was being "helped", especially during and after the Moscow Tchaikovsky Piano Competition when a figure appeared to him and told him he would win (*Psychic News*, February 24th 1980). Further evidence came to him in the early Seventies through EVP (electronic voice phenomenon) - introduced to him by Robert Mayer - and other forms of "concrete" evidence. He was in contact with many relatives, composers and other people who had passed over and held in-depth conversations with them. He asked many questions and accurate answers were given, which he verified in encyclopedias. One particularly powerful force came through to him that proved to be Beethoven. Lill had one or two musical examples given to him, including a fragment of the scherzo of Beethoven's 10th Symphony which was recorded in 1980 on Hugh Burnett's television programme *Spirits from the Past*. The 1929 edition of the *Grove Music Dictionary* under the section on Beethoven actually prints this theme and quotes it as existing in one of Beethoven's notebooks. It is impossible to know whether Lill had unconsciously seen this extract and memorised it or had indeed received the same fragment from Beethoven. He also received poetry, literature and messages in foreign languages and a great sense of humour was conveyed. He feels that he continues to be helped by spiritual forces:

> "Last night it was very hot and uncomfortable, but the force was still available. You are able to think materially and look around but you are aware of this huge incoming force which is a power without limit."

> "Our two minds intermingle, but normally it's just a tremendous sensation which goes beyond any drug - a complete thrill when you're feeling inspired. Perhaps a comparatively rare thing, but you are nearly always aware

of being in safe hands and the more you go into dangerous
territory, the more help there is."

He agreed with my suggestion that this was in effect a semi-trance
condition but added that the spiritual forces needed an intermediary
in the physical world through which to communicate with others. The
problem with music, that most intangible of the arts, is that human
physical senses are conditioned to maintain bodily functions and
survival. He feels that the tragedy of Beethoven's deafness may have
aided him in his "destiny of greatness as a composer". Lill also talked
very lucidly on general spiritual matters and he explained that his
words and views came to him from the spiritual dimension. I asked him
"Does your playing improve through spirit contact with Beethoven?".
He replied:

> "Let's get one thing clear, it's not just Beethoven and it's a
> power that is available to all living people. It's not just me.
> If people just took the precaution of having a peaceful mind
> rather than rushing around trying to escape. You can be a
> channel through which this force works without limit."

His beliefs in reincarnation were expressed in less narrow terms than
the generally accepted idea of a cycle in which the individual continues
to be incarnated in different forms. Thus a temporary physical life is
just part of a spiritually-based existence which is eternal. He spoke
about Rosemary Brown at some length since he had supported her
claims very publicly during the controversy that surrounded her music.
He spoke of Brown being totally sincere and "on the right path" but
he felt she simplified her musical communications because of her own
lack of musical ability. However, he believed it was phenomenal how
she so captured the style of the composers rather than just the notes.
I accused Lill of not having played Brown's music in public, unlike
Howard Shelley, Peter Katin, etc., and he responded that he didn't feel
the music was exactly as the composers intended since it had been
simplified. Because of our earthbound minds, he believes that no one
could be a completely clear channel. He used the analogy of having
one hundred people speaking to you on one phone line simultaneously.
He admitted to having learned the Beethoven-inspired Sonata in E
minor that Brown sent him and commented:

"A lot of it is very good. I've learned to hold my tongue since the press is so sensationalised and greedy and once you put your neck out and play something, even though you may know it's very genuine, they are going to attack you like a bunch of hounds."

His final comments about Brown were that he felt she had been chosen by the spirit world because she was not well educated and could not have therefore written such pieces unaided. He told me: "Perhaps I haven't done her justice by not playing those pieces and perhaps I should have. I've admired them." Lill stressed that he believes that spiritual help is available to anyone who can allow themselves a little peace of mind for internal prayer or meditation. He feels that present day society's addiction to media fashions and general disposability is proving disastrous to our spiritual and psychical growth and he explains his reasons with lucidity and intelligence, as well as wit and humour. He does not denigrate the massive amount of hard work that physically needs to be given to achieve a solid technique but he believes having acquired these tools a receptive mind can tap into inspiration from the world of spirit.

It could be argued that the wide range of terms used to describe the possible source of 'inspiration' are in fact differing interpretations of the same process. If one is willing to substitute the word 'inspiration' with terms such as 'God', 'Divine force', or even 'super-consciousness' then the compositional sources of music, both past and present, could be very similar. Organised Spiritualism does not appear to enter the lives of contemporary professional musicians, but in the lives of musical mediums it can play a leading role. I decided, therefore, to investigate the claims and attributes of such people.

During the 1970s, several mediums claimed to be in contact with deceased composers and to be the channels for these composers to communicate their music, but there was often a lack of information available concerning these people. For example, Mrs Karin Harms of Copenhagen claimed to be receiving original Chopin works and held concerts in Denmark to promote this music. However, only one brief source could be found concerning her work (Kenner, 1973). On occasions works were published with varying degrees of success. One such composer was Clifford Enticknap who believed that he was a channel for Handel's music. He claimed that their relationship developed on Atlantis where Handel was known as a great teacher called Joseph Arkos and that prior to this he was on the planet Jupiter with some other 'great' composers. (It might be wondered whether some of his vocabulary used words from Handel's pasticcio of 1739 entitled *Jupiter in Argos*.) Enticknap further believed that in the eighteenth century he had been a female pupil of Handel and stated that this had been confirmed to him when a medium told him that Handel was by his side. Enticknap has written a four and a half hour oratorio called *Beyond the Veil*, of which seventy three minutes have been recorded by the London Symphony Orchestra and the Ambrosian Chorus with Leslie Fyson as the baritone soloist ('Spirits from the Past', BBC television August 12th 1980). Evidently Enticknap had considerable confidence in the value of the music since he financed the recording himself. I have only heard part of this recording but the music itself is hardly worthy of Handel's name. It is more a pastiche of his style and the words are absurdly inappropriate: "He showed his genius at the keyboard, when not much more than a little child, and later he amazed the world by the very incredible speed with which he wrote his music." (*Out of this World*, 1989).

In any study of twentieth century musical mediums the one name that stands apart is that of Rosemary Brown and it is therefore felt to be important to provide details of her life to disclose any possible sources of her alleged mediumistic or musical ability. During a period of approximately twenty years she produced a stream of music allegedly dictated to her by a variety of dead composers whom she claimed appeared to her visually. Not only was music conveyed to her, but also works of art, poetry and learned discourses by scientists and philosophers such as Einstein and Bertrand Russell.

The first time Brown saw Liszt she was about seven years old and she was already "accustomed to seeing the spirits of the so called dead" (Brown, 1971, p.13). She did not recognise him until much later but remembered his long white hair and sombre robes. He told her that when she grew up he would come back and give her music. She soon realised that these visitations and other psychic abilities separated her from other people and she mainly kept them to herself to avoid ridicule. She continued to see spirits and display ESP whilst attending the local grammar school to which she had won a scholarship. Hints of mediumistic activity or at least an interest in such matters can be seen from Brown's own comments about her mother's psychic tendencies and her grandfather having worked with Sir William Crookes during his investigations of mediums (Brown, 1974, p.48). She took a broad view of religion and tried out various denominations and even became an active member of the Theosophical Society. Brown's mother played the piano occasionally and the radio was sometimes tuned in to "easy listening" programmes. She attended ballet classes as a child and she would therefore have come into contact with some of the lighter classics used for such classes. This possibly prompted a desire for piano lessons that she received for a "year or so" (Brown, 1971, p.48) until financial constraints forced them to cease. In her teens she had two terms of piano lessons and finally a year's further lessons from 1951-2 after the upheavals of World War II. During this time she claimed her psychical gifts helped her to avoid bombs on several occasions when premonitions prompted her to take different routes or avoid certain places. I was employed as a telegraphist...this supplied yet another valuable acquisition which was nimbleness of fingers developed throughout many a long hour at teleprinter keyboards" (Brown, 1974, p.66). She was married in 1952 to a fellow Spiritualist and journalist and their brief relationship (he died in 1961) was a happy one producing two children. During the period of his illness, poverty was a major factor in their lives and Brown's mother also died at this time. She now became even more interested in Spiritualism and was invited to play the organ for Balham Spiritualists' Church, a role that required a considerable amount of practice since there were several services each week. In March 1964 Brown was convalescing after an accident in the school kitchen where she worked when Liszt appeared to her very vividly one afternoon and took over her hands as she played the piano "as easily as putting on a pair of gloves" to produce music that was not of her own creation. (Brown, 1986, p.20). During one of these practices, she was overheard playing a piece that had been given to her by Liszt and she was accordingly invited to play to the Wimbledon branch of the Churches Fellowship for Psychical Studies. Word soon spread among the Spiritualist movement and mediums named other composers whom they 'saw' with Brown, including Beethoven and Rachmaninov.

She soon began to write down these pieces at Liszt's dictation and he introduced other dead composers to her. Chopin was the next to make contact and he was followed by a veritable stream of others as follows: Bach, Beethoven, Berlioz, Brahms, Debussy, Delius, Grieg,

Handel, Monteverdi, Mozart, Poulenc, Rachmaninov, Schubert, Schumann (Robert and Clara), Scriabin, Strauss (Johann), Stravinsky, Lennon and Gershwin. She claimed to have written over six hundred compositions since 1965, mainly for piano, but a notable exception was a string quartet movement dictated by Brahms and broadcast by the Dartington Quartet in October 1969. Brown claims that Liszt became insistent that the music should be conveyed to a wider audience and Sir George Trevelyan, a member of the Church Fellowship, provided the contact by showing some of her scores to Mary Firth who directed music courses at a college for further education. Firth was impressed with them and they started up a fund for her. At the time Brown was working in a school kitchen and she gratefully accepted the offer to pursue her compositional activities. However, feeling under increasing pressure because of her funding she resigned it in March 1970. There had been an unpleasant falling out between her and her patrons since the latter voiced some doubts as to the music's authenticity. However, the previous few years had allowed Brown to make contacts in the world of the media and she was interviewed for *Woman's Hour* in 1967. She started receiving piano lessons again to be able to play the composers' music to a higher standard. A recording contract was made with Philips, employing the services of the pianist Peter Katin, and the BBC prepared to make a television programme as well as a Radio 3 broadcast with Geoffrey Skelton and Daniel Snowman in May 1970. By this time she needed the services of a manager, Barry Krost, to handle all her bookings which included a late night television show in Dublin and articles in numerous newspapers and journals including, *Der Speigel*, the *Listener*, *Musical Opinion*, and the *Radio Times*. Responding to claims that she was 'suffering' from cryptomnesia, she allowed herself to be studied by Professor Tenhaeff, Director of the Institute of Parapsychology at Utrecht University, Holland. In 1971 she claimed that an analysis of her music by Stan Kelly of the mathematics department of Warwick University provided strong evidence of a correlation between Brown's 'Chopin' compositions and Chopin's known music (Brown, 1974; Parrott, 1978). In 1973 further support was given by John Lill, Richard Rodney Bennett and others and in the same year she went to France to promote her first book and make television and radio broadcasts.

In 1986 she published her third book *Look Beyond Today* which featured the songs 'Look Beyond Today', 'Love is all we ever need to know' and 'Just Turn Away' allegedly communicated by John Lennon. He appeared to her as he was in his early thirties, as do most of her composers, although some appear at a younger age. His son Julian refused to be involved with these songs and Bill Barry, an expert on Lennon lyrics wrote: "John never wrote songs as bad as that" (*Psychic News*, March 8th 1986). Brown's book is useful in providing fresh material about her communications, especially where changes in outlook have occurred. She mentions that over six hundred compositions, including an unfinished opera, had been transmitted by 1986 and that in addition to the Philips recording a German recording had been made (Intercord 160.1819 *Musikmedium Rosemary Brown*). She gives details of concerts in venues such as the Queen Elizabeth Hall, the Purcell Room and the Wigmore Hall, and of appearances on radio programmes such as *Start the Week* with Richard Baker. Musical communications were still very evident, with advice allegedly given by Debussy for Richard Rodney Bennett, via Brown, concerning his performance of a Debussy prelude. Bennett felt that this advice had to emanate from some source other than Brown's own knowledge. A piece called 'Henrietta' was dictated by Fats Waller and an unspecified item by Gershwin. The entertainer Gracie Fields communicated with Brown and provided her with a song about which no details are available. A particularly striking event concerning one Viktor Ullmann who died in Auschwitz is recounted in some detail. He wrote an unfinished opera in the concentration camp, Theresienstadt in Czechoslovakia, called *Der Kaiser von Atlantis* with the libretto by a fellow prisoner Peter Kein who was also killed. A copy of the score was conveyed to Kerry Woodward, the Director of the Netherlands Chamber Choir, who spent some time with Brown. Without seeing the score she gave him advice concerning amendments and changes with specific bar references which were conveyed to her from the departed composer. Kerry Woodward made the changes she suggested since he felt they were needed and the work was performed on the BBC (*Psychic News*, March 10th 1979).

A growing number of non-musicians appeared to Brown in the latter part of the century. These included friendly conversations with Diana Dors and her husband Alan, Douglas Bader, and poetry from Emily Bronte, Elizabeth Barrett Browning, Rupert Brooke, William Blake, Samuel Taylor Coleridge, John Keats, Edward Lear, Percy Shelley, William Wordsworth and Sir John Betjeman. She intentionally did not specify which poet wrote which poem since, she stated, she did not want the critics to cross-examine her as the musical critics had previously (Brown, 1986). In addition to music she received long philosophical explanations of the spirit world from Bertrand Russell; essays for musicians from Sir Donald Tovey; two plays: *Caesar's Revenge* (performed at the Edinburgh Fringe Festival in 1978) and *The Heavenly Maze* from G. B. Shaw; psychology from Jung; paintings from Debussy, etc., (Brown, 1986). Brown also started adult art classes with a friend of hers and artists including Samuel Palmer, Turner, Blake and Van Gogh started to communicate more strongly. She was befriended by the mother and father of Andrew and Julian Lloyd-Webber and she relates a psychometry test she undertook at their house with a pair of scissors previously belonging to Beethoven. A story is told of how Julian Lloyd-Webber came to Brown for healing when specialists could not cure an injured finger and on another occasion when a kidney stone needed moving (Lloyd-Webber, 1984).

Taking into account these numerous events, Brown must have been incredibly busy during this period as she was apparently communicating with many musicians, artists, poets and philosophers as well as undertaking some healing. Supporters of Brown tend to be aware of some of her musical works and know little of the entire range of contacts she claims. Her life seems to be filled with paranormal experiences and in a final section of her book *Look Beyond Today* (1986) she gives details of the fairies that apparently inhabit her garden; twenty-foot tall angels and little green men. She also mentions that an uncle saw the 'Angels of Mons' at the famous World War I battleground and that Jesus and the saints have been known to appear to her.

In 1975, the composer Alan Hovhaness orchestrated the first part of her Beethoven 'Symphony' using Brown's piano score. Many of her compositions have been described as 'lightweight' in content and brief in duration. She responded to the latter criticism in 1971 with pieces of greater length, e.g. a sonata from Beethoven in C minor consisting of 528 bars. She does not attach dynamics, tonal markings, phrasing or other performance details because of a lack of technical musical knowledge. In fact, Mary Firth found her to be most 'unmusical' (Parrott, 1978).

Her alleged contact with Sir Donald Tovey received differing interpretations of its authenticity. Tovey was known to hold

74

Spiritualistic beliefs during his lifetime, being convinced that the spirit of Schumann directed Jelly d' Aranyi's production of his posthumous violin concerto - traced to the vaults of the Prussian State Library after being lost for eighty years. He dictated, from the spirit world, the introduction to Brown's first record and David Togarth made an analysis of Tovey's language. His conclusion was "practically every test ended in Rosemary's favour. I would be forced to accept the text as authentic Tovey if I had to judge it purely on its literary merits". When he first read the text his reaction was "excitement mingled with astonishment" (*Psychic News*, May 9th 1970). However, the Tovey scholar and Professor of Music at the University of Edinburgh, D. R. B. Kimbell, did not find the alleged Tovey writing convincing. In private correspondence (May 21st 1996) he wrote: "...the style, the choice of imagery and allusion, the rigour of the argument is not his (i.e. Tovey's). In fact, I find the whole enterprise pretty un-Toveyan."

The authenticity of Brown's music has aroused a considerable amount of controversy. Her original supporters Dr and Mrs Firth went on to claim that it was simply an absorption of the styles of the composers but they later withdrew those remarks (Brown, 1984). Vernon Harrison, a member of the Liszt Society and the SPR, felt her Liszt pieces were "not good enough to carry conviction that they emanate from the sources to which she attributes them...but they are too good to dismiss lightly" (Parrott, 1978, p.13). He was especially impressed with the Liszt item 'Grubelei' which was partly dictated on May 29th 1969 in the presence of a BBC television crew filming *Mrs Brown and the Composers*. The producer Peter Dorling spoke of her "muttering away" whilst taking down the music in what appeared to be literal dictation. Colin Wilson confirmed that the music could have been composed by a skilled musician but Rosemary Brown was certainly not such a person.

Stan Kelly's previously-mentioned analysis of her music in comparison to known compositions produced positive results. He felt that the accusations that some of her music was trivial in nature would probably be made of such composers as Beethoven if parts of his notebooks were presented to experts. Perhaps of most importance to the acceptance of Brown's music has been the endorsement given by leading professional musicians of the twentieth century. These have included Hephzibah Menuhin who has suggested that the music seemed to come from the composers' early days; Leonard Bernstein who was particularly impressed with her Fantaisie Impromptu from Chopin; and Humphrey Searle who praised the Moment Musical in G minor from Schubert. Speaking of 'Grubelei' he stated: "It is the sort of piece Liszt could well have written, particularly during the last fifteen years of his life" (cited in Parrott, 1978, p.38). Robin Stone and Howard Shelley have played her music, the latter stating her 'Schubert' contained the composer's 'essence'. Derek Watson was impressed with her knowledge of Bruckner whom she saw clairvoyantly and Richard Rodney Bennett stated that it was impossible to produce such music fraudulently. Two of Brown's most creditable allies are the pianist John Lill and Ian Parrott the Professor of Music, University College of Wales who has written a book about her music (Parrott, 1978).

Other musicians have been more cautious or totally unconvinced, as in the case of Denis Matthews. Writing in the *Listener*, June 26th 1969, he described her music as mainly "charming pastiches" with naive manifestations of style. He claimed that her Beethoven 'largo e maestoso' movement was a vague memory of the 'largo e mesto' from the D major Sonata op.10 no. 3 with a mis-remembered 'maestoso' instead of 'mesto'. Her Bach prelude based on the C minor from *The 48* loses its harmonic progression and a Chopin study is a "pale shadow" of op.10 no. 4 in C sharp minor. In short, Denis Matthews suggested that Brown was re-creating compositions using her own conventional skills and not tapping into a psychic source.

Brown admitted to a personal preference for nineteenth century composers and has expressed a desire for Dvorak and Tchaikovsky to contact her, but they have not been forthcoming. This could be significant in challenging those who would dispute the veracity of Brown's claims as conscious fraud would surely lead her to use those composers she favours? It could be argued that the essence of nineteenth century music is harmony and despite this many of her dictations rely on melody, e.g. Grieg's 'Shepherd Piping' and Schumann's 'Longing'. She further admits that with at least two of the works, Debussy's 'Danse exotique' and 'Le Paon', she was left to write in the accompaniments herself, hence the use of harmonies that lack technical sophistication.

In an attempt to see if she could produce music outside her own musical tastes, Scott Rogo, a musician and psychical investigator, asked for a Monteverdi madrigal, a Machaut choral piece or best of all a dodecaphonic piece by Schoenberg or Webern. She claimed that she needed to be on the same wavelength as the composer and could not oblige. Rogo was disappointed with the similarity of the forms of the music (i.e. often ternary) and the over-use of sequences in the melodic line and symmetrical measurement in the barring and phrasing.

The conductor and composer Andre Previn described some of her music as "third, fourth or fifth rate Liszt" (Parrott, 1978), but Geoffrey Skelton felt "the psychic possibility at least deserves examination" (*Listener*, July 10th 1969). A review of her Piano Album (published by Paxton, 1974) prompted the comment: "Inspired is about the last word one would use of these pieces after trying them on the piano. They sound flat, thin and naively imitative..." (Horder, 1981).

Rosalind Heywood created a psychological profile of her own devising that suggested Brown was driven to the automatic production of material beyond her normal capacity by the frustration she felt at her unused artistic mind. Interestingly she pointed out that Brown's automatism developed after the death of a close member of the family as has been the case with other mediums like Mrs Verrall and Mrs Willett who were well known in the first half of the century. Furthermore, the claim of taking dictation took the direct responsibility away from the mediums who were then only passing on what was being given to them. However, the musical testing (Firth) and the psychological investigations (Tenhaeff) revealed neither musical/artistic talent nor psychological abnormalities. Some journalists have suggested that she received huge amounts of secret music tuition to achieve her results but they have not been able to substantiate these claims. She admits to having received piano tuition at the times previously mentioned and that is all.

In an attempt to research further the perceived worth of Rosemary Brown's music, I arranged on several occasions for a recording of her 'Consolation' dictated by Liszt to be played immediately before an authentic 'Consolation' by Liszt: no. 3 in D flat major. The audiences consisted of amateur music lovers who declared a preference for classical music. They were not told the order of the pieces beforehand. On each occasion they were virtually unanimous that Brown's piece was a pastiche of Liszt's music and the authentic piece was genuine Liszt. My own studies of her pieces similarly found them to be lacking in characteristic textures and details. I sent a copy of Brown's Prelude in F sharp minor (Brown, 1977) and a recording of an Impromptu (Brown, *Phillips, 6500 049*) allegedly dictated by Chopin, to the Chopin expert John Rink, Music Department, Royal Holloway College, University of

London. He felt that both pieces were texturally and formally weak and although displaying some characteristics of Chopin's music, could not be viewed as in any way convincing.

My study of a Scherzo (Brown, 1977), supposedly dictated by Beethoven, revealed a lack of structure which was again suggestive of pastiche. I forwarded the work to the Beethoven scholar Barry Cooper, at the Music Department, University of Manchester and he felt it was not written "in a style that could be mistaken for genuine Beethoven". His further comments are worth quoting in full:

> "The Scherzo contains thin, unimaginative and unvarying textures, and a lack of rhythmic variety or sense of continuity between phrases. There are several cases of poor part-writing, although elementary grammatical errors such as parallels have largely been avoided. [The piece does not] reveal any skill in motivic development, such as can be found in virtually all Beethoven's major works (and most of his minor ones), and it seems incoherent in form. It often strays far beyond Beethoven's harmonic/tonal style, while completely failing to rise to his level of contrapuntal and motivic subtlety. It also differs from Beethoven's other scherzos in never using a single staccato sign (indeed it is conspicuously short of articulation marks except in bars 13 -16)."
>
> (private correspondence, October 1996)

Brown's 'Le Paon' was played on the piano by a research student in the presence of Eric Clarke, Music Department, University of Sheffield and myself. We agreed that the music was, at best, a pastiche of Debussy's work and bore no resemblance to an authentic Debussy composition. Another student (Ms Emma Stow) undertook a musical comparison of an intermezzo written by Brahms and an identically-entitled work by Brown allegedly dictated by Brahms. Her conclusion stated:

> " ...in the light of the metrical, rhythmical and interval analyses the Rosemary Brown 'Intermezzo' would appear to be both far more simplistic and also very different in

compositional style and does not seem to possess the kind of distinguishing features found in Brahms' music."

(Music Department, University of Sheffield)

It would seem that Brown's spirit clientele has increased considerably since the early contacts with Liszt and Chopin and since 1986 she has remained increasingly out of the public eye. The last communication (written) I received from her was in November 1993 when she wished me success with my research but declined to be interviewed because of a "number of chronic health problems". In a private letter to the author Peter Underwood in 1996 she stated that she still felt that journalists were "swiping at her". Rosemary died on November 16th 2001 and her unpublished manuscripts are held in the British Library.

My own opinion of Brown's music agrees with the view that the available works are lacking the inspiration and 'feel' of the composers named by her. There is too much emphasis on melody at the expense of harmony, and ideas/motives are not developed sufficiently. A large number of Brown's works have not been published and she did not prove amenable in providing access to them despite many requests. From the music currently available it must be concluded that there is very little evidence of original music being dictated to her from the sources she claims. The question of the origin of her inspiration, and why she feels dead composers have contacted her in particular, will be discussed at the essay's conclusion in the context of the further examples which follow.

In an attempt to find further examples of musical mediums to research, a number of advertisements were placed in relevant newspapers and magazines such as the *Psychic News* and the *Fortean Times*. These advertisements asked people who believed that they were receiving music from discarnate sources to contact me in confidence. Similarly, establishments with access to mediums and knowledge of such matters were approached. Some of these, such as the Spiritual National Union and the Institute of Spiritualistic Mediums, proved to be most helpful. The Society for Psychical Research and the College for Psychic Studies were extremely helpful in providing further contacts.

A questionnaire was devised according to the guidelines set out in Wiseman and Morris (1995) but suitably modified to incorporate musical aspects of any alleged mediumship. This was sent to those people who either claimed a spiritual source for their music or were undecided about its origins. An audio-cassette was included with the questionnaire on which to make any desired recordings accessible. The aim of the questionnaire was to try to ascertain whether there were any trends and similarities to be discovered among the people who claimed to be receiving music from the spirit world. Where examples of music or performance were available, analyses of them would be undertaken. During the period 1994-1996, sixteen questionnaires were posted to appropriate people, of whom only two did not respond.

There is little of significance to be determined from the virtual evenness of distribution of the sexes, except perhaps to highlight the fact that although mediums are generally assumed to be female, a greater number in this study were found to be male. This is not generally true of the Spiritualist Church where members are predominantly female. A large proportion of the participants were born in the 1930s. This means that the majority of them have now reached the age of retirement and it would seem that this could be a factor contributing to the development of their abilities. The lack of day-time paid work may allow the time and mental freedom for previously stifled attributes to become more highly developed. One only has to attend any of the hundreds of Spiritual churches scattered across the whole country to notice the preponderance of people in their sixties and above, and although there are younger mediums beginning to appear on the Spiritual 'circuit' this does not seem to be common with musical mediums. The exceptions to this hypothesis are the alleged communicators with John Lennon, one of whom declined to complete a questionnaire, but who was nevertheless interviewed and provided music purporting to originate from Lennon.

Several of the participants described themselves as music teachers or performers, but non-musical careers such as a librarianship, the civil service and chartered accountancy were also declared and the majority of the participants had attended secondary or grammar schools, achieving O levels and A levels in a variety of subjects. Some had also attended professional courses after school or in connection with their professions but nobody claimed to possess a degree in any subject. However, the most noticeable differences could be seen in the musical education received, which ranged from none at all to diplomas from various London colleges of music. Most participants claimed at least an interest in music at an amateur level and perhaps a few piano lessons as a child.

Clairvoyance, clairaudience or similar skills were claimed by <u>all</u> the participants, but they varied in their explanations of the actual source of their abilities. For instance, one referred to her power as 'seership', but she did not provide any definition as to what exactly she meant by the term. Another explained, at length, his belief in 'worlds within worlds' meaning the co-existence of physical and spiritual planes. Some individuals felt a bonding directly with particular spirits, e.g. with Novello and with Caruso, and when this occurred the manifestations reflected the nature of the contact.

The most favourable conditions for spirit contact were peace, quiet and safety and two mediums needed to be alone to achieve this. One mentioned the problem of communication when sceptics were present. Two singers spoke of a 'buzz' of nervous energy indicating the presence of spirit but there was unanimity amongst the participants in agreeing that an external force, for which most used the word 'spirit', was guiding them and providing <u>proof</u> of the continuation of the spirit or soul after physical death. They believed that the music that was being dictated to them, or the guidance and influence on their performances was providing tangible evidence of this.

Several of the musical mediums were interviewed and recorded, others provided manuscripts of their music. A few examples of case studies follow below:

Case Study No.1

The existence of this lady (whom I shall refer to as H.) was brought to my notice via the December 24th 1994 issue of *Psychic News*, page 5, where an article by Rita Smith was published concerning H.'s musical mediumship and alleged channelling of various composers. I arranged a mutually convenient time with her husband (G.) for a meeting. I arrived at their home and noticed the brass plaque on the outside wall proclaiming G. to be a qualified herbalist. I was shown into a comfortable lounge and noticed a large electronic organ in one corner with a small tape recorder beside it. On the walls were photographs and photocopies of Tchaikovsky, Jerome Kerne, George Gershwin, Noel Gay, Dorothy Fields and Wagner. The organ was a Yamaha keyboard with printer and all the equipment seemed to be of quite a high quality if somewhat out of date. Despite H. being the communicating medium, G. dominated the interview and he obviously enjoyed playing the organ a great deal as he illustrated at length H.'s tunes which were contained in large scrapbooks filled with printouts from the keyboard printer. His own accompaniments consisted of vamping with a constant heavy electronic vibrato, somewhat obliterating the true nature of the tunes. The print outs were difficult to read because of small print and incorrect rhythmic groupings. H. admitted that if she was distracted, for instance by the phone or visitors, and left her finger on a note too long, it came out as a repeated note when it was not meant to be.

H. claimed that in about 1991 when her husband had been writing a musical, she heard a voice telling her that she would be given music and the voice identified itself as Jerome Kerne. Two days later the spirit of Tchaikovsky appeared saying "I long to bring my music back" and then Gershwin also made contact. The composers only produced melodies and no harmony was provided. I queried this situation since harmony, form and orchestration are an integral part of most classical composers' work but I was told that their simple tunes were enough to prove existence in the spirit world, this being the composers' reasons for making contact. They played me a tape of one of the melodies that had been made to sound quite attractive through the skills of a professional arranger who added suitable harmony and rhythmic indications. However, it did not resemble the music of Tchaikovsky from whom it was claimed to have been channelled. G. told me: "It is to bring relaxation, peace and tranquillity to the world and to help children to sleep." Schubert and Stephen Foster were mentioned as providing H. with melodies, and examples were played by G. on the organ with an inappropriate accompaniment. They often commented on how the composers wanted orchestral arrangements made of the pieces and hinted that since their paid arranger only produced synthesised accompaniments, they would like me to arrange some of the music for orchestra, especially the tunes they referred to as "Tchaikovsky's Symphony".

I transcribed several pages of the computer printout into more legible notation - literally hundreds of lines of music - and noticed how similar many of the melodies were in intervallic content, i.e. diatonic scales and arpeggiated triads. Rhythmic notation was omitted since H. had previously mentioned rhythmic problems. The examples dictated to her by Tchaikovsky and other composers followed similar melodic lines. After they had been suitably transcribed they formed what could be described as simple diatonic tunes and bearing no resemblance to Tchaikovsky's music.

I contacted H.'s arranger on the telephone and he agreed that if H. and G. wanted their music arranged he would undertake the work as a commercial venture, for his usual fee. (In 2004 two CDs of the music were made under a different name with synthesized accompaniment professionally enhanced.) However, he added that he felt H. and G. to be a "batty" couple. I also sent copies of the music to Professor Edward Garden, Emeritus Professor of Music, University of Sheffield, an expert on Tchaikovsky's music. He was very scathing about it:

> "None of this lady's stuff has anything more to do with T. than it has to do with any other nineteenth century composer, really…He (Tchaikovsky) always thought out his melodies, harmonies and orchestration simultaneously. Separation of these elements being unthinkable."

(Private correspondence)

It would appear that H. is genuine in her belief that she is being contacted by the spirits of dead composers. This belief is strongly encouraged by her husband who is an enthusiastic amateur musician himself. The reasons for her desire to channel music may well include a subconscious wish to participate in her husband's music-making and a Spiritualistic belief in survival after death. In themselves her melodies, especially without proper rhythmic groupings, provide no such proof and a request for at the very least some harmony to be incorporated into them, made by myself on several occasions, was not responded to.

Case Study No. 2

The Society for Psychical Research sent me a copy of a letter they had received (dated January 26th 1993) from a man, whom I shall refer to as L., writing about his experiences of "psychic vibrations". He stated that mediums had seen the spirit of Caruso and Mario Lanza standing beside him and that he wished to talk to someone with appropriate knowledge about this situation. This led to the first of several interviews with L. on February 1st 1993 as well as the making of a joint television documentary about his claims for a Dutch television company (Tenfold). I have also performed with him in an amateur concert that I conducted and he has spoken and sung at lectures that I have attended and organised. He has always proved very co-operative. The opulence of his manorial abode was very impressive and I was made to feel very welcome by L. and his wife. L. possesses an extravertant character, has a good sense of humour and a flamboyant appearance. He spoke at length in the first interview about the vibrations or the "buzz" that he feels when he sings which he claimed was the joining of his spirit by the spirit of Caruso and Mario Lanza to produce the power and tone that his voice possesses. He spoke of tests at Addenbrooks Hospital, Cambridge, that registered a volume of one hundred decibels when he sang, which he believed might be the cause of a partial deafness in one ear. In response to my questioning about why Caruso in particular was his alleged channel, he claimed that mediums had seen Caruso with him at Spiritualist churches and that he clairaudiently heard Caruso give him instructions when practising. He quoted further examples that he believed to not be coincidences, but to be communications from the spirit realm: "My son is now getting on for thirty and I called him Enrico. I don't know why...(it was) before I was aware of spiritual things...and when I write his [Caruso's] signature, it's almost identical. I didn't realise this until recently."

He spoke of his singing studies with Professor Pasqualino Pappano in Italy but although he admitted to having worked hard at developing his voice, he stressed that he had received very little tuition and none for the previous fifteen years. L. was obviously keen to exploit his voice, having spoken of various concerts in Spiritual churches, performances in the Royal Albert Hall and a private performance for Lord Harwood at the Coliseum in London after he had contacted a national newspaper about his voice. He had written to Pavarotti, Carreras and Harry Secombe offering to sing for them, stressing "I'm not doing it for material gain", but received no replies and was upset by this rejection. He mentioned how he offered to sing at a hospice to heal or help the inmates but was again refused permission. L. expanded on his healing abilities, mentioning that his music was to help people. Two examples he quoted were a blind person in Majorca who could see again after he had laid hands on him and another person who had received relief from cancer. However, he could not provide details regarding the identities of these people for further research since he claimed to have lost the information.

L. told me his goal is that: "The world should know there's more than this life" since he feels that much of the crime and cruelty committed by people might cease if they believed they would be held accountable for it after physical death. He also expressed a feeling that people who were suffering would receive solace from the knowledge that the spirit would continue but without the physical torment. "I want to become famous," he said, for the purpose of spreading his message. "I feel I could be the best tenor that ever lived," he added.

When the interview had finished, L. agreed to sing for me and we retired to his beautifully decorated music room in which was a grand piano. He sang to a backing tape but on other occasions one of his sons accompanied him on the piano. He produced an immensely powerful sound and stated that he could sing twenty-two to twenty-four difficult arias one after the other without a break, since he was being joined by Caruso and Lanza.

Soon after the first interview I arranged for him to sing at Stansted Hall in Essex for a group of mediums and Spiritualists but on the condition that Caruso should not be mentioned until after his singing and the comments of the audience had been received. The assembled company sensed several spirit presences, of which Gigli and Lanza were the most prominent. After John McCormack and Richard Tauber had also been mentioned, Caruso's name was stated to L.'s obvious pleasure. Since this time, L. has appeared on the *Big Breakfast Show, The Paranormal World of Paul McKenna, The Magic and Mystery Show* and other popular television shows. Articles have been written in *Psychic News* (April 23rd 1994 and March 30th 1996) at his request.

Different lines of research were undertaken to try to establish the basis of L.'s claims and the authenticity of the phenomenon he displayed. Initially, accounts of Caruso's life were read and recordings of his voice were listened to in order to make me as familiar as possible with details which might prove to be significant. L. provided me with a copy of a letter from Victor Morris, the Head of Auditions for the English National Opera, which was sent to him after his aforementioned audition there. It spoke of his "marvellous Italianate voice in very fine fettle" and he continued "...you make some very exciting sounds, which can thrill an audience". However, he felt that musicianship was lacking and that therefore regular coaching would be necessary before entry into operatic roles could be undertaken. "You are therefore limited to concert work, singing songs and arias on television and in clubs." L. mentioned that he had sung in the Royal Albert Hall but he could not remember the date or the year. I therefore contacted the archivist there and spent a morning sifting through the programmes for the previous thirty years of music performances but we were unsuccessful in finding any reference to L. in the extensive material contained there. I was also unsuccessful in acquiring a hospital report on the tests undertaken on L.'s voice. L. assured me that he had given his permission for the hospital to allow me access to these documents but every time I telephoned they denied that such permission had been granted.

I enquired whether L. possessed a curriculum vitae and after repeated requests his wife finally sent me a copy. It contained a considerable amount of information about L.'s life and training. The opening paragraph mentioned him being known as the 'Cockney Caruso' and also told of him playing football for West Ham and Charlton football clubs. I contacted the archivists of both clubs and they informed me that no such person had played for their teams. The musical training specified was considerable, with study under Harold Hammond, John and Ida Dickens, Pasqualino Pappano in Florence and for three years in the USA under Alma Pedroza. The list of concert venues was also very impressive, including the Hollywood Bowl, Carnegie Hall New York and the Las Vegas Hilton (with Liberace). Television appearances were similarly impressive including an NBC one and a half-hour documentary on Australia's Channel Seven and the *Russel Harty Show*. It has not been possible to verify these claims. When L. appeared on the television programme entitled *The Paranormal World of Paul McKenna* the producers arranged for a spectrograph to be made comparing Caruso's top notes - taken from authentic recordings - with L.'s. I felt this to be somewhat irrelevant since L. was not claiming that his voice was the same as Caruso's but that the spirit was inspiring his own voice. However, I acquired copies of the spectrographs and although some similarities can be detected, they provide no positive evidence of a vocal identity. My suggestion of a third tenor's voice being used for spectrographic comparison was not acted upon. A member of the SPR suggested that L. should be asked to seek from Caruso some proof of identity, perhaps via a piece of information about his life unknown to current sources or a hidden letter which could be duly found by an impartial investigator from information provided by Caruso to L. However, he was not willing to undertake this task since he states that the spirit contact cannot be used in such a manner.

Tapes of his voice have been played to a number of musicians and they have generally agreed that he has a powerful tenor voice but that it lacks the 'polish' that a voice such as Caruso's possessed. His pronunciation of Italian is very anglicised in much the same way as foreign accents are often caricatured by English-speaking people and his intonation can be faulty to an extent that one would have thought spiritual help would eliminate. Although L. claims that whenever he sings he receives spiritual help, he also prefers a warming up period like any non-Spiritualist singer. L. is a sensitive and likeable person and his financial success from his business dealings would indicate that he has no need of the income that he might derive from exploiting his musical mediumship. However, he does seek public recognition and one needs to question whether the reasons are for self-aggrandisement or a genuine desire to spread his message of life after death. The most probable explanation is a combination of both answers. In one respect he expresses genuine motives to improve the world we live in by the knowledge of continued existence in a spirit form but he may not also be aware of more egocentric motivation. His powerful tenor voice has been achieved through much hard work and training and with further tuition he could become a professional tenor in his own right without the need for spiritual intervention. If L. believed that Caruso and Lanza inspired him in the sense of motivating him to sing, one could accept his beliefs. He has not, however, provided evidence of a sufficiently verifiable nature to advance a paranormal explanation for his abilities and since the death of his wife in 1997 he has not undertaken further public performances. However, I heard in December 2003 that he might be prepared to take up singing again.

Case Study No. 3

I received an answer to an advertisement I had placed in a December 1993 issue of *Psychic News* from a lady, whom I shall refer to as G. She claimed to be a musical medium with "indisputable proof" that she was being helped and inspired by Ivor Novello. I replied to her letter and we arranged to meet in London for a chat on January 28th 1994. The conversation flowed freely about G.'s alleged communication with Novello. She obviously knew a great deal about him since she spoke of giving lectures of a non-psychic nature about his life and music to various amateur societies around the country. She also told me of contact with Elgar, Noel Coward, Coleridge Taylor and the poet Christina Rossetti. She produced large colour photographs allegedly showing spirits in various outdoor places, which I was unable to locate without prompting. G. also mentioned sittings with a Nottingham-based medium (Lee Lacy). He had been instrumental in introducing the alleged spirit contacts to her and guiding her towards developing her own psychic gifts to make direct spirit contact herself. She told me that Novello communicated in a strange way. He did not seem to be dictating to her while she was composing, as was the case with Rosemary Brown's compositions, but rather the spirit indicated that obscure sources of Novello's music would be found to provide similarities between his music and hers. She quoted several examples of this occurrence but when questioned about her claims of contact with Elgar, she admitted that this was only via the medium she used. I was impressed by her knowledge of music, albeit as an amateur, and she later sent me a copy of one of her pieces - 'Kenwood House' - and an article she had written for the magazine *Here and There* dated November 1990 called 'Ivor Novello's Scottish Lament'. I also acquired copies of *Psychic News* dated September 26th 1981 and April 26th 1986 which contained articles on G.'s musical mediumship. These confirmed what G. had told me concerning Novello's method of communication. One such example was the 'love theme' that was played between the scenes in Novello's musical *Perchance to Dream* that G. later found in her composition. She claimed to have written her piece before hearing the Novello theme or seeing it in the score. There were no significant similarities between the two themes but more of an attempt to see similarity when there was none to be heard. The simple nature of a descending melodic scale-like pattern starting on the dominant and finishing on the tonic could be heard in Novello's piece but the harmony did not underly this in G's theme.

G. referred to a light flashing when she made mistakes in her scores which was only visible to her. She has written about non-verifiable coincidences that she believes provide further proof of Novello's continued existence in the spirit world. G. seemed to be unhappy about the continuation of her gift of musical mediumship. In a private communication to me she wrote: "Quite frankly I'm very disillusioned with the whole thing - the expense, slogging away at composing - to what end? I don't know what satisfaction Novello is getting but it's certainly getting him very little publicity. What puzzles me is why Novello cannot use his powers in this direction...However, this in no way detaches from the fact that Novello has <u>indisputably</u> linked with me personally. But what for?" Since G. has received quite a considerable amount of musical training and is a prominent member of a Spiritualist church in the same area as that which Rosemary Brown used to attend, it is perhaps not surprising that she might believe in a channelling link with one or more composers. Her choice of Novello might well have been brought about simply by her enjoyment of his music. The music itself does not provide evidence of spiritual contact since it merely contains quotes of Novello-like passages which could easily have been inserted unconsciously by G. herself.

Case Study No. 4

An article in *Psychic News* dated March 23rd 1996 gave information about a musician/chartered accountant, whom I shall refer to as M. He spoke of the spirit of the dead composer Arnold Bax visiting him when he worked on a score. We met on the evening of April 1st 1996. M. lives with his wife in a very fashionable block of flats and he arrived straight from his office. M. spoke at length about his early life and love of music and how his hopes of composing or performing professionally were frustrated when his parents insisted he took up a post as a chartered accountant. He talked enthusiastically about having obtained as a young man a Licentiate in organ playing from Trinity College of Music, London, and also of his various compositions. He reminisced about his move to Spain with his wife and about the concerts that were held there. Despite his love of Bax's music, it was only after his enforced return to England as a result of financial pressures that an incident occurred that brought Bax to the forefront. M. spoke of a chance visit to a public house in Storrington, Sussex (the White Horse Inn). He told me:

> "On a very wet evening, having become rather soaked in the search, and to my great surprise, we drove outside the pub quite by chance. I couldn't resist the opportunity to nip in and book a room. The young lady told me that we could use Arnold's work room which had been made into a hotel bedroom. She slept along the corridor in his bedroom where she looked after her own child. In asking her about Arnold Bax, she told me about her room and how it had such a "live" atmosphere with furniture being mysteriously moved from time to time, and a door, normally closed with furniture up against it, suddenly being left open. Our arrival on the fifth of November 1986 was close to his anniversary three days later."

Whilst having a bath he claimed to have seen the repeated impression of a Bax-like figure standing over him and he could not sleep that night because of "an almost flashing energy which made the air literally mobile". M. also referred to a piano composition of his own written in 1987 called 'Arnold's Ghost'. On the anniversary of Bax's death on October 3rd 1995 he felt instructed to extend this piece into a full-scale orchestral work. He continued: "I have rarely worked so hard at a piece, seemingly driven and instructed." M. spoke of receiving clairaudient instructions about parts of the music which his own conscious thoughts queried, through his academic training, but which nevertheless fitted into the score when he tried out parts on the piano. He completed the score of his one movement symphony on January 27th 1996 and Bax has not appeared since. M. talked enthusiastically about other psychic matters claiming an interest in, and knowledge of, many subjects including astrology, the chakras and the use of crystals. His main musical interest was in Bax but he also spoke of Vaughan Williams appearing on one occasion, though providing no music.

I found information about the White Horse Inn connected with the ghost of Arnold Bax (Playfair, 1985) and on telephoning the establishment, the landlord informed me that events were often celebrated there in memory of the composer and that they display some memorabilia. M. has spoken of a desire to return there but in a telephone conversation (October 1996) he spoke of Bax's influence having seemingly departed from him. I sent a copy of M.'s 'Symphony' to Antony Payne, an expert on twentieth-century English music and specifically Bax. He found the score most interesting and confirmed that, to his knowledge, M. had not plagiarised any of Bax's known works. He felt that parts of the work showed great similarities to Bax's music, especially in terms of the orchestration and that it had been very well written. Payne believed that the symphony had, at the very least, been written by someone who was well versed in the music of Bax and that it warranted further study. The music that M. composed has the distinction of being the most professionally produced of all the case studies and there are signs of original Bax-like characteristics within the score. However, it is important to stress that M. had received training in composition and freely admitted to being obsessed with Bax and his music. It was certainly not beyond his ability to write a fairly extended full orchestral score in the style of Bax without recourse to spiritual intervention and because of this it is difficult to verify whether the instructions M. believed came from the spirit of Bax may have emanated from his own unconscious. His belief that the dead composer was communicating with him may well have encouraged him to work at the piece with greater enthusiasm than he would normally have displayed.

Case Study No. 5

I received a letter from a self-styled "Composer of Classical Music" whom I shall refer to as W. dated October 12th 1993. It stated that music in Chopin's style started to flow through W.'s own writing and he asked for a meeting to expand upon this. The letter also mentioned that since the age of twelve, W. had been aware that "Chopin's music reached out and touched me". There was no mention of psychic matters. I duly contacted W. and visited him on November 24th 1993. I was immediately aware of his 'nervous' energy and it took little prompting for him to sit at the piano, which was decorated with reproduction Chopin memorabilia, and play some of his works. He spoke of constantly having melodies running through his mind which he had to write down and which even interrupted some of his teaching: "I began to notice that I was composing a great deal of music all in the Chopin style. I am certain that in my other life I was born in the 1800s." He explained further: "All my music comes on the spur of the moment. If you think about writing a piece of music it never comes from the soul." Psychic and spiritual subjects did not feature in our conversation since W. was not claiming direct contact with Chopin in spirit, but more of a binding to him as part of his own destiny. I studied the music W. gave me and having listened to his tapes I felt that the music bore little resemblance to Chopin's music other than in terms of pastiche. I sent copies of two of W.'s most representative pieces (Nocturne in D flat major and Prelude in A minor - see appendix L) for analysis to a leading expert in Chopin's music - John Rink, Music Department, Holloway College, University of London. He felt that both pieces were very poor indeed and were totally unlike Chopin in terms of progressions and developmental line. He believed that W. had either consciously or subconsciously tried to copy two of Chopin's works (Nocturne opus 27 and Prelude in C minor) and had failed to provide anything like Chopin's variety of texture. Rink became quite agitated at one part of the Prelude that he referred to as "offensive". Although I would not condemn W.'s music quite so forthrightly, it certainly does contain passages in which the harmony is particularly unlike Chopin. He concluded that W. was either completely self-deluded or was indulging in chicanery by presenting his music as Chopin's.

Case Study No. 7

In May 1995 another alleged musical medium, whom I shall refer to as T., replied to my newspaper advertisement for contact to be made. He sent me several pieces of his music that he claimed were dictated by a variety of well-known composers including Beethoven, Rachmaninov and Schubert. T. also sent me a cassette tape of him playing some of these pieces and he completed the questionnaire I sent him in detail, even writing separately about his methods of communication with the spirit world.

I learned from our correspondence that T. was a self-taught pianist with a grammar school education, who had taught himself theory from the Associated Board's *The Rudiments of Music*. He spoke of having written ten pieces, mainly for piano solo, and having collaborated with Beethoven on a serious sonata. He informed me that he had hoped to be a spiritual healer and he was therefore surprised when he had heard clairaudiently the words of Rachmaninov telling him: "Time to try a little composition" (private correspondence). He would appear to have witnessed other psychical activity since in his letters he wrote of "a spiritual journey which lasted months". His experiences included poltergeist manifestations, astral projection, clairaudience and clairvoyance but he concentrated on his musical activities and wrote of contact with spirits being achieved in two different ways - direct and indirect.

Of the direct mode he wrote:

"The direct form requires a relaxation more profound than can be achieved by meditation and therefore it only happens rarely. It can only be rarely that any of us can be both deeply relaxed yet intensely aware. In my case, this particular circumstance can only arise when I have risen to full consciousness from the sleep state but not moved my body, nor opened my eyes. I am then in a receptive state. The direct method is the most exciting because one hears the music clairaudiently. One hears everything, the flow of the music, the tone of the instrument(s), exactly as clearly as if the music were being played there in the room."

Of the indirect:

"The indirect method is less reliable because the subconscious mind can interfere. However, it is the only regular way of maintaining a collaboration with a composer. One has to relax, meditate and then keep one's mind open to musical ideas. These come usually as no more than phrases. They do not have the absolute clarity and certainty of music heard by the direct method. The music is cobbled together little by little. Often one gets the outline first, the substance being added later. I usually begin by knowing the genre of the piece, perhaps its title and the name of the composer who is providing the tuition."

(private correspondence)

T. was not surprised by some of my questions about whether composers' styles develop further in their spiritual existence or, if not, at which stage of their development they communicated. He felt that the musical medium "could not win" in this situation, since elementary music might indicate a lack of development or the medium's own knowledge being used and an advanced style might not be recognised as the named composer. He hoped that he might "be able to tune into the source of inspiration directly without the composer as an intermediary" (private correspondence).

I visited T. at his house when we were both engaged to make a brief television documentary about his work and on this occasion I also met his partner. He told me that T. practised the piano for "hours" every day and that he was really obsessed with his classical music. T. felt that he was being urged by spirit to compose more discordant music and he wondered if Scriabin might be trying to make contact. On being questioned about his religious beliefs, he denied affiliation to any Church including Spiritualism and he spoke of being "spiritual without being religious in the conventional sense". I received a copy of T.'s 'Beethoven' sonata and found it pleasing to listen to but lacking developmental strength. For the purposes of making the aforementioned television documentary, the services of a professional pianist were secured to play the first movement of T.'s 'Beethoven' sonata. He further corroborated my view by stating that in places the music had a Beethoven feel to it, but that formally and in some places harmonically, it was quite different. On the same programme the American conductor Paul Lipari claimed it to not be anything like Beethoven but more akin to silent movie background music. I sent a copy of the same to John Lill and he spoke of the music giving him "mixed impressions like various people on the phone at the same time" (private correspondence). I sent the same piece to Barry Cooper, who had looked at other pieces for me before, and he felt that this piece suffered from the same faults as the Rosemary Brown Scherzo. In addition, he stated it could only be compared to "very early Beethoven" since it further lacked any sophistication in the use of tonality and finally: "It is impossible to believe that Beethoven himself had a direct hand in composing it" (private correspondence October 1996). Parts of the whole sonata were played in the Music Department of the University of Sheffield where Professor Eric Clarke felt the piece bore no resemblance to Beethoven's music at all, showing no development of form or harmonic ideas.

It would seem from the evidence collected and my own experience of T.'s music that it is not directly dictated by dead composers. T. is undoubtedly a sensitive person who is a very enthusiastic amateur musician and pianist. A combination of these circumstances may well encourage him in his composition and the choice of composers reflects his own preferences in the classical piano tradition.

The majority of the musical mediums researched seemed to be absolutely genuine in their belief that dead composers were attempting to bring new music into the world through their intermediary mediumship. Further to this, the majority did not seek financial gain from their efforts although several sought public recognition for their gift. Some of the mediums went to great lengths to underplay the extent of their musical training but there were examples of childhood piano lessons and large amounts of practice time in adulthood - often several hours each day after retirement from full-time employment. It could be argued that at this stage in life a gap in their emotional and physical lives was being alleviated by such activity. A sense of urgency may also have been experienced as life's span neared its conclusion.

A possible reason for the claims of spirit dictation could be a desire for a feeling of personal importance since an amateur musician writing a pleasant piece of music does not have the impact on friends or the general public that the claim of divine intervention does. Humility may have denied the mediums the conceit of naming God as their direct source and Spiritualism could provide a convenient alternative. Furthermore, criticism of the music could be deflected towards the spirit composer or transmission problems rather than needing to be responded to on a personal level.

The music was mainly of a good amateur quality, with the exception of M.'s Bax work which was of a superior quality, but none compared favourably with the music of the composers who were alleged to have dictated it. In their own defence, mediums stated that the transmission from the spirit world to the material world, as well as the limitations of their own brains hampering the process, had a detrimental effect on the music. However, on some occasions the music or performance were felt to be exactly in accordance with the spirits' wishes and yet the results were still unconvincing.

Whether the professed beliefs of these musical mediums is grounded in self deception, fact or deliberate fraud, it is clear that they have nevertheless achieved results which they could not have normally been expected to given their training and musical knowledge. They have been inspired by their beliefs to devote considerable amounts of time and energy into producing music and have received little in return for their efforts other than ridicule.

It would seem from past and present sources, such as various editions of the *Grove Dictionary of Music*, that musical mediums, despite the claims of the Spiritual establishment, have not achieved a high enough standard of composition or performance to be acclaimed by professional musicians. The exception is Rosemary Brown who has received some support for her music. To a large extent they bring about this comparison themselves by entering the 'domain' of the professional musician. If the mediums' claim was one of being 'inspired by' the composers concerned rather than one of being 'dictated to', then the musical establishment might accept their music rather more willingly. At present it would seem that most of the musical mediums encountered could equally have the psychologist John Sloboda's assessment of Rosemary Brown applied to them: "There is no evidence of the 'vision' that her composers had in such abundance in their lives" (Sloboda,1994).

Paranormal Manifestations of Music

In studying the claims of musical mediums, the music allegedly communicated entered the minds of the percipients without an external sound source. However, the manifestation of 'paranormal' music presents the possibility of music from an unknown origin being heard by individuals who make no claim of mediumship, or even recorded by physical instruments for the purposes of direct analysis. In discussing 'ghostly' music it is necessary to define what is meant by such terms before presenting the variety of manifestations encountered and discussing the possible reasons for the word 'paranormal' being applied to them.

In writing about ghosts and apparitions, there are immediately problems of terminology. For example, 'spectres', 'phantoms', 'spirits' and 'entities' are all words that may be used to describe the phenomenon of paranormal manifestations, but in an imprecise way. The difficulty with definition can be further exacerbated when words apparently change their meanings or interpretations according to time and fashion. Perhaps the most commonly used terms for paranormal visual manifestations of human beings are 'ghost' and 'apparition'. Professor H. H. Price's (Wykeham Professor of Logic, University of Oxford) definition of a ghost is: "A visible but non-physical entity closely resembling a physical human being either living or dead" (cited in Underwood, 1993a, p.117). This definition presents two problems: First it assumes that the 'ghost' can only be perceived visually and second it proposes that a ghost can be that of a human being who is either living or dead. I would argue that a ghost need not be experienced solely visually and that it is also useful to distinguish between manifestations of the living and the dead, confining the use of the term 'ghost' specifically to the latter, implying also that it excludes inanimate objects. The word 'apparition', however, may encompass phenomena relating to that which is living, dead or inanimate and can be used as a general term, with other words, such as 'ghost', having a more restricted meaning.

One might believe that the industrialism of the nineteenth century and the urbanisation of the countryside where traditions were better maintained, would have eroded or annihilated beliefs in apparitions but this was not true. In 1862 the Ghost Club was founded to investigate authentic claims of ghostly phenomena and in 1886 *Phantasms of the Living* was published by the SPR, exploring seven hundred and two known cases of apparent spontaneous ESP, including examples of crisis apparitions (Gurney, Myers and Podmore, 1886). However, the major investigation by the Society was the 1894 *Census of Hallucinations* which was distributed to over seventeen thousand people throughout Britain. It asked: "Have you ever, when believing yourself to be completely awake, had a vivid impression of seeing or of hearing a voice; which impression as far as you could discover, was not due to any external physical source?" (Sidgwick, 1894). Of the seventeen thousand replies, about ten percent answered affirmatively to the question, one in twenty admitting to having seen a realistic apparition and one in thirty to having seen the apparition of a recognised person. Later, in 1948, the Cambridge criminologist and psychical researcher Professor Donald J. West undertook a survey to explore people's experience of external psychical phenomena. From one thousand five hundred and nineteen replies, fourteen percent answered affirmatively. In 1975 the parapsychologist Erlendur Haraldsson conducted a national survey in Iceland asking whether people had ever perceived or felt the nearness of a deceased person. Thirty-one percent replied affirmatively (Haraldsson, 1991). People of all ages, cultures and degrees of intelligence seem to witness such phenomena.

Although many alleged apparitions may be hallucinatory in origin, some are ostensibly veridical in that they correspond to events outside themselves in a way for which no ordinary explanation seems feasible. Collectively perceived apparitions and apparitions connected to a specific location which are recognised by persons without any knowledge of the 'haunting' provide puzzling examples. Crisis and death-bed apparitions can also convince their observers that they have had paranormal encounters.

It is possible to see how throughout history the essential characteristics of apparitions have not changed apart from those particular features that belong to their period of origin, e.g. dress. The range of possible explanations for the origins of apparitions in their various forms include theories based upon religious belief, reincarnation doctrines, fraudulent activity and physical hallucination amongst others. Perhaps mankind's fear of death and subsequent annihilation has encouraged many of the concepts of post-death survival, including reincarnation and Spiritualism. Firstly, one might consider the widely-held Spiritualist belief in post-death survival resulting in spirits capable of appearing as ghosts or communicating with the living through a medium. If this is viewed as the only source of apparitions then it does not encompass the many examples of apparitions of the living and nor does it take into account cyclic/periodic ghosts that appear at specific times or dates, apparitions of animals or of inanimate objects, or time slips of complete events. However, it is widely accepted in Spiritualist groups that spirit contact, with its need for a medium to be present, is different from witnessing ghostly phenomena.

The theory of cyclic ghosts suffers further from the changes made to the calendar in Britain in 1752 when the date was moved eleven days forward and by the changes made by Pope Gregory in 1582 who decreed that October 5th should become October 15th to bring the equinoxes into alignment. Despite these changes, some authors would have us believe that cyclical appearances continue on the same date across these calendar changes (e.g. Underwood, 1993a). Similarly, one wonders how ghosts traditionally appearing at midnight cope with the clocks being moved forwards or backwards according to the changes in British Summertime!

Undoubtedly, many apparitions can be accounted for by natural phenomena in much the same way that many UFOs have been registered when planes or astronomical activities have provided a solution to sightings. Electrical and plumbing sounds are often quoted by the susceptible as indicating 'ghostly presences' and people who do not live in rural areas and are not acquainted with the foibles of old buildings or of certain animals may well interpret natural sounds as having a paranormal origin.

Misinterpretation of natural phenomena is understandable but there are times when deliberate fraud appears to have been involved in the production of supposedly paranormal events. The large numbers of photographs of apparitions have been almost totally discredited and claims of physical manifestations of spiritual ectoplasm in the nineteenth and early twentieth centuries have ceased after the countless examples of fraud that were uncovered or admitted to. The possibility of intentional fraud has to be considered either for monetary gain, such as when a 'haunted' public house attracts more custom, or for reasons of practical joking.

Another factor to be taken into account may be the problem of faulty memory through the human ageing process. Appearances of allegedly deceased people have sometimes been found, after investigation, to have taken place before their death and not after (Wilson, 1995). A combination of false memory and legend can allow fact and fiction to combine into a new hybrid reality. Furthermore, cerebral ischaemia can produce hallucinations (of apparitions) in people who seem to be in otherwise good health (McHarg, 1982).

Sources also provide a range of alternative theories and possible explanations for the appearance of apparitions (see Stokes, 1987). Peter Underwood favours the 'electronic impulse wave theory' according to which brain waves become more active in extreme stress and at a certain level produce a telepathic image that is capable of being picked up by someone else. This perceptual capacity may eventually fade away if people do not maintain it by experiencing the impression (Underwood, 1988). Myers, an early founder of the SPR, believed apparitions to be a "manifestation of persistent personal energy" (Myers, 1903) which possibly meant some sort of spiritual energy and Sidgwick believed this presence could be perceived by a suitably sensitive person. The later researcher, G. N. M. Tyrrell, published a book *Apparitions* (1953) containing sixty-one cases in which he argued that apparitions were telepathic hallucinations emanating from the subconscious. Other theories have included astral light, hybrid beings created from dead persons' spirits, thought forms (tulpas) and even alien manifestations from other dimensions.

There would seem to be three main questions that need to be explored in differentiating these theories:

- Do apparitions reside solely in the percipient's mind?
- Do apparitions exist outside the percipient's mind (e.g. tulpas), despite being caused by it?
- Do apparitions manifest from an external source?

Perhaps the greatest difficulties arise when one attempts to define apparitions with reference *exclusively* to one of these explanations. For centuries there have been countless reports of sightings by groups of people; many photographs have been taken; animals' behaviour has been affected by such entities; physical objects have been moved etc. It seems too simplistic to claim that all these cases were either fraudulently reported or were solely the product of the percipient's mind. The reports of cyclic hauntings and apparitions that were unknown to the observer would seem to indicate that the human mind was not conjuring up such entities in every case, but neither can it be claimed that every example originates from an external source (Wilson, 1995).

It is necessary to explain at the outset exactly what will be excluded under the title of musical 'apparitions' and what will be included. For the purpose of this essay, séance manifestations will not generally be discussed since the previous essay mentioned these. The word 'musical' has excluded cases involving sounds generally believed to be of a non-musical nature, e.g. door bells and servants' bells, but church bells have been included since they have a greater propensity for musical interpretation. The human voice has been included only in a singing or chanting capacity. Spoken dialogue, screams and other non-musical utterances have not been included. The term 'musical apparition' has been taken to indicate the presence of music with or without an apparitional performer in a situation that would suggest that its physical production was implausible.

This research is not the first to explore incidences of music being heard without an apparent physical sound source. An exploratory study of apparitions was made by the psychical researcher Ernest Bozzano which included examples of deathbed music being heard as well as examples of musical mediums, telepathic music and musical hauntings (Bozzano, 1923). However, more recently two large-scale studies of such phenomena were carried out in the nineteen sixties and seventies by the late American psychic researcher D. Scott Rogo under the titles of *NAD* volumes one and two (Rogo, 1970; 1972). In these studies, Rogo investigated case studies from people in Britain and the USA who claimed to have heard 'transcendental' music or, to use his own words, 'music of the spheres' (Rogo, 1972). The term 'NAD' is derived from the "Tantric Yogi doctrine of superhuman music" (Rogo, 1970, p.17). His conclusion provides, he believed, evidence for post-death survival in a psychic ether, i.e. a different dimension from which this music emanates.

> Possibly the oldest surviving musical treatise is the *Musica Disciplina*, which was written by Aurelian of Reome in the mid ninth century. Aurelian mentions instances of the hearing of 'angelic music': "...there was a certain monk of the monastery of St Victor...Holding vigil by night before the porch of the church, he heard a choir of angels singing the responsory...one night coming out of his own house adjoining the wall of St Alban's basilica, he heard a harmonious choir of angels singing the word 'Alleluia' with Psalm 148 up to the end of the Psalter..."

> (cited Godwin, 1987, p.96)

These separate incidents of the hearing of angelic choirs are far from the only sources from antiquity and further examples could be added from Hebrew texts: "...Nine angels who sing by night sing down on all those who can sing..." (cited in Godwin, 1987, p.61). The German mystic Heinrich Seuse (Henry Suso) (c.1295-1366) wrote about hearing inner music in a similar way to the English mystic Richard Rolle (d. 1349) in the *Fire of Love*, but he also spoke of hearing music from an angelic source outside himself: "...it seemed to him in a vision that he heard angelic strains and sweet heavenly melody; and this filled him with such gladness that he forgot all his sufferings..."(cited Godwin, 1987, p.112). (Many further examples of 'angelic music' could be quoted, e.g. Godwin, 1987; Rogo, 1970; 1972.) A degree of caution is necessary in referring to such ancient manuscripts, since faulty translation may have suggested external origins for music when not intended. Further to this, the authors themselves, often of a deeply religious or mystical nature, may have externalised what was a part of their deeply-held belief system. A number of saints, including St Chad, St Joseph of Copertino, St Veronica Giuliana and St Guthlac (Rogo, 1970), either heard celestial music or it was heard by others at their deathbeds. However, there has been a dearth of accounts of choirs of angels being reported in the last few centuries apart from sporadic mentions. One modern recording which has been suggested by an Italian source - Bacci and Capitoni - as having a possible angelic origin was made recently as part of an electronic voice phenomena or EVP experiment (private correspondence).

Historical references to musical apparitions or hallucinations have not been limited to choral phenomena as can be attested by an alleged statement made by the religious reformer John Calvin on December 9th 1562 when, according to Theodore Beza, who succeeded him as the leader of his organisation, he heard on this date "a very loud sound of drums used in war", even though no such instruments were nearby (cited in Inglis, 1985, p.50). At the same time and unknown to him, the Huguenots were suffering a defeat at the Battle of Dreux.

The most famous instance of inexplicable drumming is undoubtedly the phenomenon known as 'The Drummer of Tedworth' (or Tidworth) which allegedly produced poltergeist characteristics, but more importantly for this study also gave rise to music from an unknown source. A detailed account was provided by the Revd Joseph Glanvill, a chaplain to Charles II and a Fellow of the Royal Society, in his *Saducismus Triumphatus: Full and Plain Evidence Concerning Witches and Apparitions* (London, 1681, but first published in 1666). He wrote that in March 1661 (or 1662 since there is confusion concerning the actual dates) a beggar named William Drury annoyed the townsfolk of Ludgarshall on the outskirts of North Tedworth in Wiltshire by his incessant drumming and general harassment of the people. He was arrested and placed in gaol by the magistrate John Mompesson and his confiscated drum was removed to the magistrate's house - the local manor and now the site of Zouche Manor. Immediately, poltergeist events broke out including the drum playing by itself. Scratching sounds were heard, beds were shaken and other phenomena were witnessed by a number of people. Mompesson took the precaution of burning the drum but the sounds of drumming continued to be heard including military tattoos and specifically the jig 'Roundheads and Cuckolds go dig, go dig'. Drury meanwhile had been freed from gaol but on re-offending had been re-arrested and sentenced to transportation on charges of vagrancy and witchcraft. He escaped but was not heard of again. However, the manifestations at Mompesson's house continued and the case became celebrated enough for a Royal Commission to be sent to investigate it, whereupon the disturbances ceased, only to return after the commissioners' departure. It appealed to the populace's imagination sufficiently for a broadside ballad, dated 1663, to be published about it (cited in Price, 1993, pp.391-393). In

1716, Joseph Addison wrote a comedy about it called *The Drummer or the Haunted House* and in more recent times Edith Sitwell wrote a poem - *The Drum* (Selected Poems, 1936, London).

Even before the resurgence of interest in 'supernatural' matters that the nineteenth century gothic revival caused, castles had long been associated with hauntings and poltergeist activity, usually of a visual nature. This is reflected in works of literature such as the ghostly characters in Shakespeare's *Hamlet* and *Macbeth*. The alleged re-enactments of tragedies that were enclosed in their walls has lent support to the theory that events could be trapped in time and under certain unknown circumstances might be played back to a present day observer. In short, what has become known as 'the stone-tape' theory - a popular concept of paranormal recording and replaying.

Evidence for musical apparitions has been more difficult to discover, since the more spectacular stories and legends have not been of a musical nature. Very little information was provided for another seventeenth century haunting where drumming was allegedly heard. Concerning Castleconnell Castle near Limerick in Eire a letter of 1640 states: "For news we have the strangest that ever was heard of enchantments in the Lord of Castleconnell's Castle, four miles from Limerick, several sorts of noise, sometimes of drums and trumpets, sometimes of curious musique [sic] with heavenly voices" (cited in Rogo, 1972, p.33). A. R. G. Owen, the psychical researcher, believed this to have a more earthly origin stating: "The phenomena mentioned in the letter doubtless started as crude jokes played by the Irish to take a rise out of their Anglo-Irish masters" (Owen, 1976, p.33).

I have decided to discuss musical apparitions in terms of their locations - castles, churches and abbeys, palaces and country houses, inns, other buildings and outside locations. A final section investigates, where possible, the people who have witnessed such phenomena. Having researched the available literature on apparitions, a number of castles were indeed discovered to have reports of musical apparitions associated with them and for ease of access it was decided to remain within the UK for detailed investigation.

The evidence for music having been heard in strange circumstances was sometimes very weak, relying on perhaps one anecdotal reference, e.g. Abergeldie Castle in Aberdeenshire is reputed to possess the ghost of Kittie Rankie who was burned as a witch after having been imprisoned in its cellars: "...in the mid nineteenth century...the ringing of bells were said to haunt the cellars..." (Spencer, 1992, p.135). The original reference for this story has not been provided other than another author being named. There is a similar lack of evidence for Gight Castle's "ghostly piping" (*Folklore, Myths and Legends of Britain,* 1973, p.465) and Loch Nell Castle where even the instruments are not specified - "ghostly or fairy music has been heard" (Hippisley Coxe, 1975, p.165). Booklets intended for tourists have often promoted ghost stories, especially when the town or city advertises 'ghost walks'. Edinburgh Castle is referred to (Matthews, 1993) in one such guide as being the starting place for a tunnel under the High Street that is haunted by ghostly bagpipe music and the beating of spectral drums can evidently occasionally be heard in the castle itself.

Even greater problems were encountered when several different sources were available since the information was often of a highly contradictory nature. It was therefore decided to contact the present owners or managers of a number of castles throughout the UK to enquire whether any information was known concerning past or present musical anomalies. Seventeen castles were chosen after having been identified in written sources as harbouring musical ghosts or apparitions, of which eleven proved helpful in casting further light on the legends and provided recent, well-informed opinions on the alleged phenomena. For instance:

<u>Cortachy Castle, Kirriemuir, Angus</u>.

The legend of the drummer of Cortachy has received many different interpretations:

> "The seat of the Earls of Airlie, it is haunted by the ghost of a fine young drummer boy who was caught 'in flagrante delicto' with Lady Airlie. He was seized, boxed up in his own drum and flung off the highest tower to his death. Since then drumming is supposed to be heard outside the castle when one of the family is about to die."
>
> (Brooks, 1990, pp.215-216)

> "...when the sound of the drum is heard, a death in the Ogilvy family may surely be expected...The original drummer appears to have been the messenger of some hated chieftain...the Ogilvy of that time had the drummer

104

stuffed into his own drum and flung from the topmost battlements of Cortachy."

(Harper, 1994, p.254)

With this and other contradictory information available it was particularly helpful to receive an explanatory letter from the Factor of Lord Airlie:

"...Legend has it that, in the seventeenth century during one of the frequent clashes between the Ogilvy family and Clan Campbell, a Campbell drummer boy was sent to Cortachy under a flag of truce. He was immediately slaughtered by an Ogilvie of the time and hung out of an upper window in his own drum. The legend is that when the death of an Earl of Airlie is imminent, the drum will be heard. There is no record of it having been heard at any other time, but there is some anecdotal evidence that, when the present Earl's grandfather was killed at the Battle of Diamond Hill in the South Africa War in 1900, the drum was heard by a member of the family, who was at that time a guest at Achnacarry Castle at Spean Bridge. I was, myself, present at Cortachy on 28th December 1968 when the present Earl's father died; there is no evidence of the drum having been heard in the days leading up to the event."

(Private correspondence, September 10th 1996)

Herstmonceaux Castle, Hailsham, East Sussex.

Another drumming legend has been quoted in many sources as manifesting in this castle:

"Ghostly drum music is frequently heard on the battlements of Herstmonceaux Castle and a nine-foot tall phantom drummer has been seen. The ghost is that of a previous lord of the manor who beat a drum in order to frighten the prospective lovers of his young wife."

(*Folklore, Myths and Legends of Britain,* 1973, p.202)

"The Drummer's Hall has long been reputed to be haunted by the ghost of a giant drummer...and the figure is said to have been seen striding along the battlements above the Great Hall, beating a drum and sending showers of sparks cascading from his incandescent drum sticks."

(Underwood, 1971, p.94).

I received a letter from the Operations Director of the castle who informed me: "We have not had any reportings of musical phenomena, ghostly music, etc." (private correspondence, September 12th 1996). Once more it would appear that either the story was a hoax from the very beginning or the apparition no longer manifests there.

Duntrune Castle, Kilmartin, Argyl.

It would be a mistake to assume that the majority of hauntings have been perceived as drum music. The Duntrune phenomenon has been described as piping:

> "The piper played his pipes to warn returning MacDonalds, and the Campbells, robbed of their prey, seized the piper and slashed off his fingers...the sound of his piping continued for centuries...100 years ago [1893?] a skeleton was unearthed, with all the fingers missing...No set pattern, but October seems the favourite month and early evening the usual time [for the haunting]."

(Underwood, 1993b. p.164)

> "...a piper...managed to warn the invaders by playing 'The Piper's Warning to his Master'. Campbell of Duntrune then chopped off his hands...(Another version says a piper on a nearby hill played 'The Campbells are Coming')...when it [the castle] was being restored quite recently they discovered, under the kitchen floor, two skeleton hands. The piper's ghost haunts the tower and this is where some still hear the sound of his warning'."

(Hippisley Coxe, 1975, pp.163-164)

I received a letter from Robin Malcolm of Duntrune Castle who knew of the legend but stated: "I have never heard 'ghostly' music, nor my wife, nor anyone I know, present or past. There was a service of exorcism about 1870. Prior to that, I suppose paranormal music was a possibility" (private correspondence, 1996).

What can be learned from these three examples and are there any similar circumstances or attributes in the other cases? Firstly, it might seem that the writers about alleged hauntings need to verify their information more correctly to avoid contradictions. The original sources of stories were virtually always omitted. Several accounts seem to have been re-worded and repeated in subsequent books with a little embroidery by new authors. It is perhaps not surprising that the traditional Scottish love of pipes and drums should appear prominently in the musical hauntings comprising four examples from the total of eight contacted.

Music/instruments were reported as follows:

type of music	no. of examples
bagpipes	3
drums	3
'music'	3
chanting/ singing	2
harp	2
pipes/whistle	2
trumpet	1
piano	1
organ	1

The reporting of the piano was quoted in one source only (Underwood, 1993b) for St Donat's Castle in Wales. It now houses the United World College of the Atlantic and a letter from them informed me: "We have no knowledge of any ghosts, musical or otherwise" (private correspondence, September 18th 1996). Similar private correspondence refuting the present existence of musical ghosts was received during September and October 1996 from:

- The Administrator of Culzean Castle, Maybole, Ayr. (See Underwood, 1993b for alleged modern manifestations and witnesses)

- The Administrator of Bodiam Castle, E. Sussex. (See Underwood, 1984 for precise date of haunting, i.e. Easter Sunday)
- The Duke of Argyl, Inverary Castle, Argyl. (See Underwood, 1993b for claims of harp music being heard by former dukes)
- The Keeper of Tower History (Dr G. Parnell), H M Tower of London. (See Underwood, 1984 for claims of religious chanting in 1978)

Dr Parnell's letter was particularly interesting since he had obviously enquired further into the matter: "I have consulted one or two colleagues who have worked here since the 1960s, but they can add nothing".

- The Custodian of Richmond Castle, North Yorks.

Whilst denying any personal knowledge of 'ghostly' music, a leaflet was enclosed with the correspondence that tells of the legend of a drummer boy who was trapped in a tunnel between castle and nearby Easby, but whose drumming then mysteriously stopped. Some say that "ghostly drumming is sometimes heard" (Bord, 1990, p. 153).

Despite mentions of paranormal music being heard in current literature, replies were not received from:

- Ewloe Castle, Clwyd. "...a recent custodian has heard ghostly singing" (Bord, 1989, p.83).
- Balcomie Castle, Fife. "...the man was found dead, since when the sound of his whistle has often been heard around the castle" (Brooks, 1990, p.211).
- Fyvie Castle, Aberdeen. "...a phantom trumpeter...ghostly activities are being reported here all the time" (Underwood, 1993b., pp.173-174).
- Odiham Castle, Hants. "...the clear notes of some piping instrument have been heard" (Underwood, 1996, p.21).
- Taunton Castle Hotel, Taunton. "...from somewhere in the depths of the building...there comes the sad sound of violins" (Mead, 1994, p.40).

The manager of Culcreuch Castle, Fintry, Stirling sent printed information about ghostly harp music and a piper. Curiously the only previous source that I had discovered had not mentioned the harp music (Mead, 1994). Since the enclosed literature made quite specific claims, i.e.: "The Phantom Piper is heard so often that two independent groups of scientists have attempted to establish a natural cause for the sounds" (hotel leaflet), I decided to visit the castle which has now been converted into a hotel, for the purposes of conducting my own research on site. I stayed, with a colleague from the Ghost Club Society, for two nights (March 25th/26th 1997) in the allegedly haunted 'Chinese Bird Room'. Members of staff knew of the legends but had not witnessed anything themselves. However, we were told stories of guests having to leave the room early because of 'unpleasant' experiences and feelings there. A tape-recorder was set up for part of the first night which only succeeded in recording the 'clanging' of water pipes and a certain amount of noise from outside - nothing of a musical or paranormal nature. The manager of the hotel informed me that the stories of the castle were inherited from the previous owner, one Hercules Robinson, and "we created a story" (D. Littlefear, manager) from the information supplied. However, he stressed that many people had since experienced phenomena in the castle. On the second night, after an unsuccessful sèance during which nothing of significance occurred, a video camera was used to record any activity during the remainder of the night. Nothing paranormal was recorded and we departed the next morning not having discovered anything of an anomalous nature.

A combination of the often remote location of castles, together with the understandable air of mystery they invoke, would seem to promote the continuation of legends that were often started to keep intruders away. Present-day owners maintain such legends when it is good for business. Comparable advertising is found in the large number of claims for famous personalities to have stayed in various properties, e.g. "Dick Turpin stayed here". It is not surprising that a population that is witnessing the gradual decay of its historical sites and legends should wish to maintain past traditions of which castles provide striking evidence. A less sceptical viewpoint could claim that only suitably 'sensitive' people are able to experience genuine paranormal phenomena that lie outside of current methods of perception, both human and mechanical, and that in a busier, more technological society these too are declining in number.

There are very few towns or cities in Britain that do not contain an abbey or at least one church and on the outskirts can occasionally be found the ruins of such places. The buildings are often hundreds of years old and music will have almost certainly been used as part of the tradition of worship since their inauguration. Church decorations have illustrated biblical scenes with angels, often playing musical instruments, and with pictures of heaven and hell. Even the smell of some buildings - especially if incense is used regularly - can induce an altered state, by contrast with the outside world. Churches are often used for events of great joy and sadness, such as marriages and funerals, and if one accepts that an extreme set of emotions can imprint themselves in an unknown way into a building's fabric, then churches must be investigated as a possible source of such activity.

The literature of haunted properties contains many references to churches and abbeys (notably McEwan, 1989) and examples of alleged paranormal music are referred to in a number of sources. One of the earliest well-documented cases was reported in the *Journal of the Society for Psychical Research* (*JSPR*) in December 1915 and concerned the Abbey of Jumieges in France. The ruined abbey was visited by a family of four (mother, father, brother and sister) at about 3 p.m. on July 6th 1913 when it was reported:

> "I suddenly became aware of the sound of a large number of men's voices which seemed to come from the open space on our left where the few scattered stones marked the site where the monastic choir had been. The singing was very soft; the air was quite familiar; I remember saying to myself twice: "I am imagining this! I am imagining this!" and then the music 'left' my attention as I heard my father exclaim: "Why, there are the monks singing!"...I was so struck with the strangeness of the thing that I determined to pretend I had heard nothing, until I learned from my companions if their experience had been the same as my own. I found this was the case, and we agreed that the voices were chanting "Vespers" - that is to say, they were chanting a psalm in Latin. We tried to think of possible 'natural' explanations, but the present parish church was a kilometre and a half from there - so the caretaker told us - besides which, if the sound had come from there, we should have heard it for longer than a few seconds...I wrote an account of this shortly after it took place."

(Ernestine Anne, cited in *JSPR*, December 1915, pp.119-120)

This account was corroborated in writing by the other members of the family and further enquiries confirmed that there was not a community of monks in the vicinity. They could have actually heard monks singing who were concealed from their view in some unknown place but one might query the short duration of the music if Vespers were truly being sung. A collective hallucination seems unfeasible since each witness evidently heard the music separately without initial reference to each other. In a typical collective hallucination one person indicates a presence - usually visual - and then others present claim to see it. It seems at least possible that the family actually witnessed a paranormal 'playback' of music from a different time.

The literature of haunted churches and abbeys in Britain where music had been heard was consulted, and letters were sent to all of these establishments to enquire about recent activity or general awareness of the phenomena. Thirty-eight examples were discovered, exclusively in England with the exception of Iona in Scotland where "ghostly music and bells have been heard" (Bord, 1990, p.175) and the chapel ruins of St David's, Wales where "Ghostly hymn-singing is said to be heard" (Bord, 1990, p.99).

The quality and quantity of information regarding musical hauntings varied considerably. Some were extremely vague with perhaps only one reference from the available literature. "Avenbury Church: Haunted by ghostly music" (Hippisley Coxe, 1975, p. 94) is one such example. Others, including Borley Church in Essex and Beaulieu Abbey near Southampton, were very well documented. Information regarding the time and date of the occurrences were mainly omitted or mentioned simply as "at night" but more precise data were given regarding the nature of the music. Some authors used the term 'chanting' whereas others used 'singing' or 'a choir was heard'. Some places contained a variety of musical manifestations and the categories can be classified as follows:

types of music	no. of examples
chanting / singing / choir	16
organ playing	10
bells ringing	9
unspecified music	4

solo soprano	2
trumpets and drums	1
horns	1

The single example of trumpets and drums being heard was at Fotheringhay Church in Northampton in 1976, when a local schoolteacher and his wife approached the church believing that a rehearsal for a concert of medieval ceremonial music must be happening inside. On entering they found the place to be empty but continued to hear the music as they returned to the churchyard gate (Dening, 1996). With subsequent research it was found that on that precise date (allowing for the revisions of the Gregorian calendar) in 1476, the bodies of Richard, Duke of York and his son Edmund were interred in the family mausoleum situated there at the same time of day as the teacher's visit. Further examples have been reported of ghostly chanting there (Dening, 1996) but my letter to the incumbent did not receive a reply. I visited Fotheringhay Church on the anniversary of this event to try to record any paranormal music and noticed the relatively close proximity of the road and other buildings suggesting that a car radio or music from a private dwelling may have given rise to this story.

Before investigating the more common manifestations such as chanting and organ music, the solo soprano heard at St Peter's Church, Babraham, Cambridge, is worth consideration since I made contact with the organist of over forty years, Mr C. Ingrey. He was interviewed by the *Cambridge Evening News* (appeared October 31st 1989) concerning his having heard a soprano voice in the church when it was completely empty. He later learned of a previous organist, who had died in 1933, whose wife had been a soprano. Mr Ingrey claimed that other people had felt a 'presence' in the church. I asked him on the telephone (February 17th 1997) whether he had heard the voice on more than one occasion and whether he recognised the 'aria' that she was singing. He replied that this was the only time that he had heard the voice but that he had smelled female perfume on other occasions. He did not recognise the aria since it was just a few seconds of singing. Nothing has happened of a paranormal nature recently (February 1997). A solo soprano voice was also heard at Langenhoe Church, near Colchester, Essex, in the 1940s and 1950s but the church was demolished in the

1960s. However, it was quite extensively investigated at the time and no definite evidence was found to prove or disprove paranormal manifestations (see Underwood, 1971; McEwan, 1989).

The inclusion of horns being heard refers to a single account (McEwan, 1989) when the organist, Mr R. Rowland, of St Dunstan's Church, East Acton, London, heard the sound of two horns ringing out just as he reached the sign for the horn stop in his music. I received a letter from the present vicar who has not heard of any paranormal music associated with the church, but he did mention that a previous incumbent exorcised the place to remove the presence of some "unearthly friars". Avenbury Church was one of the places where the nature of the music was not specified. I received a letter from the Revd Prebendary W. Gould with an article attached concerning Avenbury Church from an unnamed local newspaper dated May 16th 1991. It mentioned that organ music has been heard occasionally since 1896 but that the church is now derelict. A previous vicar, the Revd Archer-Shepherd, provided this possible explanation: "Some telepathic or auto-suggestive, or other natural cause may have acted on their auditory nerves, setting up sensations which were transmitted by the brain into external sounds."

Ten different examples of paranormal occurrences of organ music were reported in religious buildings:

- Borley Church, Borley, Essex.
- The Cathedral and Abbey Church of St Alban, St Albans, Hertfordshire.
- Caistor Church, Caistor, Lincolnshire.
- Lutton Church, Lutton, Northamptonshire.
- St Andrew's Church, Norwich, Norfolk.
- St John's Church, Torquay, Devon.
- Cressing Church, Cressing, Essex.
- St Mary's Church, Bowers Gifford, Essex.
- Hassingham Church, Norfolk.
- St Crux Church, York.

Both the church at Borley and St Albans Abbey will be discussed later since they have both been written about extensively with claims of different types of music being heard. The other churches have only produced organ music as their alleged paranormal musical manifestations. The evidence varied, with only one reference found for the last six examples quoted and therefore letters from incumbents were particularly useful. Replies were received that denied all knowledge of such activity although suggestions were made that local lads might have been playing pranks or as one reply suggested: "Air remaining in pipes can be expelled by the movement of mice, of which we have many. We are also in a very isolated setting which fuels the imagination" (private correspondence with Mrs Choules, Church warden to St Mary's Church, Bowers Gifford, Essex, September 14th 1996). I was informed that St Crux Church in York had been demolished and the Hassingham reference was unsubstantiated after several requests from the initial source. The church at Caistor in Lincolnshire was mentioned in several books and comments included:

"In the church a ghostly monk plays the organ, and his music has been recorded on tape" (Hippisley Coxe, 1975, p.141) and "The local church has long been reputed to be haunted by a monk who plays the organ...there were footsteps echoing through the empty church and loud and clear notes from the church organ" (Underwood, 1971, p.44). A letter to me from Mr D. Naylor, an organist, provided a possible explanation to the phenomenon:

> "The 'ghostly' music to which you refer is easily explained. Many years ago I regularly went to play the organ late at night without switching any lights on, except for the console. You can imagine, therefore, how the rumours started, especially with a boarding school close by! There have, of course, been no subsequent tales reported."
>
> (private correspondence, September 23rd 1996).

A similar explanation was provided to alleged 'ghostly' organ music in St John's Church, Torquay: "There was at that time an almost blind parish clerk who used to play the organ for his own amusement without bothering to put on the lights!" (Revd B. G. Burr cited in McEwan, 1989, p.29).

There are many legends concerning bells in folklore - warding off evil spirits, warning of storms and even providing healing properties. Minsden Chapel in Hertfordshire was built in the fourteenth century and was traditionally associated with Alice Perrers, a mistress of Edward III who was involved with occult practices. It soon fell into decay but was leased by the historian, Reginald Hine who vowed: "After my death and burial I will endeavour, in all ghostly ways, to protect and haunt its hallowed walls" (R. Hine cited in Underwood, 1971, pp.170-171). Most sources quote directly or indirectly Underwood's account of the music: "...ghostly manifestations usually begin with the toll of the lost bells of Minsden and as the sounds die away the figure of a monk is seen...After a moment the strains of sweet and plaintive music fill the air..." (ibid).

The local librarian informed me that there had not been any recent musical manifestations to her knowledge and one wonders whether the howling of the wind in a ruined and atmospheric setting may have lead to such accounts. The traditional date of the haunting is Hallowe'en when the weather might well be inclement and 'trick or treaters' may be in evidence. When I visited the site, in April 1997, the local publican confirmed that "youngsters like to fool around there at Hallowe'en" and there were signs of human activity in the form of empty alcohol bottles and other debris.

Incidents of chanting or choirs singing were reported in the following buildings:

- Beaulieu Abbey, Hampshire.
- Borley Church, Borley, Essex.
- The Cathedral and Abbey Church of St Alban, St Albans, Hertfordshire.
- Winchcombe Church, near Cheltenham, Gloucester.
- Whitby Abbey, Whitby, N. Yorkshire.
- Spinney Abbey,Wicken, Cambridgeshire.
- St Mary's Church, Hendon, London.
- Fountains Abbey, Yorkshire.
- St Mary's Church, Beaminster, Dorset.
- St Mary's Church, Reigate, Surrey.
- St John's Priory, Poling, Sussex.
- Denny Abbey, Chittering, Cambridgeshire.
- Pyrford Church, Pyrford, Surrey.
- Lawford Church, Colchester, Essex.
- St Margaret's Church, East Wellow, Hampshire.
- Whalley Abbey, Clitheroe, Lancashire.

The latter ten examples cited rely on one reference only and these were often unsubstantiated. For example, Fountains Abbey in Yorkshire where "…a ghostly choir has been heard chanting in the Chapel of the Nine Altars by numerous people on many occasions" (Hippisley Coxe, 1975, p.136). I received a letter from Mr M. Newman, the Regional Archaeologist for the Yorkshire region, who informed me: "...while it [the Abbey] is open to the public, Gregorian chant is played through a public address system. This latter fact is sometimes overlooked by some visitors" (private correspondence, October 1st 1996).

Similarly, a single account appears in a booklet by a local Essex historian and psychic researcher, Mr W. Downes, who writes about Lawford Church, near Colchester:

> "As she got nearer to the church she was amazed to hear a full choir heartily singing, despite the fact that she was certain that the local choir had been disbanded 'for the duration'. Yet here was a fully lit church with a choir singing at eleven o' clock at night. Something was definitely wrong, so she went along the path to the south door of the church and tried the handle, but found that it was locked. Suddenly she became aware that the singing had stopped and the lights were no longer alight...she became frightened and ran home."

> (Downes, 1992, p.50)

I received a letter from the Rector of St Mary's, Lawford who stated: "We have had some 'ghastly' music in our time but I am not aware of anything 'ghostly' (private correspondence, September 10th 1996). I spoke to him on the telephone (February 22nd 1997) and he confirmed that he believed that it was "fiction".

I received a more positive reply to my enquiries about Denny Abbey in East Anglia where plainsong had been reported as being heard amongst the ruins (Harries, 1974). The existing and previous custodians both claimed to have heard a distant chanting and although willing to concede that it was music travelling from surrounding areas, they agreed that the place seemed to possess a heavy atmosphere. Mrs Cooke, the custodian, also stated that she has occasionally been asked by visitors whether she has been playing music there, when she has not, since they have heard something (private correspondence September

19th 1996). I visited the site in person in April 1997 and spoke to Mrs Cooke who was very keen to show me exactly where she had heard the music and to explain how it could not be heard elsewhere. She described herself as being sensitive to such manifestations and spoke of other psychic-related events happening to her.

Beaulieu Abbey in Hampshire is well represented in references to monks chanting and although the present owner, Lord Montague, has not witnessed them himself, his sister Mrs E. Varley heard chanting in her teens: "I was sitting by the window of my room quite late at night when I heard it. It was very clear and quite loud enough for me to pick up the notes of the chant...when I sang the tune the next day to someone staying in the house, they recognised it as Gregorian chant" (cited Brooks, 1990, pp.42-43). The Curator of the Motor Museum, situated on the site, has also allegedly heard "the sounds of monks chanting" (Bord, 1990, p.27). I was invited by the Ghost Club to attend an all night investigation of the ruins in January 1994 and myself and six other members spent the night at various vantage points where the monks had been seen or heard. No phenomena were perceived apart from one member hearing chanting coming from the ladies' toilet. I investigated personally and found it to be the whirring of an electric fan heater and nothing like the Gregorian chant suggested! A sèance was held which similarly provided no evidence of the paranormal and the members of the group departed at about 5 a.m.

I was almost guilty of self-deception when visiting Bolton Abbey in Yorkshire, in October 1993, which does not have a history of musical mysteries but does have stories connected with it of 'ghostly' monks being sighted. On entering, with a fellow investigator, what appeared to be an empty building, the sounds of monks chanting were heard by both of us. I recorded this with a video camera only to find a few moments later that the cleaner, who was in the vestry, was playing a tape of plainsong while she undertook her duties. Had we fled in terror another story of a haunting would have been added to the literature.

Information about musical hauntings at St Albans Abbey were quite well documented and a reply was received to my request for further material. There are various stories concerning musical phenomena reported at the Abbey. One involves a bell tolling in the belfry when the bells had been removed during World War II; another tells of the organ playing by itself and a "glorious burst of singing" (Puttick, 1994, p.13). A well-documented case occurred prior to this concerning the *Albanus*

Mass of Robert Fayrfax, Master of the King's Music during the reign of Henry VIII. To commemorate the four hundredth anniversary of Fayrfax's death, the Mass was performed in a concert at the Abbey on October 20th 1921. It was after this event that Canon George Glossop claimed to have heard the music previously "in the middle of the night on more than one occasion" (Puttick, 1994, p.15). His wife vouched for his sincerity and his daughter also claimed to have heard the same music. There have been several other reports of choral music being heard from the Abbey at about 2 a.m., the most recently quoted taking place in 1983 (Carrington and Thresher undated). A letter to Dr B. Rose, the Master of the Music at the Abbey, prompted the reply that he knew of the story but having been at the Abbey for nine years, he had received "no experience of any 'ghostly' music" (private correspondence, September 25th 1996).

It is generally believed amongst psychic researchers that Borley Rectory (which burned down on February 27th 1939) on the Essex/ Suffolk border, was the most widely written about and researched haunted property of the early twentieth century. The well known researcher Harry Price called it "the most haunted house in England" (Price, 1940). Apart from servants' bells ringing inexplicably in the rectory, there were no manifestations of a musical nature there. However, the church opposite has long been a focus for claims of such activity. In 1937 when the rectory was being constantly investigated, reports were also made of paranormal activity coming from the church: "He told Mr Glanville [a psychical researcher] about his son, aged nineteen, who when returning from work about a fortnight before, had heard singing and chanting coming from the church as he passed it. The church was locked at the time" (Tabori and Underwood, 1973, p.160). Further examples at various times of day and night include an account from another investigator, Mr J. May who related: "I heard soft notes and chords from the organ...a jumble of atonal chords" (ibid.). Experiments to produce notes from the organ with trapped air in the pipes proved fruitless, but at least one of the times the organ was heard two local boys were the cause since they later admitted to a prank (ibid.). Between 1970 and 1972, numerous investigators claimed that music had been recorded but it has not been possible to trace this music if it actually existed. In 1985, a faint type of chanting was heard (cited in Downes, 1993) and Handel's 'Largo' (from *Xerxes*) was heard from within the church which was empty and with the organ console locked (ibid.). I wrote to the present incumbent and did not receive a reply but I have visited the church on a number of occasions during a period of about twenty years, sometimes remaining outside the church for most of the night. I have only been able to record the natural sounds of nocturnal rural life and an infrequent motor vehicle.

Apart from the statements of comparatively few people there has been little evidence of music of a paranormal nature being produced in religious buildings. A combination of suggestive minds, natural causes or pranks have probably brought about many of the reportings. The music has reflected the nature of the music that one would expect to hear in such places, i.e. singing/chanting, the organ, bells, etc.

Continuing the procedures adopted for castles and churches, it was decided to investigate palaces and country houses where anomalous music had been reported. The self-imposed limitation was to restrict examples to Britain, but since one of the most controversial events of this nature took place at Versailles in France, it seemed appropriate to discuss this case also.

In 1901, the Principal and Vice-Principal (Miss C. A. E. Moberly and Miss E. F. Jourdain respectively) of St Hugh's College for Women, Oxford, visited the Palace of Versailles as sightseers. Whilst there they decided to visit the Petit Trianon, the house and garden that Louis XVI had given to Marie Antoinette in 1774 but they became lost and depressed. They observed various other people including "a middle-aged lady in a summer dress, sitting on a seat on the lawn [and] a French wedding party" (Moberly and Jourdain cited Coleman, 1988 p.16). They later learned that the date of their visit coincided with the sacking of the Tuileries on August 10th 1792 and they wondered whether the place might be haunted. The ladies returned to the Petit Trianon in January 1902 and on this occasion whilst alone, Miss Jourdain witnessed people and scenes that vanished when she focused on them; the topography was also different to her recollection of 1901. Her account provides many interesting visual details of anachronistic dress but it is her comments about hearing music that are particularly relevant to this study:

> "...faint music, as of a band, not far off was audible. It was
> playing very light music with a good deal of repetition in it.
> Both voices [spoken] and music were diminished in tone,

119

as in a phonograph, unnatural. The pitch of the band was lower than usual. The sounds were intermittent..."

(Jourdain, 1902 cited in Coleman, 1988, pp.30-31)

She also referred to a "band of violins" later in her book (cited in Sidgwick, 1911, pp.353-360) entitled *An Adventure*. The authors used the pseudonyms 'Morison' and 'Lamont' to protect their identities in Oxford. Further research revealed that no bands had been allowed to play at the Petit Trianon or at the Palace in winter until 1907 but the psychical researcher Mrs E. Sidgwick mentioned that soldiers often exercised in the vicinity and the music may have had a military source (Sidgwick, 1911). Miss Jourdain attempted to write out the music (Bod. MS. Eng. misc. C257, p.130).

In 1908, both ladies searched through a large amount of unpublished music at the Conservatoire de Musique in Paris and discovered similarities in several period pieces, notably: *Dardanus - Oedipe a Colone* no. 6 by Sacchini; *Rigaudons- Le Marechal Ferrand* 1767 by Philidor; and *Le Roi et le Fermier* by Monsigny. (Moberly and Jourdain, 1910, cited Coleman, 1988, p.50). The musicologist Ian Parrott was particularly impressed by their account and firmly believed in the music's paranormal origin. He opposed the sceptical viewpoints expressed by such renowned musicians as Ernest Newman and Sir Malcolm Sargent. He defended the claim that she could not have remembered eleven bars of unknown music after just one hearing by proposing the idea that she was attuning directly with someone's memory from the period and was therefore able to maintain the piece in her mind. The SPR published several viewpoints in their journal *(JSPR* Volume 44. no. 734/5/6. December 1967; March 1968; June 1968) with both sides of the problem argued, and the prominent psychical researcher Andrew MacKenzie devoted a chapter of one of his books (Mackenzie, 1982, pp.124-156) to the subject. Here he cites the story of a Mr Crooke who had heard "old music" at the same location played by a string band when no band was present (ibid., p.135). On examination it would seem that probably a combination of faulty memory by the ladies, a little embroidery of the facts and the misconception of natural events as paranormal events may have lead to the mystery of the 'ghosts' and 'ghostly music' of the Petit Trianon.

It was hoped that more recent accounts might be discovered in the following palaces and country houses in Britain that claimed to possess paranormal music:

- Sandford Orcas, Sherborne, Dorset.
- The Treasurer's House, York.
- Sawston Hall, Cambridgeshire.
- Hampton Court, Middlesex.
- Leith Hall, Aberdeen.
- Lyme Park, Cheshire.
- Old Soar Manor, Kent.
- Nanteos Mansion, Aberystwyth.
- Levens Hall, Kendal, Cumbria.
- Combe Manor, Berkshire.
- Purse Caundle Manor, Dorset.
- Willington Manor, Bedford.
- The Queen's House, Greenwich.
- Cotehele House, Cornwall.
- Beauchief Hall, Sheffield.
- Barcaldine House, Strathclyde.
- Calverley Hall, Leeds.
- Hope House, Little Bursted, Essex.
- Marks Hall, Kelvedon, Essex.
- Hyde Hall, Great Wigborough, Essex.
- Colne Priory House, Earls Colne, Essex.

The music was of a varied nature, with chanting, bells, pipes and drums, the piano, the harpsichord and spinet all being reported. Most of the cases were only reported in a single reference and repetition of stories without further research was apparent in the remaining examples. However, one story deserves special attention since it seems to provide clear evidence for the possibility of a paranormal occurrence in the Treasurer's House, York. A local historian and archivist, John Mitchell, has dedicated much time and research into this event and writes of it:

> "The most remarkable story of the hauntings in York in recent years must surely be the events which were recorded by Harry Martindale in the early nineteen fifties...Harry, an apprentice aged about seventeen, had been working in one

of the cellars (of the Treasurer's House), installing piping for central heating. He was standing on a short ladder when he first heard the sound of a trumpet...the sound drew nearer and nearer, and suddenly the figure of a horse came through the wall...Harry fell from his ladder to the earth floor in a state of confusion and shock...On the back of the horse was a man dressed in Roman costume, and behind him came a group of soldiers...Shocked and trembling, he rushed up the cellar steps to the ground floor. Here he stumbled across the curator who, noticing his agitation, said: "You've seen the Romans haven't you?". This remark was of great comfort, as Harry then realised that he had neither been seeing things nor was going out of his mind. He was later astonised to find that two other people had also left accounts, giving identical details."

(Mitchell, 1996, pp.69-70)

If one is to believe this account, then it would certainly seem that an event took place in the cellars of the Treasurer's House that is inexplicable in terms of being 'mind' generated. The full account gives further details of a dog not wishing to enter the area and also of Harry's descriptions of the soldiers being authenticated by expert historians. He evidently provided details of their costume and appearance that would only have been known to scholars who had specifically studied the period in depth and this was almost certainly beyond the capabilities of a plumber's teenage assistant.

Since first-hand research of such an exhaustive nature was not available for the other properties, letters of enquiry were sent to their managers or owners and ten replies were received. All denied knowledge of such manifestations in recent times but one, Levens Hall in Cumbria, enclosed a leaflet about previous legends. The author J. A. Brooks informs one (Brooks, 1990) that the hall contains visual ghosts and he promotes the story concerning a priest who had heard a harpsichord being played which was "wreathed in light" despite a power cut taking place at that time. The priest identified the music as a "Grand" that the owner, Mr Robin Bagot, played and which was a particular favourite of Mrs Bagot. However, Mr Bagot was away on business at Cockermouth at the time. I received a letter from Mr Bagot's son with information which told me that over thirty years ago

Mr Bagot was "seen and heard playing his harpsichord when he was, in fact, in Keswick" (private correspondence, September 11th 1996). This provides further complications, since the priest did not claim to have seen Mr Bagot and there was a discrepancy between the names of Cockermouth and Keswick as the business venues. The legend of Levens Hall has not appeared, to my knowledge, in any other literature about the paranormal and since further recent manifestations have not occurred, the incident remains a mystery unless the story was invented to provide extra atmospheric charm to an already imposing building.

The only other reply to confirm the existence of paranormal music at any time was Barcaldine House in Scotland. It is a sixteenth century building that has been converted into a hotel. Peter Underwood writes of a "Blue Lady...when she has been sighted music is invariably being played" (Underwood, 1993 b., p.144) and he also mentions frequent sightings having taken place in 1989. The owners R. D. H. and J. C. Campbell contacted me (April 22nd 1996) and told the story of a piano being played by a lady dressed in blue. The communication began: "On a particularly wild and windy night..." concluding "...none of the Campbells of Barcaldine have 'met Harriet' yet!". I have the feeling that this story is told without the slightest belief in its authenticity since its exaggerated and stereotypical style seems somewhat deliberate.

The degree of vehemence with which the paranormal music has been denied varied between the correspondents. For instance, Lyme Park in Cheshire reputedly possesses a ghost that: "causes the sounding of distant bells" (Underwood, 1984, p.170). However, a letter from the Education Officer, Ms K. Atkinson informed me "...some authors have 'embroidered' the stories of our ghosts. I do assure you I know of no paranormal music at Lyme in the last six hundred years" (private correspondence October 15th 1996). Similarly, Cotehele House in Cornwall is said to contain "plaintive music" in the oldest part of the house (Underwood, 1983 p.20) but the present administrator assured me that "no such phenomena have ever been recorded here" (private correspondence undated [1996]). One famous example is that of Hampton Court which has been recorded as possessing "ghostly music...the sound of piano playing from empty rooms" (Underwood, 1984, p.124). However, a letter from Mr S. Edwards, the Deputy Curator, Works of Art, informed me: "Although there are a number of traditions concerning ghosts at Hampton Court, none can be recalled here that involve musical phenomenons [sic]" (private correspondence, December 2nd 1996).

Disappointingly, no one replied to my letters from the two places that have received several written reports of paranormal music, namely Sandford Orcas Manor in Dorset and Sawston Hall in Cambridgeshire. I have therefore been guided by the available literature. Sandford Orcas Manor - a Tudor building - was investigated in 1966 by three researchers from the Paraphysical Laboratory (now obsolete) and their leader Mr Benson Herbert claimed "there is a prima facie case for the house being haunted" (cited in Legg, 1969, p.36). This investigation was brought about by the claim of the tenant, from 1965-1979, Colonel Claridge and his wife, that they were witnessing a number of visual manifestations and one of a musical nature. The latter consisted of harpsichord or spinet music that seemed to emanate from the gatehouse. The owner of the house, Sir Hubert Medlycott, testified that from 1916 until 1964 his family, who were in residence, had certainly witnessed nothing, but despite this Colonel Claridge maintained that an increasing number of ghosts were appearing. I telephoned the present incumbent Sir Mervin Medlycott (February 27th 1997) to enquire whether he had witnessed any paranormal music but he did not return my call. It is likely that the alleged activity ceased with the departure of the Claridges, thus implying that either the Colonel was the focus of the disturbances or that he invented the story himself to arouse interest in the house that was open for a fee to the public.

Sawston Hall in Cambridgeshire was re-built in 1584, the original having been burned down in 1553 as a reprisal against the Huddleston family for protecting Mary Tudor from an attempted assassination. Numerous ghosts have been reported as well as spinet or harpsichord music, which was first reported by Mrs Huddlestone in 1930. Some time later a guest enquired "What is that tinkling music I keep on hearing ?" (Poole, 1995, p.14) but it should be noted that a harpsichord was kept at the time in an unused room (ibid.). Underwood cites several persons as having witnessed phenomena there (Underwood, 1993b.). More recently, during the filming of *The Nightcomers* (an adaptation of Henry James' *The Turn of the Screw*), two security men maintained that "Music had been playing in the chapel" (Forman, 1985, p.87) when it was deserted. It is possible that the guards let their imaginations deceive them, taking into account the scary nature of the film being made at the hall. Investigations were held there during

February and March 1983 by members of the Cambridge University Society for Psychical Research but no event of any significance occurred. A few seconds of music was recorded, the source of which could have been a radio signal being picked up (Cornell, 1984). The building is currently used as the Cambridge Centre for Languages and no recent paranormal musical activity has come to my attention. With reference to the harpsichord music that has also variously been referred to as the spinet or virginals, it seems strange that the music was not reported until 1930 if the manifestation was active before then.

The literature on alleged paranormal music occurring in palaces and country houses generally made claims that were not substantiated by present day owners or managers. If the manifestations happened at all in the past, it would seem that recent reports have not been made. It is possible, perhaps, that human beings are no longer capable of perceiving such phenomena through the distractions inherent in a materialist society. Alternatively it may simply be that superstitious belief, which can lead to naive acceptance of supposedly paranormal events, has lessened within an age that demands reason and explanation.

A degree of caution is especially necessary when investigating public houses and hotels since commercial interests can influence landlords and managers into exaggerating or inventing phenomena to secure a greater clientele. In practice this does not seem to have occurred since landlords and managers seem to have considered that fear of the paranormal is equally likely to have an adverse effect on business. The available literature was consulted and ten establishments were discovered that contained the appropriate criteria for investigation. Four of these were only referred to in one source - Guy Lyon Playfair's *The Haunted Pub Guide* (Playfair, 1985) - and the remainder were from a variety of books:

- The Prince of Wales, Kenfig, Wales. (Organ music)
- The Crown Hotel, Poole, Dorset. (Piano music)
- The White Hart, Chalfont St Peter, Buckinghamshire. (Violin music)
- The King's Arms, Peckham Rye, London SE 13. (Singing)
- The Ferry Boat Inn, St Ives, Cambridgeshire. (Music)
- The Talacre Arms, Holywell, Clwyd. (Piano music)
- The Angel, Lymington, Hampshire. (Piano music)

- The Crown and Horseshoes, Enfield, London. (Bell sounding)
- The Waggon and Horses, Sheffield, Yorks. (Violin music)
- The Black Horse, White Roding, Essex. (Piano music)

(The Castle Hotel, Taunton, Culcreuch Castle Hotel, Fintry and Barcaldine House, Strathclyde have already been mentioned.)

The landlords or managers were all contacted by post and none of them replied, which came as a considerable surprise. The following possible conclusions were reached. The letters may not have been received or were lost; it was felt that acknowledgement of any phenomena would either be detrimental or of no consequence to their trade; there was genuinely nothing about which to reply; or the enquiry was not treated as a serious one. I therefore sent a second letter to the above places in the hope of contact being made. I received one reply only, from the general manager of the Angel Inn, Lymington, Hants., who informed me that there was no activity of a paranormal nature occurring there at present and that the only story he knew was "two geriatric spinsters claim to have bore witness to a piano playing itself a merry little ditty in the style of Noel Coward" (private correspondence, April 1997). In the circumstances the available literature had to be relied upon, with the exception of the Prince of Wales, Kenfig, concerning which a documentary television programme had been made (*Out of this World*, BBC1, shown July 30th 1996).

References to piano music vary from pianos that play by themselves (the Crown Hotel, Poole; the Talacre Arms, Holywell; and the Black Horse, White Roding) to piano music being heard when there was no piano present (the Angel, Lymington). The Crown Hotel piano music is normally reported (Legg, 1969) as a single note, which could easily have been a string breaking inside, and the Angel's piano was evidently only removed the day before the alleged manifestation, thus suggesting a mis-remembered date may have been the cause of the claim. Pranks on public house landlords may well have taken place in the other examples of piano music and also in the mysterious ringing of the bell of the Crown and Horseshoes. An old time sing-song emanating from the cellars of the King's Arms, Peckham Rye, may well have had a similar origin.

One of the two stories of violin playing has only been found in one reference where a customer recalled a landlord moving out of the

Waggon and Horses, Sheffield because of "that ruddy ghost playing his violin upstairs" (Salim, 1983, p.39). However, the violin playing at the White Hart, Chalfont St Peters, has been referred to in several sources. The story is told of a previous landlord, Donald Ross, who died in the 1920s, playing the violin in the bar during his tenancy and on the night of his death. Various tales are told, especially concerning a couple who ran the pub in 1989, heard the violin music and soon departed (Brooks, 1990). The author Guy Lyon Playfair adds a final paragraph to his account of the story where he states that: "Phantom music turns up fairly often on haunting cases. Nowadays, I suspect many examples of it go unnoticed because the witnesses assume it to be a neighbour's radio" (Playfair, 1985, p.14).

The final example of music allegedly being heard paranormally in a public house concerns the Prince of Wales, Kenfig, in Mid-Glamorgan. In 1982, an electrical engineer, John Marke, and an industrial chemist, Allan Jenkins, undertook an experiment to investigate "the landlord's claim to have heard ghostly voices and organ music in the pub" (Bord, 1992, p.191). They connected electrodes to a stone wall in the public house, hoping to obtain a recording of anomalous music and having fed twenty thousand volts through it, they placed tape recorders in the locked room for four hours overnight. They claimed that various sounds were recorded, including organ music. This apparently amazing discovery was not brought to public attention until the organ music was played on the television programme *Out of this World* and the experiment was repeated with the involvement of various BBC sound experts. The alleged organ sounds bore no resemblance to any organ and rather sounded like some form of electronic distortion. The BBC Workshop engineer, John Hunt, was suspicious of the various sounds he heard and referred to the organ music as sounding like feedback. Another public house in the neighbourhood also started claiming that spoken voices could be heard but it was pointed out by the BBC engineer that these were almost certainly radio broadcasts that had been tampered with. The two original researchers were joined by another BBC engineer to conduct an experiment but all they recorded were a few 'bangings' - as if someone was banging on the wall, floor or ceiling.

There were further examples of paranormal music that have been written about that do not fit into the previous categories. The places concerned are:

- The Theatre Royal, York.
- An unidentified house in Lawrence Street, London.
- The Old Rectory House, Burford, Oxford.
- 50 Berkeley Square, London.
- The Camberwell Palace Theatre, London.
- Weston Vicarage, Weston, Yorkshire.
- Willington Mill House, Northumberland.
- An unidentified house in Walton on Thames, Surrey.
- An unidentified cottage in Stainland, Halifax.
- A Victorian house in Southend on Sea, Essex.
- Wheel Cottage in Thundersley, Essex.
- Sundial Cottage, Prestbury, near Cheltenham.
- An office in Peter Street, Manchester.
- An unidentified house in Humber Avenue, Coventry.
- Elm Vicarage, Wisbech, Cambridgeshire.
- Dickmountlaw Farmhouse, Arbroath.
- Dockacre House, Launceston, Cornwall.

It was difficult to contact all the places mentioned since several had either not been identified fully or had been demolished. Only two buildings (The Old Rectory, Burford and 50 Berkeley Square, London) were referred to in more than one source from the literature. There seemed to be no consistency in the type of music manifested, which included chanting, bells, piano playing, violin music, flute music, the sound of a spinet and bugle calls.

The place with the most references was the Old Rectory at Burford, Oxfordshire. It was said that "...the sound of singing near the monks' old graveyard, and the tolling of a bell at 2 a.m. are reported" (Hippisley Coxe, 1975, p.88). The building, which was part of a medieval priory, is now lived in by the chaplain and other parts are inhabited by Roman Catholic nuns. A letter requesting further information from me was not replied to and neither was a similar letter to the incumbent of Elm Vicarage where a phantom bell has been heard (Hippisley Coxe, 1975). Another supposedly haunted vicarage was to be found at Weston in North Yorkshire. The phenomena occurred during the incumbency of Charles Tweedale who was discussed in the previous essay. He made several references in his diary to paranormal music phenomena taking place:

"...we began to have musical sounds and instrumental manifestations of varied import....a strain of music began to sound from the top of the wardrobe. It was most beautiful, and the tone something like that of a musical box. It played a delightful air twice over, concluding with a fine chord. Nothing was seen. There was at that time no musical box in the house."

(cited May 31st 1909, Tweedale, 1940, p.37)

Tweedale also spoke of other people hearing music. About his wife he wrote "...she heard a violin playing from inside my study...when I was not in the house" (ibid.). On another occasion he wrote that his wife and a servant both heard the tune 'The Anchor's Weighed' being played on the violin. It would seem that nobody was actually playing and there was no gramophone in the house. Many further examples could be cited (see Tweedale, 1940, pp.37-56). Tweedale's obsession with Stradivarius violins has already been discussed and it is likely that his imagination or the instruments actually being played accounted for much of the activity related. I visited Weston in August 1996 and spoke to an elderly man living in a manor house located next to the church. He informed me that people in the community had thought Tweedale was "round the bend".

It was not possible to acquire present day comment on the Camberwell Palace Theatre since it was demolished in 1966, but according to the 'Gaiety Girl' Ruby Miller, she heard music there at a time when the building was deserted: "I paused when I reached the orchestra pit to listen to the pianist, who was playing some music he had written...at the same time I heard an orchestra playing circus music, apparently on stage" (cited Paul, 1985, p.94). The theatre's part-time fireman, Alfred Goswell, also spoke of an occasion when he had heard a note played repeatedly on the piano when the building was empty (ibid.). The other theatre allegedly containing paranormal music is the Theatre Royal, York which according to Peter Underwood: "...has a frequently seen Grey Lady and the unexplained sound of chanting" (1993a, p.79). I spoke to the administrators of the theatre on the telephone (March 6th 1997) and they knew no details of chanting.

Two offices were mentioned in the literature. The unidentified building in Peter Street, Manchester was said to be "haunted by thin piping tunes heard by many people" (Mitchell and Richard, 1983, p.83) and 50 Berkeley Square, London was claimed to have been the scene of a bell ringing in the 1870s (Underwood, 1971). I received a note from the current occupant informing me that he had not heard of any musical phenomena, though, he added flippantly "a certain tuneless humming sometimes emanates from various offices at dull moments" (R. Hardy, private correspondence undated [1996]).

The remainder of the properties to be researched were private houses, some of which were not identified by the authors, and a farmhouse in which it was alleged that the sounds of piping could be heard under the hearthstone (Hippisley Coxe, 1975). The house in Lawrence Street, London, where hymn singing occurred, despite the radio being turned off (Hallam, 1975); a house in Walton on Thames, Surrey, where piano notes, bagpipe music and pealing bells were heard (Price, 1993); and another in Humber Avenue, Coventry, where piano strings were plucked (Michell and Rickard, 1983); will all remain mysteries unless further evidence is forthcoming. To this list can be added the unidentified cottage in Stainland, Halifax, where an apparition was described as "...having a white face, sunken eyes and long flowing white hair...the figure was apparently playing a violin" (Spencer, 1992, pp.113-114). Another cottage mentioned, in Thundersley, Essex, was said to have been the focus for bugles sounding during the night at the time of the full moon in the 1960s (Payne, 1995). This was linked to a legend of two sons who were believed to have contacted their mother from the dead by such sounds during the night. My letter to the present owners was not replied to and neither was my letter to Sundial Cottage, Prestbury, where it is said that a ghost is heard playing the spinet (Brooks, 1992). I was more fortunate with Dockacre House in Cornwall since the owner of many years, Mrs Buckridge, replied to my letter concerning ghostly flute music sounding whenever a death is about to occur in the house (cited in Underwood, 1983). Although she believed that paranormal occurrences did take place in the house, she felt that they were not of a musical nature and believed the flute music legend to be untrue.

Concerning the remaining two properties, a hand-bell ringing was reported at Willington Mill House (Price, 1993) but the property had been demolished some time before. A harmonium being played in a Victorian house in Southend on Sea was reported (*Psychic News* January 1956, cited in Payne, 1995) but the property was not identified and further details were not available.

The evidence for paranormal music in this selection of properties probably constitutes the weakest of any section, despite the claims of some of the authors about the authenticity of the cases.

There were many instances of paranormal music being allegedly heard when a building was not the focus of attention, largely in natural and general locations. The following details these examples.

Seascapes

Location	Nature of Music
off coast of South Hayling Island, Hampshire	sunken bells
off coast of Dunwich, Suffolk	sunken bells
off coast of Nigg Bay, Eastern Highlands	sunken bells
off coast of Aberdovey, Gwynd	sunken bells
off coast of St. Ives Bay, Cornwall	sunken bells
off coast of Forrabury, Cornwall	sunken bells
off coast of Mount Bay, Cornwall	sunken bells
off coast of Senen Cove, Cornwall	sunken bells
off coast of Walton on the Naze, Essex	sunken bells
off coast of Pendor Cove, Cornwall	singing

Lakes and pools

Location	Nature of Music
Marden Pool, Herefordshire	sunken bells and singing
Rostherne Mere, Cheshire	sunken bells and singing
Llangorse Lake, Powys	sunken bells
Cole Mere, Ellesmere, Shropshire	sunken bells
Tunstall Pool, Norfolk	sunken bells
Llyntarw Clatter, Powys	singing
Glen Esk, Angus	singing and piping

Rivers, broads and creeks

Location	Nature of Music
Bosham, West Sussex	sunken bells
Llandyssul, River Teifi, Dyfed	sunken harp
Hickling Broad, Norfolk	drumming

Wells

Location	Nature of Music
Oundle Well, Northamptonshire	drumming
Harpham Well, Yorkshire	drumming

Bridges over water

Location	Nature of Music
Woodford Bridge, Redbridge, Essex	bell
Nun's Bridge, Hinchingbrooke	drumming

Over/under hills/mountains

Location	Nature of Music
Twm Barlwm, Risca, Gwent	organ
Cley Hill, Warminster, Wiltshire	singing
Sithean Beinne Bho'idhich, Skye	music

Other locations

Location	Nature of Music
Unspecified, Stow on the Wold	singing
Open farmland, Edgehill, Warwickshire	drumming
St. Nectan's Glen, Cornwall	bell, organ and chanting
Country lanes, Liphook, Hampshire	flute
Cave, Cricieth, Caernarvon	piper and two fiddlers
Unspecified, Bayham, Kent/Sussex border	chanting
Middle Hill Wood, Broadway	sunken bell
Carin Kyle Rhea, Loch Alsh, Skye	music
Charlotte Square, Edinburgh	piano

The same problems of lack of verifiable sources and single references were encountered in this section as in the preceding categories. It is clear from the list that sunken bells constitute the greatest number of incidents of alleged paranormal music in natural settings and with the exception of the bell sounding under Middle Hill Wood at Broadway in Worcestershire, all the examples are under water. The most common reason for the bells being submerged was as a result of villages and, in particular the local churches, being swept out to sea as land and cliffs crumbled through erosion. It has been claimed that the bells can still be heard tolling. For instance, the sunken village of Dunwich off the coast of Suffolk has been written about in such terms and I visited the current village on the coast. The curator of the local museum felt it was possible that the tides might occasionally move any bells that may be below the sea resulting in the clapper striking the bell and causing a sound to be heard. However, he believed it to be even more likely that music from natural causes, even other churches further along the coast and shore, may well give rise to the illusion of the sounds emanating from beneath the sea. This interpretation was somewhat different from the written reports discovered which stated: "...the sunken church bells ring to warn of impending storms..." (Bord, 1990, p.79) and in another report: "The phantom bells, for some reason, are most often reported just before Christmas and frequently late at night" (Underwood, 1984, p.97). Other sources (for instance, *Folklore, Myths and Legends*, 1973) repeated these claims which also contained alleged sightings of ghostly figures on the shore. Only single references were found for the remaining examples of sunken bells under the sea. These were from Bord (1990) and Underwood (1983) for the majority of cases and Payne (1995) for the bells of Walton on the Naze.

The legends attached to sunken bells in lakes and rivers are of a different nature since they contain a number of contrasting characteristics. It has been claimed (mainly in Bord, 1990) that bells have been stolen by mermaids - Marden Pool and Rostherne Mere; by Vikings - Bosham Bell Hole; and by the Devil - Tunstall (*Folklore, Myths and Legends*, 1973). An earthquake allegedly caused the bells of Llangorse to sink into the lake and at Cole Mere the locals' cursing at the difficulty of recovering the bells after Cromwell's troops had submerged them caused them to sink forever below the surface (Bord, 1990). It has been claimed that all these bells can be heard at various times of the day and year but actual firsthand accounts or recordings have not been made available. In this respect, tales of drumming are similarly unverified. It is possible that the Drumming Wells of Oundle and Harpham have acquired their 'musical' reputations through a combination of the wind and an enclosed space causing drum-like vibrations. Natural causes may also be responsible for the drumming heard at Hickling Broad where the legend of a drowned drummer boy trying to summon his lover lends further power to the imagination (*Folklore, Myths and Legends*, 1973).

An example of drumming where practical joking was admitted to occurred at Hinchingbrooke Bridge, where an airman from a nearby RAF base "marched up and down the banks of Alconbury brook, drumming deep into the night" (Forman, 1985, p.61). However, the alleged drumming that occurred after the Battle of Edgehill (1642) in Warwickshire was examined seriously in the seventeenth century. A month after the battle had taken place it was reported by local shepherds that the sights and sounds of the battle, including drumming, were still being re-enacted. King Charles I came to hear of this and duly sent several officers to investigate. They interviewed the shepherds and even witnessed the battle themselves on two occasions before returning to the King, who interpreted the sign as a portent of his eventual success in the Civil War! (Smyth and Stemman, 1981). The original source for this story was published by Thomas Jackson, London in 1643 and was reprinted in 1860 as an appendix to Lord Nugent's *Memorials of John Hampden, his Party, and his Times.*

Other references to 'music' are similarly difficult to examine since, in both cases, on the island of Skye, fairies are said to be the performers (Hippisley Coxe, 1975). The post graduate science course director at the University of Edinburgh, Alastair McIntosh, brought to my notice the 'faerie music' legend associated with 'the hill of the pipers' on the Isle of Harris:

> "It was said that at certain times one could lie on the hill and hear the music of piping deep within. In recent years a new mains sewage system was being installed ...and the digger broke through into a multi-chambered souterrain buried under the hill. One of the passages ran down to the sea and ...on stormy days the crashing of boulders on the beach was communicated through the chamber to create a 'tinkelling' sound."

He continued:

> "I frequently delight in playing my penny whistle in remote locations outside and often muse as to the extent to which distant walkers will take it as evidence that the faeries are still alive and well."

(private correspondence, August 10th 1993)

Mermaids are said to be responsible for the singing heard at Pendor Cove, Cornwall, and Rostherne Mere, Cheshire, and at least on one occasion practical joking has been evident:

> "The Reverend Robert Hawker of Morwenstow...About the year 1825 he decided to test the power of the mermaid myth by swimming to an offshore rock near Bude, on the north coast of Cornwall. Naked to the waist and with a shining tail of oilskin wrapped about his legs, he combed his tresses of seaweed, preened himself in a mirror and began to sing, all in the light of the full moon. Large and awe-struck crowds gathered to watch this remarkable phenomena, which continued for several successive nights until finally wearying of his performance and discovering that he had a sore throat, the Mermaid of Morwenstow suddenly burst into the strains of 'God save the King' and plunging from the rock, disappeared into the sea."

> (*Man, Myth and Magic*, Volume 5, p.1814)

It is possible that other musical legends of the sea may have been caused by the mistaken identity of marine life such as seagulls and seals, such as the sirens of Greek mythology that almost caused the downfall of Odysseus in Homer's *Odyssey*.

Examples of musical manifestations where water is not a prime factor are fewer in number and insubstantial in content. The single reference for Bayham simply states "chanting heard" (Hippisley Coxe, 1975, p.69) and the reference to Stow on the Wold is similarly imprecise: "Poltergeist activity...mellowed into singing" (Bord, 1992, p. 326). An example where nature in the form of the wind, wild life or water may not have been responsible can be found in the report of inexplicable piano music being heard in Charlotte Square, Edinburgh. This case relies on a passage from an Edinburgh tourist guide book (Matthews, 1993) which admits that the music is so similar to a modern piano that it is often mistaken for one. In truth that is probably exactly what it is!

It would seem that natural locations fare no better than buildings in providing the researcher with verifiable accounts of music of a paranormal origin or, ideally the music itself. It is possible that the locations themselves do not produce or enhance the situations whereby paranormal music may be witnessed but that they help stimulating the imaginations of suitably sensitive people who are able to perceive it.

Having discovered that locations only seemed to influence the music heard in terms of association with the setting as in cases of sunken bells off-shore and organ music in churches, it seemed possible that the focus for these alleged manifestations might be the people who witnessed the phenomena. Scott Rogo's two studies of people claiming to have heard 'astral' music (Rogo, 1970; 1972) provide some data about the differences in the music heard by diverse groups of people. Saints and deeply religious people often perceived bells and sacred vocal music, but his case studies generally seemed to confirm a broad range of people from widely different social and cultural backgrounds experiencing a similarly wide range of musical phenomena. Although he received in excess of a hundred replies to his advertisements for witnesses of paranormal music to contact him, his request, which was published in *Psychic News*, would have automatically attracted a readership favourably disposed towards psychic matters. Some of his cases were taken from *Phantasms of the Living* (1886), an in-depth investigation into apparitions of living people allegedly appearing at certain times, which was instigated by the Society for Psychical Research.

I placed similar advertisements in paranormal-biased newspapers and magazines: *The Psi Researcher*, *The Fortean Times*, *Psychic News* and the newsletters of the 'Noah's Ark Society' (a Spiritualist organisation) and the 'Ghost Club'. I also placed an advertisement in a non-paranormal biased newspaper - *The Essex Chronicle*. Despite the naturally limited circulation of the former newspapers, I received several accounts of alleged paranormal music having been heard, whereas the *Essex Chronicle*, with a circulation of 45,000 copies each week (April 1997), provided me with only one reply. Seventy-five per cent of the letters were written by women and all the respondents appeared to be in sound mind and of at least average intelligence.

Having read of Patrick Moore (the astronomer) being witness to an anomalous musical experience with a group of friends, I contacted him for further information: "Suddenly there was a sound of music - not a tune, but concerted, rippling chords, not random...The lid of the piano keys was closed and nobody was around..." (St Aubyn, 1996, p.115). In correspondence with me, he confirmed that he had no explanation for this event that occurred as he had reported.

Witnesses mainly expressed surprise at hearing the music which they described as varying from being quite specific (e.g. 'The Harry Lime Theme' played on an organ), to indistinct, e.g. "like an orchestral version of Heaven" (private correspondence)). All these people were alone at the time of the manifestation and in either quiet ("middle of the night"), remote ("on a mountain") or relaxed ("in the bath") locations. With the exception of a larger number of women than men having allegedly perceived the music and a predisposition towards belief in the paranormal being conducive to such activity, the general population would appear to hear this type of music only very rarely.

Present day and historical sources inform one that music has been heard and continues to be heard in situations where it appears impossible for such music to exist because of the absence of performers. A study of locations has indicated that the music is often appropriate to that which would be performed if physical musicians were present. In order for cases to be documented it would seem that in the majority a human presence is necessary actually to witness the music. There would appear to be very few records of machines having tape-recorded music in locations where humans were not present, although this might be considered for possible future experiments. One such example was reported to me by Alan Gauld (Department of Psychology, University of Nottingham) concerning a tape-recording of harpsichord music made during the night at Carnfield Hall in Derbyshire when nobody was present and such an instrument was not in the house. The recorder was placed on a time switch but unfortunately the music faded after two to three months (private correspondence with Gauld, July 1997). Some cases of reported paranormal music were undoubtedly fraudulent in origin consisting of claims made for financial gain or for practical joking. One such case was reported by Peter Underwood:

> "Some 'phantom music' was brought to my attention by a leading psychical research society...several investigators were convinced that the music was paranormal...I made a preliminary visit and thought I could hear faint music. I found that the very next room was full of music. I then heard different music from another room."

On investigating an arm chair belonging to the host, he found several buttons which when depressed produced music from different parts of the house. When the owner of the house was confronted with this discovery he replied: "...I've had a lot of fun meeting all sorts of interesting people...I've never claimed it was ghostly music; people came, heard the music and told me it was 'paranormal'" (Underwood, 1996, p.10).

Some genuinely reported cases may have had a similar origin without the witnesses' knowledge. Mistaking natural sounds for paranormal music or even distant radios and other music sources certainly allowed further cases to be included in the literature. However, there are examples where none of these explanations would seem to be acceptable and one has to question whether music with a paranormal origin was occurring and, if so, from where it originated. An example is the alleged music from the site of the Battle of Edgehill during the English Civil War. Rogo believed that such music was impossible to prove: "When a person hears transcendental music, it is impossible to verify that the percipient did actually hear it" (Rogo, 1972, pp.18-19). He was convinced that the music could only be heard inside the percipient's brain and did not rely on an external sound source. Therefore, it could not be recorded. However, he did not believe that it was manufactured by the brain but that it existed in a different dimension from that which human beings can perceive with their 'normal' senses. Medical conditions do not seem to explain percipients' experiences. Sufferers from hearing problems (tinnitus, etc.) are acutely aware of their deficiencies and would be unlikely to confuse paranormal music with their ailments. One such case was brought to my notice in 1994:

> "One night as I was settling down to sleep, I became aware of hearing music. I suffer from tinnitus and thought what a pleasant change it was to hear [instead of] the usual rushing water and whistling that I usually get. It sounded like an orchestra...I can only describe the music played as heavenly..."

> (Mrs B. Murkoff, published in *Enigmas Magazine,* November/ December 1994).

Similarly, it is probable that psychological problems of hearing 'voices' or 'music' would recur sufficiently for them to be diagnosed and treated medically (David Smith, 1992; Gordon, 1997). If a solution to the enigma of paranormal music is to be found, it may be discovered by further study of the brain. However, it may be possible that such activity can occur in the brain without the percipient being aware of it, though there is as yet no research which would support such a claim. Perhaps the nearest one comes to this in conventional science is the work of American neurosurgeon Wilder Penfield who discovered that electrical stimulation of the sensory cortex produced sensations which the patient could immediately discuss, since a local anaesthetic was all that was needed for the incision. One woman was able to hear music and "when Penfield stimulated the same point thirty times, she heard the familiar melody again each time, beginning at the same place. She could even hum in accompaniment" (W. Penfield, cited in Blackmore, 1993, p.212). It is therefore possible that some people's brains receive similar stimulation in either unknown or even random situations that cause the paranormal music to be heard in at least some of the circumstances encountered. However, this suggestion may not apply to all the accounts of anomalous music and one must remain open to Rogo's notion that the music is genuinely beyond human comprehension.

Prologue 2

This series of essays proposes to bring together information from two different disciplines that have not been yoked together before in pursuing the study of music and witchcraft. A number of scholars have devoted time and energy to the meaning of paganism and witchcraft in Europe since 1400, including Robin Briggs, Ronald Hutton, P. G. Maxwell-Stuart and James Sharpe. With such a difficult subject, given its multitude of different interpretations it was to be expected that a number of varying as well as similar viewpoints would be expressed by these and other academics. However, this was not the case and a large degree of agreement was encountered in the works studied. There was unanimous disapproval of the Egyptologist Margaret Murray's views on the origin of witchcraft as the survival of an ancient pagan religion (Murray, 1921). Briggs refers to her views as "complete nonsense" (Briggs, 1996, p.37) and Hutton demolishes her arguments stating that "she ruthlessly ignored in her sources anything which did not support her case" (Hutton, 2000, p.196). Having agreed that Murray was wrong, one needs to investigate whether her statements about large-scale meetings of witches (covens) had any truth in them. Hutton affirms that the word 'coven' was not used "in the earlier material" and is a Scottish word that appeared during the sensational trial of Isobel Gowdie in 1662 (Hutton, 2000, p.100). P. G. Maxwell-Stuart draws attention to the alleged Sabbats. Maxwell-Stuart emphasises that these Sabbats were referred to as 'synagogues' - "a reminder of the anti-Semitism which was rife at the time" (Maxwell-Stuart, 2001, p.19). The reasons why these tales were invented were variously attributed to torture, psychological fantasy, delusion or ancient shamanistic traditions. The lack of official torture in England led to less lurid details being

140

extracted from the hapless victims and the emphasis during English trials seemed to be on local maleficia and the use of familiars rather than demonic orgies - the only exceptions being sporadic mentions in the Lancashire trials and in East Anglia during Matthew Hopkins' period of activity in the seventeenth century. The historians Scarre and Callow draw attention to relationships with the Devil being more prominent in Scotland and Europe than in England until the arrival of Hopkins also (Scarre and Callow, 2001, pp.5 and 27).

One has been led to believe that there were not groups of people who met together to indulge in an alternative religion, despite what the torturers may have extracted from their victims. However, there are still questions to be asked as to how many people were accused of witchcraft, who they were, what were they accused of and why. Again, there is broad agreement between the scholars selected. There have in the past been fanciful claims of the numbers of executions, including thirteen million by Zsuzsanna Budapest and a much-quoted nine million originally made by the nineteenth century suffragist Matilda Gage (Purkiss, 1996, fn. 23, p.28). Radical feminism has also linked the so-called 'Burning Times' to the Jewish holocaust of the twentieth century. However, reputable scholars seem to put the figure at around forty thousand between the late fifteenth century and the end of the seventeenth century. In England the numbers were relatively small and five hundred executions has been suggested, with the worst record coming from Essex, especially during Hopkins' period of activity from 1645-1647 with possibly over one hundred executed (Sharpe, 1996, pp.111, 125 and 129), but acquittal was also relatively common.

It is generally believed that women formed the vast majority of people executed for witchcraft; however Briggs suggests men constituted a possible twenty five per cent in Europe, rising to a high in Iceland with ninety per cent (Briggs, 1996, pp.260-261). Although numbers varied in different districts and at different times, there is no doubt that the majority were indeed female and they were mainly over the age of fifty. There are many reasons why this may have been. Women's place in the home and on the domestic front gave them access to knowledge that men did not share. As midwives and mothers they had an understanding of healing and knowledge of the human body that they might use for evil purposes, especially if they no longer had families of their own through death or having remained unmarried. Through a hard life of either constant, dangerous childbearing or hard physical work, women would often have an ugly appearance beyond their fifties and if mistreated they would almost certainly have been bad-tempered and somewhat eccentric. Typically outliving men, especially during times of war, they would have found themselves alone and poor. Their imposition on the village community would have not been welcome but to refuse them alms may have caused fear or guilt and the lack of available medicine would have rendered their services necessary at times. There are a number of possible reasons why they were accused and Scarre and Callow (2001) alluded to a number of factors including:

- Judicial gullibility and clerical fanaticism combined with witches' intellectual weaknesses.
- Different interpretations of the Bible according to Protestantism or Catholicism, but both being anti-female.
- The merging together of heretics and witches notably in the *Malleus Maleficarum* with its blatant misogyny.
- The advances of printing to allow the dissemination of information.
- The 'snowballing' effect of torture resulting in further convictions especially where central government was weak and local zeal was infectious.
- Women being viewed as more susceptible to the Devil, being theoretically more lustful and in practice socially disadvantaged.
- The period being particularly eventful in terms of wars, famines, plagues, and religious and state upheavals.
- The rise of the Devil and fears of the Anti-Christ.
- A certain amount of sadism with the excuse that witchcraft was a *crimen exceptum*.
- The possibility of actual *maleficia* taking place.

Briggs places witchcraft firmly in its social and cultural context believing that "...the pliable figure of the witch can be manipulated to fit the spirit of each age" (Briggs, 1996, p.5). He highlights the problems of using information from trials and contemporary reports and the definitions that they produce as well as including instances of the hereditary dangers of having a previously convicted witch in the family and the importance of folklore and fantasy. Within the ideology of the time, the supernatural was perfectly rational and most people did not believe in chance but more likely fate dictated by God, the Devil's input or the beliefs of the ancient (usually Greek) philosophers and astrologers. Miracles and the supernatural when it was part of the Church were from God, but outside of this domain the same event would be interpreted as coming from the Devil. Briggs stresses the village as the main setting for witchcraft outbreaks and that witch-finders needed support - and payment - for their services.

Before investigating witchcraft in approximately the last hundred years, perhaps one should inquire why witchcraft declined and finally died out. It would be easy to make a sweeping statement along the lines that the Enlightenment and Age of Reason ensured the finale demise of trials for witchcraft in the eighteenth century. However, men believed they were being just as rational in the previous hundred and fifty years when they were killing the agents of Satan in their thousands and the term 'Enlightenment' would have meant nothing to anyone at the time. The processes that led to the end of the witch-hunts were varied and gradual. Changes in judicial procedures had already begun in France in as early as 1640 and the centralisation brought with it removed the power and zeal that less important officials had been able to wield. This spread to Germany where the universities demanded extra caution before instigating witchcraft trials and the use of torture was declining. The costs of undertaking trials were increasing and it was therefore cheaper for towns or villages to not prosecute people on flimsy evidence.

There had always been scepticism about the claims of witches, famously from Reginald Scot in his *Discoverie of Witchcraft* (1584) but also by others such as Johan Weyer in *De Praestigiis Daemonum* (1563) and Balthasar Bekker in *De Betoverde Weereld* (1692-3). However, with the gradual increase of urbanisation and wider horizons of intelligence, the previous hold of superstition was beginning to weaken, at least in the non-rural areas. Even the stage plays of the seventeenth century tended to promote a more sceptical response from their audiences and the personification of witches was used as part of a general exploitation of the supernatural together with fairies, ghosts etc. Dramatists' main source for their work was Scot's *Discoverie of Witchcraft*, which has already been mentioned in relation to scepticism (Purkiss, passim).

Historians tend to agree about many factors concerning early modern witchcraft. They are unanimous in condemning the simplistic views that have been so often been promoted in the past, namely:

- Witchcraft was part of a continuing pagan religion.
- Women met in large covens for orgiastic demon worshipping.
- Millions of them were burned at the stake.
- The 'Burning Times' stemmed from the Inquisition and was promoted by Christianity through misogynistic men.
- Midwives were targeted because of jealousy from male doctors.
- The state became involved because of the large amounts of money that were to be made from confiscated property.
- The Enlightenment brought it all to a sudden end as man became more rational.

Although some of the above may have been true, in a few cases there are a large number of other factors that need to be taken into account concerning the rise and fall of the myth of collective witchcraft. Scholars also agree that it is a difficult problem to unravel because of the wide areas involved in both geographical and chronological matters. However, the 'classic' early modern stereotype of the witch was a female who was poor, malevolent and demon worshipping.

In *The Triumph of the Moon* Ronald Hutton traces the development of witchcraft and provides a great deal of evidence for its origins (Hutton, 2000). He illustrates that the language of modern paganism originated in German Romanticism in the late eighteenth century with a fusion of a love of the ancient Greeks' perceived culture, nostalgia for the past and a desire for unity between people, culture and nature. Gradually an idealised rural landscape was emerging of happy village life with maypoles, games, dances and 'wassails' all contributing to a concept of 'Merrie England'. (See Georgina Boyes, *The Imagined Village*, 1993, p.63 passim.) Nineteenth-century England turned increasingly towards the ancient Greeks for inspiration and for a while this form of paganism was acceptable to an overtly Christian country, since the Greek philosophers were believed to possess a moral code that was acceptable within the Christian ethos. By the end of the century, ideas of freedom, self-indulgence and ancient knowledge were arising and the formerly minor deity Pan was being seen as the spirit of the English countryside. The influential work of Sir James Frazer, *The Golden Bough*, promoted a belief that paganism underlay and informed all Western religion. Kenneth Grahame, Thomas Hardy and Rudyard Kipling also promulgated a sense of idealised pagan rusticity and later the works of D. H. Lawrence (*The Rainbow*) and Robert Graves (*The White Goddess*) continued to promote pagan images. The literature of the period was not the only influence that was to result in the modern Pagan movement. Eighteenth century secret societies such as the Freemasons or 'The Craft' used numerous ceremonies, tools and claims of ancient traditions that were later to be incorporated into modern Paganism. In the following century, groups such as the Rosicrucians and the Golden Dawn organisation incorporated concepts from the Kabbala and magic influenced by the occultism of Eliphas Levi and the Theosophical writings of Helena Blavatsky. In the late nineteenth and early twentieth century, Woodcraft movements developed and Robert Baden-Powell started the Scouts movement in 1907. These groups emphasised the essential goodness of the material world to varying extents and although they included few 'actual' pagans, they introduced certain non-Christian elements without opposing Christianity itself.

Another influence on the modern Pagan movement, and specifically witchcraft, were the meetings of Charles Godfrey Leland with an allegedly Florentine witch, Maddelena, culminating in his book *Aradia* in 1899. The work combined witchcraft and cunning craft as well as giving both an ancient pagan descent. This alleged 'witches gospel' tells of the mating of Diana with Lucifer to produce Aradia who goes to Earth to teach witchcraft (Hutton, 2001, pp.142-147). Alex Sanders made the opening of his documentary film *The Legend of the Witches* this same story and so the myth survived to the latter part of the twentieth century. Another direct influence on the modern scene was the magician Aleister Crowley, who promoted techniques of ritual magic and veneration of an ecstatic goddess. Pagans also acknowledge the work of Dion Fortune (Violet Firth), who promoted the same phenomena. For instance, *The Goat-Foot God* (1936) and *The Sea Priestess* (1938).

Margaret Murray's works provided a very big impetus towards the rise of modern Paganism and witchcraft. Her works had the stamp of authority from the Folklore Society via Sir Lawrence Gomme and the University of London via Karl Pearson, both of whom had pioneered the idea in England that paganism had survived as witchcraft. Her views of the practice of a persisting pagan witch religion both promoted the concept of a horned 'God of the Witches' and paved the way for Gerald Gardner to reveal an actual witch religion. She wrote the foreword to Gardner's influential book *Witchcraft Today* (1954) and thus was born a new native British religion. Hutton traces Gardner's foundation of the religion upon the influences previously mentioned, adding his (Gardner's) own predilections such as scourging and naked rites. In 1949 he had already published a work about witchcraft in the guise of a novel *High Magic's Aid*, but in 1951 the Witchcraft and Vagrancy Acts were repealed, thereby allowing witches to advertise their existence. During this time there were upheavals in the public's perception of Wicca that stemmed from links with Satanism promoted by the press for commercial reasons, while Montague Summers and Dennis Wheatley conveyed similar false impressions in their books such as *Witchcraft and Black Magic* (Summers, 1965) and *The Satanist* (Wheatley, 1990). Vandalism of churches and grave desecration were blamed on witches. In a more positive way Doreen Valiente and Patricia Crowther provided an intellectual and glamorous approach to the religion and many covens started to be formed around the country independently of Gardner.

The last forty years marks the date since the death of Gerald Gardner up to the present time (2004). There were already other covens meeting before his death and one high priest was to gain considerable notoriety by his flamboyance and public openness, namely Alexander Sanders in combination with his young, blonde and beautiful wife Maxine. Their willingness to be photographed and to give press interviews brought them considerable fame and a large number of followers. One such initiate was a journalist, Stewart Farrar, who together with his eventual wife Janet went on to form their own coven in Ireland and write numerous influential books about Wicca (Farrar, 1984). Indeed it was Stewart Farrar who coined the word 'Alexandrian' to differentiate Sanders' type of Wicca from Gardner's. The impetus for Wicca was maintained during the 1970s with the appearance of journals such as 'The Wiccan' in 1974 and 'The Cauldron' in 1977 that published intelligent articles for interested readers. Alex and Maxine Sanders split up in 1975 but new people were continuing to develop the religion such as Marian Green and Lois Bourne. There was also a strong pro-reaction in the USA with feministic interpretations of witchcraft from

Zsuzsanna Budapest and a rigorous intellectual approach from Margot Adler (1997).

A number of other factors contributed to the continuing strength of the religion during the 1980s and 1990s. These fall into different categories such as books, television programmes, organisations and academic interest. Hutton mentions the novel *The Mists of Avalon* by Marion Zimmer Bradley (1982) with its Wiccan interpretation of the female roles within the Arthurian epic and the Terry Pratchett books where Wicca and magic are perfectly normal. In the 1990s, many books have been written about the history and practices of paganism, and Vivianne Crowley has drawn attention to the subject from psychology's viewpoint (Crowley, 1996). Indeed the 1990s and start of the new century has seen a huge increase in the number of books published on modern paganism and Wicca. The 1980s and 1990s also produced a number of television programmes that explored the subject of witchcraft with a favourable attitude. These included *Robin of Sherwood*, *The X Files* and *Wycliffe*. The twenty-first century has seen an explosion of similarly favourable teenage-based television programmes concerned with it such as *The Craft* and *Buffy the Vampire Slayer*.

The 'Pagan Federation' was founded in 1971 and other groups include 'The Fellowship of Isis' and 'The Children of Artemis'. In addition to these, there exist a number of pagan Druid and Heathen groups. If one is to believe the figures quoted by the various organisations, both formally and informally, then numbers are certainly on the increase. In 1996, Hutton quoted six thousand pagan Druids and about ten thousand initiated Wiccans in Britain alone (Hutton, 2001, p.400).

In the 1990s, pagans and academics have formed closer relationships. Panics over ritual abuse have been mainly overthrown and pagan chaplains can now be found in hospitals, prisons and universities. Important conferences have been held on pagan issues at King's College, London (1990), Newcastle University (1994), Lancaster University (1996) and King Alfred's College, Winchester (1997).

The academics whose works have been consulted for this work have shown a remarkable degree of conformity. From the anthropological view, Luhrmann observed the groups were "astonishingly diverse", especially in spiritual terms, and that they avoided clear-cut beliefs. Mythology and symbolism were very important in their magical practices and the power of the imagination was stressed. They possessed "relative sanity" compared to non-pagan groups (Luhrmann, 1989, p.99). Susan Greenwood argued that: "Paganism is an umbrella term for a number of diverse groups and practices...but all share a common uniting belief in communication with an 'otherworld'..." (Greenwood, 2000, p.1). Hutton also mentions the fewer rogues and saints and notably the lack of actual scandals compared to the Christian Church. He stresses the difficulties in entering a coven and the ease in which it can be left, in contrast to some cults that demand the rejection of previous links and current associations outside its own world (Hutton, 2001, pp.410-411). Graham Harvey makes comments that have often been confirmed in conversation at conferences, moots and other gatherings by many pagans. (Harvey, 1997):

- "Paganism is a polytheistic Nature religion."
- [Paganism has developed] "as a fundamentally pluralist tradition."
- "Paganism is not concerned primarily with the unusual or the supernatural, but with the miracle of ordinary life in all its facets."
- "Pagans may be the only people who accept the whole package (polytheism, seasonal festivals, nature-centred spirituality and lifestyle..."
- "The Craft attracts people because it combines the honouring of Nature with techniques for self-exploration."
- [The Otherworld] "is a dimension of the Earth accessible to those able to alter sufficiently their consciousness or perception."
- "Alongside experience Pagans value intuition."

Witchcraft fits into this list in contrast to the early modern stereotype previously mentioned. There is a complete lack of either the demonic or a sense of doing evil deeds. The divinity of Nature is stressed and ideas of being exclusively female and poor are missing. Modern witches' acceptance of polytheism and interest in self-exploration and intuition would have had no place in the early modern model.

I decided to investigate the place of music within modern paganism and witchcraft specifically because there appeared to be a lack of knowledge about this subject in contemporary and earlier sources. It received virtually no references in the extensive literature explored.

Where reference was made, it was only with passing comments, such as Luhrmann, alluding to the fact that music was used. The composer Cyril Scott stated that: "Of all the arts, music is from the occult standpoint, by far the most potent; so potent indeed that it has been instrumental in moulding thought and morals, influencing its sister arts and even to some extent history itself" (Scott, 1935, p.157). Moreover, music seems historically to play an important role in the practice of paganism and the perception of witchcraft:

> "Music…ranks so high that no understanding can reach it, and exudes such a power that dominates everything and of which nobody can give himself on account. Religious cult can therefore not dispense with it; it is one of the best means to have a miraculous effect on man."
>
> (Neubauer, cited in Flaherty, 1992, p.163).

This has been commented upon in many varied sources, for instance:

> "Music has always been an adjunct to religion, and in ancient times music has always been held to have magical powers. Music was supposed to put man in touch with the supernatural, as we see from such words as *charm, enchanter, incantation,* all of which are derived from singing."
>
> (E. J. Dent, 1965, p.19)

For the purpose of my research I almost totally excluded references to witchcraft unless they pertained to Western ideology and I concentrated on the tradition within England, for practical reasons. There were difficulties in deciding what was the definition of paganism and how broad a spectrum should be used concerning different types of music to be investigated. Since many people refer to themselves as pagans, I included their views and information when they used such a definition. I limited my research to mainly classical music (or perhaps more correctly, art-music), folk and New Age music since I did not wish to enter the realms of gothic rock and heavy-metal music. I felt that such music was more important as entertainment rather than being an actual part of religious worship. This observation is validated in an article about pagan music stating the current pagan band scene "…is not for religion, not primarily for fun, but for commerce; the record and concert promotion business" (R. Wybold, 1995, p.24).

The subjects studied were:

- The place of music in images of witchcraft before its modern revival.
- The interpretation of witches and witchcraft related activities in classical music.
- The use of music in twentieth century pagan/witchcraft rituals and the current scene.

Perceptions of the Place of Music in Witchcraft Before and at the Start of its Modern Revival

Examples linking music and witchcraft from before 1700 have been extremely difficult to find. Prior to the twentieth century, there were no audio recordings available and I have therefore had to rely on printed material referring to music or illustrations, such as woodcuts depicting supposed witches' sabbaths. (See Robbins, 1965.) Commentators on, and documenters, of witchcraft have inevitably influenced the public perception of it through their choices of imagery and emphasis. Drawing on these sources I shall present examples chronologically, beginning with the earliest documented examples of witchcraft portrayed in music.

A documented connection between music and witchcraft on stage is not encountered until the sixteenth and seventeenth centuries. A sixteenth century example of music being included in a poem is *The Faerie Queene* (Spenser, 1596, ed. Roche Jr.,1978) by Edmund Spenser. It mentions Hecate as well as a demon of lechery that rides dressed in a green gown astride a bearded goat, the latter animal often being illustrated as the embodiment of evil at witches' sabbaths. The work initially paints an evil hag-like picture of a witch causing mists and transformations and using herbs and ointments for evil purposes. A particularly unpleasant description describes one as follows:

"Her craftie head was altogether bald,
And as in hate of honourable eld,
Was overgrowne with scurfe and filthy scald;
Her teeth out of her rotten gummes were feld,
And her sowre breath abhominably smeld;
Her dried dugs, like bladders lacking wind,

Hong downe, and filthy matter from them weld;
Her wrizled skin as rough, as maple rind,
So scabby was, that would have loathd all womankind."

(Ibid., I, viii, 48-50, p.144)

However, in the second part of the poem (*II.xii*) altogether different characteristics are presented, much more akin to the seductive qualities of Circe who Homer portrayed as a powerful enchantress in *The Odyssey* and to whom there are further references. Music is also introduced of a sensuous nature to accompany the wantonness:

"Eftsoones they heard a most melodious sound,
Of all that mote delight a daintie eare,
Such as attonce might not on living ground,
Save in this Paradise, be heard elsewhere

There, whence that Musick seeméd heard to bee,
Was the faire Witch her selfe now solacing,
With a new Lover, whom through sorceree
And witchcraft, she from farre did thither bring."

(Ibid., II, xii, pp.378-9)

Witches were important in plays such as Dekker, Rowley and Ford's *The Witch of Edmonton*, Heywood's *The Wise Woman of Hogsdon*, Heywood and Brome's *The Late Lancashire Witches*, Middleton's *The Witch*, Jonson's *The Masque of Queens* and, of course, Shakespeare's *Macbeth* (Budd, 1989). This reflects a lively interest in the supposed supernatural elements of existence. There was also a high level of interest within the royal court, notably that of James I, for which context many of these works would have been intended. Other 'supernatural' characters such as devils, demons and infernal spirits also appeared in numerous masques of the period. Music is not mentioned at all in *The Wise Woman of Hogsdon* (Heywood, 1604, ed. Wilson, 1882), perhaps explained by the fact that her character is portrayed more as a cunning woman than a witch, with whom there is traditionally no musical association. In *The Witch of Edmonton*, the hag-like qualities are represented but the only music pertains to the pitch of the bells worn by a group of Morris dancers. It is possible that another character - an 'old fiddler' - may play at some instance but it is not clearly suggested in the text (Dekker, Rowley and Ford, 1621, ed. Rhys, 1949).

Shakespeare's first performance of *Macbeth* was probably in 1606 (Kors and Peters, 2001) and his interpretation of the witches was undoubtedly heavily influenced by such works as James VI's *Daemonologie* of 1597 that was reprinted in 1603 when he became King of England. It has been suggested that the Hecate scenes are not authentic but added later by Middleton:

> "...three passages (III.5; IV.1, 39-43; IV.1, 125-32) in the witch-scenes, which can be distinguished from the genuine text by the introduction of Hecate, by the use of an iambic instead of a trochaic metre, and by prettiness of lyrical fancy alien to the main conception of the witches."
>
> (Chambers cited in Hartnoll, 1966, p.40)

In *Macbeth*, Act III, Scene v, between lines 33 and 34, there is a stage direction: "Music and a song within": "Come away, come away etc." during Hecate's speech. In the following Act IV, Scene i, between lines 43 and 44, "Music and a song" is specified: "Black spirits etc." In the same scene, the word 'hautboys' (a woodwind instrument making a similar sound to the oboe) is indicated and followed by the direction of "music" to which the witches dance and vanish. Both the songs 'Come away, Hecate' and 'Black Spirits' are used in Middleton's *The Witch* but there are further complications since there are disputes concerning early transcriptions of the works (Middleton, 1994, xv). It has been suggested that Shakespeare did not include the songs in *Macbeth* and that they were added by Middleton when he was revising the work in 1609-10 (ibid., xiv). This has resulted in different editions either including or excluding the songs. Furthermore, it has been argued that the music might hold up the dramatic flow if 'enlarged resources' were necessary to perform it (Hartnoll, 1966). It is likely that the composer of the music to both the plays was the same.

The Witch was written in 1615-1616 and it has obvious affinities with *Macbeth* but lacks the intensity of Shakespeare's tragedy. Middleton was influenced by Scot's *Discoverie of Witchcraft* (Scot, 1972) and he might therefore be thought to be satirising the witches rather than portraying them as powerful prophetesses. He even quoted directly from Scot's work, notably throughout Act I, Scene ii. He was also undoubtedly acquainted with Jonson's *The Masque of Queens* (1609) that depicted witches in the first part of the masque together with 'infernal music' (Jonson cited in Kors and Peters, 2001). Jonson represented twelve hags paying homage to a "devil-goat" and their dance was accompanied by "a strange and sodayne Musique".' Their "magicall Daunce" had "contrary and backward motions, and antic gestures" (Clark, 1999, p.92). Jonson cited Johan Nider's *Formicarius* and mentioned two male witches from it - 'Stadlin' and 'Hoppo'. Middleton reintroduced the names but changed them to female witches. During the ninth charm, the 'Dame', who may be thought of as the same figure as Hecate, utters the following spell with a direct implication of music being necessary, but not specified: *"Around, around, around, around, till a music sound, and the pace be found, to which we may dance, and our charms advance"* (Ibid. p.345).

Music is mentioned at various times during *The Witch* when Hecate is present. In Act I, Scene ii, she conjures up a cat playing on a fiddle, and the witches' dance in Act V, Scene ii. The songs 'Come Away, Hecate' and 'Black Spirits' are both included in the play and one other song, 'In a maiden-time professed', does not occur during any of the Hecate or witches' appearances. It has been suggested by the musicologist Ian Spink (Middleton, 1994) that the composer Robert Johnson wrote the music to these songs because this would fit in with his time working for the 'King's Men' from 1609 onwards. The music is lively and uses big melodic leaps. Rhythmically, it is angular and lends itself to dance with suitably 'awkward' moves. It is, in some ways, a forerunner of how Purcell was to treat the same scene in *Dido and Aeneas* in 1689 and unless Shakespeare was using the songs as a humorous interlude, they would seem somewhat incongruous in these settings for *Macbeth*. Thomas Duffett, an early writer of what became known as pantomime, wrote complete parodies of plays such as *Macbeth* with stage directions such as: "Three Witches fly over the Pit riding upon Beesomes..." (Dent, 1965, p.154). Later in the seventeenth century, *Macbeth* was revived with fresh material added to it. Davenant produced one such performance in the mid-1660s with music by Matthew Locke and a further production in 1673 "in the nature of an opera" (Hartnoll, 1966, p.53). However, the music was lost and in 1694 the composer John Eccles wrote new music for the play. William Boyce published a collection of pieces allegedly by Locke, but the composer's true identity has been disputed. (Dent, 1965). Apart from music that is composed only indirectly for the play using its title or imagery, there have not been many noteworthy settings of incidental music that have survived. In the 1770s, J. Vernon, a comedian, published 'The new songs in the pantomime of *The Witches*'. J. F. Reichardt, a Berlin *Kapellmeister,* composed music for the Witches' scenes and the little-known M. P. King wrote a 'Witches' glee' in the nineteenth century (Ibid.).

Although witches do not appear in Shakespeare's *The Tempest* (except for 'Sycorax', a witch and the mother of Caliban, who does not have an acting role) nevertheless, the 1667 adaptation by Dryden and Davenant introduced singing parts for devils and spirits. The musicologist E. J. Dent takes this further in believing that "Shakespeare had himself laid down the principle that music…was generally to be associated with supernatural characters and happenings" (ibid. p.155). In addition dancing scenes for "fantastic spirits" were included that served a similar purpose to the witches' dances of other plays and masques. Much of the music by Locke, Humfrey and others has survived and been transcribed (Tilmouth, 1986) and the latter's 'Masque of Devils' could just as easily have been performed by witches reminiscent of Purcell's *Dido and Aeneas*.

Shadwell's *Psyche* was the first English work to be described as a 'semi-opera', i.e. a work for stage that did not simply consist of dramatic scenes with incidental music, but lacking the development of plot necessary to be classed as full opera. The music was composed by Locke and first performed in 1675. Shadwell claimed to have been influenced by Apuleius' *Golden Ass* that has the theme of Goddess-worship and witchcraft permeating it (ibid.). Similarly to *The Tempest*, witches are not portrayed as such in the text, but there are songs, choruses and dances for 'Cyclops' [sic], 'Devils' and 'Furies'. The Romano/Greek pantheons are well represented with Venus, Pan, Bacchus, Mars, Apollo and others. It would appear that the supernatural characters are not meant to inspire fear but are used as part of a lavish entertainment. There was a prominence of supernatural and other magical beings in Restoration theatre providing a potential for unusual music as well as a love of spectacle. Works sometimes even referred to its popularity that was governed by seventeenth century views of witchcraft and magic. For instance, Dryden and Lee's *Oedipus* (1679) mentions the audience's love of ghosts in the epilogue. (For an expansion of this see Plank, 1990, pp. 392-407.) The reasons for this popularity may have included an enjoyment of masques and the grotesque qualities of the 'antimasque'; the possibilities of allegorical interpretations; the excuse of indulging in the irrational by the use of music; and the enjoyment of 'fantastic' stage machinery and fireworks, etc. It might be argued that Jonson's *The Masque of Queens* set a precedent for future productions with its 'hollow and infernal music…with spindles, timbrels, rattles, or other venefical instruments, making a confused noise, with strange gestures' (ibid. p.395).

The small amount of surviving music accompanying early stage productions, excluding *Dido and Aeneas*, therefore provides little evidence of what could be called an established tradition of 'witch-music'. However, there were situations where music was important to enhance the stage activity. The musicologist Peter Holman makes the following point:

> "Extended pieces of concerted music were usually reserved for three situations. Ritual scenes naturally required music, whether the protagonists were Christian or pagan priests, soothsayers, enchanters or magicians, engaged in communal prayer, sacrificing to the gods, foretelling the future or summoning up supernatural beings."

> (Holman and Thompson, 2001, p.614)

Some characteristics do emerge as prevalent, for instance contemporary instruments and dances were used, but with more deliberate harmonic dissonance and jagged rhythms. Purcell's use of 'flatt' trumpets for the devils' appearances in *The Libertine Destroyed* (Shadwell 1675) may have set a precedent for Monteverdi's low brass for the Hades scene in *Orfeo*. The rapid semi-quavers, repeated notes and chromatic progressions of the 'infernal symphony' for the spirits in *Rinaldo and Armida* (J. Dennis 1698 with music by J. Eccles) provides more than a hint of how future composers were to accompany such scenes. It is always important to remember that the textual record may give only a partial and misleading representation of performances. It is possible, for example, that instrumentalists may have added their own spontaneous ornamentation. In short, the rules of music theory were being in some ways overturned just as the witches allegedly embraced misrule.

Moving away from the stage, Robert Herrick published *The Hag* in 1648 but there is no mention of music in it. There are various musical settings of the poem by Frank Bridges and an early setting by J. Liptrot

Hatton. R. Burns provides further information in his poem *Tam O'
Shanter* when the hero comes across a witches' 'sabbat' but he is not
seriously suggesting that one accepts his poem as a work of fact:

> "Warlocks and witches in a dance;
> Nae cotillion brent new frae France,
> But hornpipes, jigs, strathspeys, and reels,
> Put life and mettle in their heels,
> At winnock-bunker in the east,
> There sat auld Nick, in shape o' beast;
> A towzie tyke, black, grim, and large,
> To gi'e them music was his charge:
> He screwed the pipes and gart them skirl,
> Till roof and rafters a' did dirl!"

(Burns, 1791, p.124)

Burns assigns the Devil the job of playing the pipes to which the
warlocks and witches dance traditional folk dances rather than an
imported French court dance ('cotillion').

Goethe's *Faust* was completed in 1801 and it contains two parts
where witchcraft and music are brought together, namely 'Walpurgis
Night' and the immediately following 'Walpurgis Night's Dream'
(Goethe, translated Wayne, 1967). Dancing takes place during the
sabbath in the Harz Mountains to which one can presume music was
played as an accompaniment and in the following 'Lyrical Intermezzo'
Ariel is said to play upon a lute. An orchestra is spoken of and unusually
the bagpipes are spoken of tenderly - "sweetly now the bagpipe blows"
(ibid. p.182).

In the earlier part of the nineteenth century, folklore and the upsurge
of Romanticism combined in both literary and musical works. There
was an interest in the gothic and macabre with novels including Mary
Shelley's *Frankenstein* in 1818 and slightly earlier Samuel Coleridge
Taylor's *The Rime of the Ancient Mariner* in 1798. Byron's *Manfred*
(1817) introduces a character referred to as the 'Witch of the Alps'
but music is not mentioned during her brief appearance in Act II. The
only references to music can be found in Act II, Scene iii where the
indication of 'A voice without. Singing' is written and in Act II, Scene
iv where a 'Hymn of Spirits' is presented, but without specifying
whether the words should actually be sung and, if so, to what tune.

During the twentieth century, a number of populist writers devoted time to describing what they have believed to represent witchcraft practices and rituals, including references to music. Some held extreme beliefs about the nature of witchcraft and their descriptions of the role of music reinforce these distorted images. For instance, Montague Summers' exaggerated beliefs about witchcraft can be seen in many of his works. These reflected a desire to portray it as a real diabolic religion. Concerning the sabbaths, allegedly orgiastic gatherings of witches and demons, he writes:

> "There were often dances...the choreography of hell, awkward jiggetings and lewd leapings, the muckibus caperings and bouncings...The music well suits the movements. As there is an immortal melody and the 'Perfect Diapason' of Heaven, so is there the horrid cacophony of hell. Music may be potent for evil, unloosing hideous passions and cruelty..."

(Summers, 1965, p.284)

The author continues this diatribe against witchcraft with a comparison with Père Labat's account of voodoo in the eighteenth century:

> "A kind of madness falls upon the dancers. They ceaselessly whirl around. They tear off their clothes and bite deep into their own flesh...until finally in the darkness promiscuous prostitution holds the most horrible sway.
>
> This might almost exactly serve as a picture of the dancing at the witches' sabbat, only in place of the drums mention is made of various other instruments: violins, tambourines, flutes, rebecks, fifes and drums, hautboys, the bass-horn, a hurdy-gurdy, the Jew's harp, and (especially in Scotland) the pipes."

(ibid. p.285)

This negative view is achieved through the emphasis on extreme behaviour, frenzied music and dance allied with nudity, madness, abandoned sexual activity and general loss of control. Music is obviously vital for the dance to take place and the instruments used are common in folk traditions.

The author Dennis Wheatley can arguably be claimed to be responsible for some of the interest in witchcraft and the occult in the 1970s. His novels were, and still are, very popular and his book *The Devil Rides Out* was turned into a successful film of the same name. However, when he turns to 'fact', rather than fiction, he further distorts some of the issues concerning witchcraft. *The Devil and all his works* (1973) is most definitely not simply about the Devil but also discusses mythology, psychical research, religion and many other subjects. In mentioning the musical activities of the alleged sabbaths he writes:

"Offal was eaten and, whenever possible, the flesh of a murdered child. The band struck up, but it played no tune, only made a horrid cacophony. They danced, but back to back. Then the orgy began, and it was no matter of joyful, healthy lust...Such were the sabbaths of the sixteenth and seventeenth centuries..."

(Wheatley, 1973, pp.242-43)

Furthermore, one presumes that he means that the dancing "back to back" was a circle dance facing outwards as opposed to inwards, as the reference is to the illustration by Jan Ziarnko in Pierre de Lancre's *Tableau de l'inconstance des mauvais anges et demons*. (Reproduced in Robbins, 1965, p. 300.) This shows a circle dance and a group of musicians (in the top left corner marked 'G') playing horns, a rebec (a predecessor to the violin) and a lute-like instrument. Music and dance is again used to reinforce a stereotypically negative view of witchcraft, in this case particularly emphasising links with Satanism.

On the contrary the use of images of witches by modern witches or, in Crowley's case, a magician, present a stark contrast to the demonic depictions. The author and practising witch Doreen Valiente believed that the spirit of a dead witch contacted her and she kept a diary of the communications she received. She was told that they celebrated meetings indoors with drinking and fiddle or pipe music but that religious meetings were always outdoors. Writing on the subject of music in general she maintained: "Music has always been a magical thing, used by witches as an aid in their working" (Valiente, 1989), p.214). She also wrote that songs were sung at Esbats including *Greensleeves*, *Hares on the Mountain* and *The Coal-Black Smith*:

> "In fact, the music of the witches' Esbats and Sabbats was mainly the popular tunes of the day. In the accounts of Scottish witchcraft, there is mention of a number of lively and bawdy old ballads being sung and danced to..."

(Valiente, 1973, p.11)

The very existence of these rites has been doubted but the musicologist Bob Stewart speculates as to what the possible nature of witch music might be: "If the music described at the many well-documented witch-trials was folk music – and it could hardly have been anything else – then we can be sure that the ancient forms of antiphonal chanting and linked dancing were used in these rites" (Stewart, 1988, p.109).

In the realm of twentieth century ritual magick [sic] one finds music taking a place mainly through the interest and writings of one man - Aleister Crowley (1875-1947). He wrote a great deal about his work and also aroused considerable interest and horror, mainly concerning his sexual and drug-taking excesses. However, it is only his use of music that is of any relevance to this study and it could be argued that, since he was not a witch and hardly even a pagan, he should not be mentioned at all. He was, however, known to follow pagan gods and goddesses on occasions (Hutton, 1999, p. 41) and he has obviously had an effect on occultism, mainly through his writings. He played the piano reasonably well (a recording is available at The Museum of Witchcraft, Boscastle) and he wrote of an interest in music:

> "The violin is the most useful of all, for its every mood expresses the hunger for the infinite, and yet it is so mobile that it has a greater emotional range than any of its competitors. Accompaniment must be dispensed with, unless a harpist be available..."

(Crowley, cited in Dearn, 1977, p.12)

He used music in his ceremonies, especially when he had the services of his 'Scarlet Woman' Leila Waddell who was an accomplished violinist according to contemporary accounts:

"After a long pause, the figure enthroned [Leila Waddell] took a violin and played with passion and feeling, like a master. We were thrilled to our very bones. Once again the figure took the violin and played…with such an intense feeling that in very deed most of us experienced the ecstasy which Crowley so earnestly seeked [sic]."

(Sketch, 1910, cited in King, 1987, p.64)

Most contemporary commentators agree that witchcraft in its modern form was instigated by the activities of Gerald Gardner and the publication of his book *Witchcraft Today* in 1954 (Gardner, 1999). Its introduction by the respected Egyptologist Margaret Murray further enhanced its reputation and led to the belief that witchcraft had been continuing underground since ancient days. Gardner wrote other books including *High Magic's Aid* under the pseudonym of 'Scire' in 1949 and *The Meaning of Witchcraft* in 1959 (Gardner, 1982 and 1999). I was told by Patricia Crowther, his high priestess, that he did not use music in his rituals other than through simple chants and a few simple percussion instruments. However, he obviously believed music to have considerable power, especially in the hands of a witch. He devotes a chapter of *High Magic's Aid* to 'Music Magic' wherein the witch-heroine controls a group of soldiers intent on harming her by playing the harp:

"Morven, still playing, was peering out of the door too, but it was a soothing tune; calm and peaceful, like a balm to the mind, and concluding with a soft chord. Thur looked at her in silence. Brother Stephen spoke with conviction: 'That be witches' knowledge'…"

(Gardner, 1999, p.117)

Gardner's work was continued in many ways by the self-styled 'King of the Witches' Alexander Sanders. Indirect conversations with his ex-wife Maxine and direct conversations with an ex-member of his coven (Carol Morse) have indicated to me that he did not use music extensively in his rituals. However, I discovered an unpublished Sanders lecture in a box of his belongings at the Museum of Witchcraft in Boscastle that indicated his interest in music:

Rites and Ceremonies of the Wicca:

"...I have been humbled to have heard the majesty of his [Pan's] pipes and this is what he said to me in the music of his pipes: 'Come, come my child, dance for me...The pipes of Pan which shall forever play To [sic] help you along for another day...'"

(Sanders transcription of a lecture given in 1986, page 6 of an unsorted package of papers housed in the Museum of Witchcraft, Boscastle.)

Furthermore, there were a number of cassette tapes in the same collection linking Sanders with the music of Phillip Thornton. (Sanders recorded by Derek Taylor: *Mother Matrix an Invocation*, *The Ritual of the Cabbalistic Cross* and *Moon Magic - 2nd degree initiation*, all with music by Phillip Thornton, 1984.)

Amongst rare references in poetry and prose to witchcraft's musical characteristics is T. S. Eliot's *East Coker*. The author G. Tindall (1967) draws attention to the oft-quoted idea that the Christian Devil and the 'Hornèd God' Pan are the same person and the performer here:

"In that open field
If you do not come too close, if you do not come too close,
On a summer midnight, you can hear the music
Of the weak pipe and the little drum
And see them dancing around the bonfire..."

(Eliot, 1963, pp.196-7)

The music of Pan is magically conjured up in Kenneth Grahame's *The Wind in the Willows* when the Rat and Mole search for and find a lost baby otter:

"The merry bubble and joy, the thin, clear happy call of the distant piping! Such music I never dreamed of, and the call in it is stronger even than the music is sweet!.. Breathless and transfixed the Mole stopped rowing as the liquid run of that glad piping broke on him like a wave, caught him up, and possessed him utterly."

(Grahame, 1997, pp.112-13)

The music presented here is very different from the "whining of infernal and discordant music" (Haining, 1972, p.71) that one is often led to believe accompanies the 'Hornèd God'. The image of Pan and the effect of the music are that of protection and beauty and the altered state achieved as it "possessed him utterly" is in stark contrast to the crazed frenzy described by Montague Summers (1965). These contrasting examples illustrate the fact that music can be described as contributing to the achievement of altered states of very different types and sometimes these are expressed as comparative extremes.

Thus the music encountered enhances different situations according to the desires of the author. It can be riotous and orgiastic, perhaps reminiscent of a Bacchanalial gathering or a lively village feast where the fiddles and pipe and tabor have often been shown to be played both in terms of visual illustrations and literary representations. It can be magical and peaceful in its connection with nature and its effects on the human mind using the panpipes and harp respectively from similar sources. These cultural constructions seem to dominate the available material and finding opposing interpretations is very difficult. Of course, a limited definition of 'magic' and 'nature' is being presented here since both can also provide violent images in image and music. Rhythms can be flowing or jagged and harmonies concordant or discordant. However, in each example music can sometimes be seen to have played a meaningful role. The strongest characteristics encountered are the use of dissonance and links to folk music of the time.

The popularity of Margaret Murray's books and articles were an important factor in witchcraft's resurgence in the mid-twentieth century. Starting with *The Witch-Cult in Western Europe* in 1921, *The God of the Witches* in 1931 and culminating in *The Divine King in England* in 1954, Margaret Murray provides the most influential texts for images of music in witchcraft. Although her interpretation of witchcraft's roots has been condemned by recent academics, she nevertheless made available considerable information that may have remained unseen if it had not been for her exertions. Referring to a Palaeolithic cave painting Murray speculates quite dramatically in stating:

"The musical bow of the little masked figure of the Palaeolithic era is very primitive, the player is dancing to his own music as the Devil so often did in Scotland. The

163

flute as an instrument for magical purposes occurs in Egypt at the very dawn of history, when a masked man plays on it in the midst of animals. The panpipes, as their name implies, belong specially to a god who was disguised as an animal."

(Murray, 1962, p.84)

In *The Witch-Cult in Western Europe,* she devotes a complete section to the music used at gatherings but she cannot resist adding her own comments to the original sources:

"The music at the assemblies was of all kinds, both instrumental and vocal.
The English trials hardly mention music, possibly because the Sabbath had fallen into a decadent condition; but the Scottish and French trials prove that it was an integral part of the celebration."

(Murray, 1921, p.135)

Her interpretation of the English witches' sabbath having fallen into a "decadent condition" is more readily attributed to its likely non-existence and she does not provide any evidence for her assertions. A strongly contributing factor leading to accusations that the Scottish and French held such events was the existence of documentary evidence and descriptions elicited by torture. The greater prominence of alleged Sabbaths in European countries provided the expectation of music at such gatherings. It would seem that the music was only played to accompany dancing and singing which is a common role in folk gatherings not involved in witchcraft. The Devil was also said to participate in the musical entertainment, often as the performer on the pipes. The music was used to accompany the dancing and the 'pipes' were the instrument used in general, although Murray mentions the cittern (a guitar-like instrument) as played in England, in France the violin, and the Jew's harp in Scotland. It can be surmised that the music was almost undoubtedly played on instruments that were common in the area.

It is quite remarkable how Murray's research has been reproduced in other works and almost automatically been accepted as factual. For instance, Patricia Crowther quotes the Somerset witches' music wherein "the Man in black sometimes playes [sic] on a Pipe or Cittern, and the company dance" (Crowther cites Murray in *Lid off the Cauldron*, 1981, p.88). Although the pipe is a relatively easy instrument to play, albeit not well, the cittern would require both skill in playing as well as either knowledge in its manufacture or sufficient money to purchase one.

Murray refers to the 'North Berwick' case that directly involved James VI of Scotland:

> "The North Berwick witches (1590), when at the special meeting called to compass the death of the king, 'danced along the Kirk-yeard, Geilis Duncan playing on a Trump'."
>
> (*Spalding Club Misc.* I, 114-15, cited in Murray, 1921, p.136)

She implies here that the group of witches met to plan the King's death and then danced in the churchyard to the accompaniment of Duncan's Jew's harp playing. The explanation for this could simply be alcohol-induced high spirits. However, it could also be claimed that it represents a legitimate and necessary ritual believed to contribute to the success of the plot. The former would seem to be a more likely explanation!

The historian H. R. Trevor-Roper writes of the "macabre music made with curious instruments - horses' skulls, oak-logs, human bones, etc…" - but he does not give a source for these deliberations and he is generally not interested in musical discussions (Trevor-Roper, 1984, p.16). His views on Murray's work are made clear in a footnote where he quotes the historian C. L. Ewen: "The fancies of the late Margaret Murray need not detain us. They were justly, if irritably, dismissed by a real scholar as 'vapid balderdash'" (Ibid., 41, footnote citing Ewen *Some Witchcraft Criticisms*, 1938).

Murray's images can still be seen, albeit in modern fantasies in reworked illustrations such as the music at celebratory festivals, the "most famous of which were the May Day carols" (Millar, 1981, p.16) that were popular folk songs sung at appropriate celebrations. At these festive events groups of musicians played improvised or semi-improvised music on whatever instruments they owned.

> "The Lord of Misrule and his associates then dressed in scarves, lace and ribbons, tied bells on their legs and then, with hobby-horses, dragons and 'other antiques', this

'heathen company' danced to the sound of drums and pipes
to the local church."

(Stubbes, 1584 cited in Aldcroft Jackson, 1994, p.4)

Murray used a number of primary sources for her evidence of
witchcraft practices mainly in the seventeenth century and printed
in nineteenth century Scottish works. These allegedly provide
information about the musical activities of the witches and demons at
sabbaths and other gatherings. (For instance, Pitcairn, Criminal Trials
in Scotland from A.D. M.CCCC.LXXXVIII to A.D. *M.DC.XXIV*, 1833
and *Spalding Club Miscellany*, 1841.) The Devil or demons were often
shown in various guises involved with playing music, and the level of
musical expertise seemed to vary. According to one source:

> "Isobel Cockie of Aberdeen was accused of being at a
> Sabbath on All-hallow eve: 'Thou wast the ring-leader,
> next Thomas Leyis; and because the Devil played not
> so melodiously and well as thou crewit, thou took his
> instrument out of his mouth, then took him on the chaps
> therewith, and played thyself thereon to the whole
> company.'"

(Spalding Club Miscellany, i, 1841, pp.114-5)

This suggests that the Devil was prevented from playing and then
slapped around the face by the irate witch. However, his playing was
sometimes quoted as being somewhat better: "Thou and they was
under the conduct of thy master, the Devil, dancing in ane ring, and he
played melodiously upon ane instrument, albeit invisibly to you" (ibid.
p.149). The Devil was not always the musician as can be evidenced by
the following quotation:

> "At Tranent (1659) eight women and a man named John
> Douglas confessed to 'having merry meetings with Satan,
> enlivened with music and dancing. Douglas was the pyper,
> and the two favourite airs of his majesty were *Kilt thy coat,*
> *Maggie, and come thy way with me* and *Hulie the bed will*
> *fa*."

(*Spottiswoode Miscellany ii*, 1844-5, p.68. *Kilt thy coat, Maggie*
is reproduced from the *Skene* manuscript, 1620 cited in J. Purser,

Scotland's Music, 1992, p.123. There is a further example of a gypsy tune that allegedly contains "gypsy magic".)

A typical witches' sabbath allegedly contained music, dancing and lewd activity and one can see some of these activities where the musical accompaniment favoured appears to be bagpipes and horns from contemporary illustrations (reproduced in Robbins, 1965). These were popular peasant instruments of the medieval and early modern period in contrast to the angelic harps portrayed in church paintings and stained glass windows. Further comparisons might be made with the 'feast of fools', an often bawdy and irreverent celebration popular in the Middle Ages, where the music was of a very raucous nature consisting of "singing nonsense, a musical cavalcade, and a band that howled and clanged kettles and saucepans" (Clark, 1999, p.18). The sixteenth century French commentator N. Barnaud (1585) compared these Bacchanalian-like celebrations to the witches' sabbaths, with Bacchus being the Devil.

It was alleged that vocal music was also heard at the gatherings with intentionally crude words as a form of blasphemy: "Then fal they to dauncing, wherein he leadeth [the Devil presumeably] the daunce, or els they hoppe and daunce merely about him, singing most filthy songes made in his prayse" (Danaeus, 1575).

The number of songs mentioned by name are very few, for instance *Kilt thy coat, Maggie* and *Cummer, go ye before*, and when identified they are probably either made up or existing ditties. Apart from church music, the only other musical performances encountered would have been mainly from minstrels at fairs and other celebrations, and in taverns. The song mentioned below almost certainly falls into the category of an improvised ditty since there is no known record of the music or its title:

> "At Forfar Helen Guthrie told the court that Andrew Watson 'made great merriment by singing his old ballads, and Isobel Shirrie did sing her song called *Tinkletum Tankletum*'"

> (Kinloch, 1848, p.120)

Witches allegedly indulged in an activity that is to change the words of well known songs to either more pagan-orientated or irreverent versions:

"At Aix in 1610 'the Magicians and those that can reade, singe certaine Psalmes as they doe in the Church, especially *Laudate Dominum de Coelis*: *Confitemini domino quoniam bonus*, and the Canticle *Benedicite*, transferring all to the praise of Lucifer and the Diuels: And the Hagges and Sorcerers doe houle and vary their hellish cries high and low counterfeiting a kind of villanous musicke."

(Michaelis, 1613, p.336)

In the above quotation the "villanous musicke" is not expanded upon but one might speculate that howling to the sacred chants was what the commentator was suggesting.

With the lack of examples of music references available from British sources it was necessary to augment these with a few French examples. It has been said that "viols and other instruments" were played and at another trial in 1652 there was evidence that there was dancing to songs (van Elven, 1891). It is mentioned that in Lorraine in 1589 the instruments were very primitive and apart from small pipes played by the women, a man:

"…has a horse's skull which he plays as a zither [a plucked-stringed instrument with a sound board, but un-fretted]. Another has a cudgel with which he strikes an oak-tree, which gives out a note and an echo like a kettledrum or a military drum. The Devil sings in a hoarse shout, exactly as if he trumpeted through his nose so that a roaring wooden voice resounds through the wide air."

(Remigius, 1693, p.88)

The crude nature of the instruments again places the musical activity very much in the domain of the peasant folk traditions. However, it was not always "infernal noise" that was produced if one is to believe the next quotation:

"…they dance to the sound of the tambourine and the flute, and sometimes with a long instrument which they place on the neck and pulling it down to the belt they strike it with a little stick; sometimes with a violin…with such harmony that there is not a concert in the world that can equal it."

(De Lancre, 1613, p.127)

The cittern has sometimes been referred to as the 'English guitar' to differentiate it from the better-known 'Spanish guitar' that was probably the instrument intended in the Suzanne Gaudry trial, under Spanish jurisdiction, in 1652 (Kors and Peters, 2001, p.360). In this trial under interrogation she spoke of dancing to the music of "a guitarist and some whistlers" (Francais, *L'Eglise et la sorcellerie* (Paris, 1910), cited in Kors and Peters, pp.360-1). A group of accused witches from Somerset in the 1660s said: "The Man in black sometimes plays on a Pipe or Cittern, and the company dance" (Glanvil, *Sadducismus Triumphatus*, pt. ii, 1681, p.14).

R. Pitcairn, a nineteenth century collator of criminal trials in Scotland, provides a few references to music from witchcraft trials in sixteenth and seventeenth century Scotland. Agnis Tomson makes various statements about the music at a sabbath in 1591:

> [They] "daunced this reill or fhort daunce...[They sing] Commer goe ye before, commer goe ye. Gif ye will not goe before, commer let me...[Geillis Duncane plays] a fmall trumpe, called a Jewes trump, untill they entred into the Kirk of North Barrick...Geillis Duncane, who upon the like trump did play the faide daunce before the Kinges Majestie."

> (Pitcairn, 1833, p.217)

Illustrations would seem to indicate that the "fhort daunce" was probably a reel danced in an eight-figure pattern, and the reference to the "Jewes trump" would appear to refer to the so-called "Jew's harp". (A single pronged metallic instrument that is vibrated between the lips and uses the mouth as a resonator.)

The song referred to by Agnis Tomson as 'Commer goe ye' provides information about the type of dance being used - a circle dance with anti-clockwise ('widdershins') movement but it does not hint at the musical accompaniment. It is likely that it was either sung to any known popular melody or an improvised tune.

Pitcairn provides another reference to music from the second confession of Issobel Gowdie in 1662 where she speaks of the song 'Our Lord to hunting he is gone', but unfortunately the rest of the source is 'mutilated' (Pitcairn, III, p. 608). 'Gillatrypes' are mentioned and explained as being 'probably a dance popular among the vulgar' but usually the type of dance used is unspecified (ibid. p.606).

Reginald Scot's *The Discoverie of Witchcraft* also mentions music and dance at a gathering but draws one's attention to the 'lies' that are repeated:

> "And here some of *Monsieur Bodins* lies may be insertyed, who saith that at these magicall assemblies, the witches never faile to danse; and in their danse they sing these words; Har, har divell divell, danse here, danse here, plaie here, plaie here, *Sabbath, sabbath*. And whiles they sing and danse, everie one hath a broome in hir hand, and holdeth it up aloft. Item he saith, that these night-walking or rather night-dansing witches, brought out of *Italie* into *France*, that danse, wjich is called *La Volta*."

(I. Bod. *De dæmon*. Lib. 2, cap. 4, cited in R. Scot, 1972, p.24)

The fore-mentioned '*La Volta*' was a popular dance during the period originating in Italy and then spreading throughout Europe and containing a few risqué steps. It was "considered incredible by onlookers" (Hughes, 1952).

Although written primary source material from the early modern period is limited, it is still possible to draw conclusions from that which can be traced. Firstly, they provide evidence for the prevailing beliefs about and conceptions of witchcraft. Secondly, they give some indications of the perceived role and power of music in these contexts.

The prevailing image is that of the stereotype witch presented as a hag-like female character who indulges in licentious behaviour at gatherings that are attended by other witches and demons. These are accompanied by music and dancing, according to the writings of authors such as Montague Summers and Dennis Wheatley. If one is to believe the various staged performances previously mentioned then the music was more dissonant than would ordinarily be the case and rhythms employed tended to be more jagged to allow exaggerated dance movements. There are good examples in *Dido and Aeneas* that will be analysed in the next essay. In other examples music is shown to accompany dancing and is mainly played on folk-type instruments such as the pipes and fiddles. The choice of instruments may reinforce the argument that essentially one is witnessing an exaggerated interpretation of traditional folk events that were remembered by the accused at the time. Instruments, such as the organ and harp, associated with the Church do not appear, perhaps highlighting the schism between the Church's fear of witchcraft and its own practices. The music suggested has links with classical Bacchanalian festivities and village revels in a more diluted form. The final type of music discovered provides a complete contrast to the other categories and is found in only a minority of examples. This is music of beauty and possessing ethereal qualities as quoted in *The Wind in the Willows*. It can be argued that the characteristics of witchcraft do not apply here but in the broadest sense of paganism and the supernatural it is felt to be applicable.

References to Witchcraft in Classical Music

There is a vast repertoire of music that seeks to explore the theme of witchcraft and I therefore have had to limit the study to avoid it becoming too unwieldy. I have included some examples of paganism, especially when it has reflected the beliefs and ideals of modern Wicca, for instance in *The Midsummer Marriage* by M. Tippett. I have chosen classical music as opposed to any other type because it paints many contrasting pictures of witches in many musical genres. This does not happen so often in rock, pop or folk music where purely instrumental works about witchcraft are quite rare. The works that have been mentioned provide evidence of witchcraft's popularity as a subject for musical interpretation. The study is far from exhaustive since many works are either no longer available in print or recording, or remain unpublished and only music from the West has been included. A decision had to be made concerning what would or would not be included under the heading of 'witchcraft'. Works that used specific words in their titles, such as 'witch', 'witchcraft', 'hex', 'enchantress', etc., were an obvious choice. Similarly, characters traditionally portrayed as witches or possessing witch-like characteristics such as Circe, Medea or Hecate were also included. The references to 'Walpurgis night' and 'black sabbaths' brought an obvious implication of witches gathering together. Although these primary sources could be included without hesitation, other sources presented difficulties. For instance, *Macbeth* and *Faust* contain witches and a Walpurgis night gathering respectively but unless a text was available there were obvious problems in knowing whether the witches had received a musical personification. I decided to mention such works unless the titles seemed to indicate that the witches' scenes might have been omitted.

Other sources were referred to if the theme of the music implied supernatural activity that is traditionally associated with witchcraft or paganism in a broader sense. It seemed ludicrous to omit Weber's *Der Freischütz* from the discussion because of its lack of witches, since the 'Wolf Glen' scene, is an important contribution to the repertoire of classical music to accompany and describe supernatural activities and it also contains spell casting and the appearance of the Devil. Exceptions were also made for Stravinsky's *The Rite of Spring* and Tippett's *The Midsummer Marriage* since their themes of nature and pagan dance have a strong affinity with modern paganism and witchcraft.

I decided to explore the theme according to musical genres in chronological and geographical order within each category. The categories chosen were:

- Opera
- Vocal/choral music
- Orchestral/instrumental music

The number of examples in each category from different periods varies considerably because of the changes in prevailing repertoire. For instance, there were virtually no examples of relevant vocal or instrumental music from the eighteenth century but there were many operatic ones.

(Initially I contemplated including the research of film scores in the survey but this suggested a vast body of extra material that it was felt would have made the study too unwieldy. I therefore analysed the music to just one film, *The Wicker Man*. It was chosen because I feel it contains music that is often associated with pagan and Wiccan ideals.)

Since the birth of opera in its current form in Renaissance Italy, it has often been used as a medium to reflect human situations and emotions in exotic or unusual circumstances. Initially ancient history and mythology, especially Greek, were preferred sources from which to create exotic backdrops for universally understood intrigues and affairs of the heart. This gave the performers and producers the chance to show off their voices and inventiveness in creating lavish stage sets and costumes. Many composers put their finest talents into composing such works (e.g. Verdi, Puccini and Wagner) and librettists sometimes made politically controversial statements through fictional scenarios. For instance, da Ponte after Beaumarchais in *The Marriage of Figaro* by Mozart, and Méry and Locle after Schiller in *Don Carlos* by Verdi. It is therefore not surprising to find numerous references to witchcraft and related subjects - sorcery, magic, pagan rituals, etc. - in operatic works from the seventeenth century to the present day. Operas and semi-operas reflected the public view of stereotypical witches as seen in the literature and witch trial evidence of the time. They can also be thought of as models for later productions that included the representation of witches. One such composer was Henry Purcell. His stage works *King Arthur* and *The Indian Queen* can only be classed as semi-operas since they lack a cohesive plot and detailed characterisation but his generally acclaimed masterpiece *Dido and Aeneas* does not fail in these respects.

Purcell's opera *Dido and Aeneas* (hereafter *Dido*) was written in 1689 for performance at Josias Priest's 'School for Young Gentlewomen' in Chelsea. The libretto was by Nahum Tate who succeeded Thomas Shadwell as Poet Laureate in 1692. The original score has not survived and the earliest musical score dates from after 1750 but a libretto exists from 1689. The most authentic music manuscript is *The Loves of Aeneas and Dido*, St Michael's College, Tenbury, MS 1266 (5) (now in the Bodleian Library, Oxford), but there are also later copies, for instance a score copied by Philip Hayes in about 1780 kept at Tatton Park in Cheshire and an even later version known as the Oki Ms, preserved at the Nanki Music Library in Japan. The 1689 libretto can be found in the Royal College of Music, London (D 144) or in facsimile in *The Works of Henry Purcell,* Vol. III, rev. Margaret Laurie (London: Novello, 1981, pp. xiii-xx). There have been many arguments as to which version should be used in performance since the musical scores and librettos contain some discrepancies. The work was influenced musically by John Blow's *Venus and Adonis* (c. 1682), a three-act semi-opera with masque and dance insertions on a similar theme of requited love. However, *Dido* is far more tragic and its music more profound. A synopsis of the action is as follows:

Act I:

> Dido, the Queen of Carthage, has fallen in love with Aeneas, a Trojan prince and her companion Belinda encourages her. Aeneas enters and confirms his love for her. They go off to the hunt together.

Act II:

> A Sorceress invokes her witches and plans with them to cause the destruction of Dido and Carthage by sending an elf disguised as Mercury to tell Aeneas he must leave at once. They conjure up a storm and the disguised elf (usually sung by the Sorceress) appears to Aeneas who agrees to leave Carthage that night.

Act III:

> The sailors are about their business preparing to leave and the Sorceress and witches enter to gloat at their success planning to shipwreck Aeneas and plotting that 'Elissa' (Dido) will die that night and Carthage be in flames the next day. Dido's feelings are not comforted by Belinda and she explodes with anger believing Aeneas has betrayed her. He recants but she sends him away and embraces death.

The Sorceress and the witches (Tate actually called them "enchantresses" in the 1689 version) would appear to continue the tradition created by Davenant's 1663-4 version of *Macbeth*. Also the musicologist Edward Dent has maintained that Restoration audiences could not conceive of an opera without witches (Dent, 1965). The connections between *Macbeth*'s witches and Tate's are obvious. The language used is similar, for instance "weyward sisters" describes both groups and neither receives any degree of characterisation. However, their roles are very different. *Macbeth*'s three witches prophesy events whereas Tate's Sorceress and numerous witches take an active part in promoting the disasters; notably the Sorceress's appearance in the guise of Mercury to Aeneas demanding his departure.

(Another source of witches can be found in Shadwell's *The Lancashire Witches* (1681) (Shadwell, cited in, Budd, 1989) in which Mother Demdike provides a model for the Sorceress in her unmitigated plans for evil and similar machine effects are likewise required for the witches to fly away. It has even been suggested that the witches might represent the Catholic clergy - a source of worry to Protestant England at the time of James II (Plank, August 1990).)

The music can be categorised as follows:

- Sorceress' vocal music

- First and Second Witches' duets
- Witches' choruses
- Witches' instrumental prelude and dance music
- Furies' dance music

The Sorceress' music plays a powerful role in the opera and can be thought of as an evil parallel to Dido, even her vocal range is the same. For a different interpretation of the Sorceress' range one might read I. Cholij and C. A. Price 'Purcell's Bass   Sorceress', (*Musical Times, cxxvii* (1986) 615-18). The musicologist Wilfred Mellers draws further attention to the importance of her role:

> "The Sorceress was Nahum Tate's invention, and is a fundamentally serious creation. Her music - in the sub-dominant minor, the traditional key for *chants lugubres* – contains excruciating suspended minor seconds, angular leaps and chromaticisms; yet it is spacious and noble, in the same style as the opening of the overture, and is directly comparable with Dido's arioso in both intensity and span. On no account should the Sorceress be treated grotesquely. She must have a Circe-like grandeur, because the destructive force is a reality, like love."

> (Mellers, 1965, cited in Price, p.209)

Her opening summons of the witches, after the prelude, prepares the listener for the dark deeds to come. The sustained vocal line consists of a combination of eerie semitones, awkward leaps and arpeggio movement as she summons up her witches. She is the only character to sing recitative against a string accompaniment in the opera. The Sorceress' slow and sinister instructions, often using a repeated-note recitative style, act as a stark contrast to the lively witches' choruses. Her menacing melodic line of semitones and leaps is maintained in her announcement to Aeneas that he must leave Carthage. Her mood and music are different for her final scene since the plot has worked and Purcell chooses, in contrast to surrounding items, a bright sounding key for the glee with which she plans to shipwreck Aeneas, expects Dido to die, and Carthage burn down. This is the Sorceress' moment of success and she celebrates with music of aria-like proportions.

The First and Second Witches initially have brief interjections that revolve around what the Sorceress is singing, but they have their own duet in "But ere we this perform", which is given a canon-like treatment. Their music is lively and jolly as they conjure up a storm to send the hunting party "back to court". Their final scene contains another canon with the somewhat dubious line "Our plot has took", answered by "The Queen's forsook" before breaking into a canonic "ho, ho, ho" refrain. The witches are not given personalities within the plot but act as contrasting characters to the impressive Sorceress. Their hag-like qualities were almost certainly stressed by outrageous attire and make-up and one can speculate that the tone of voice used to sing their duets was suitably nasal and unpleasant.

The witches are given five choruses in *Dido* in addition to the Tilmouth quartet suggested between Act I and II. They are always chordal except for outbursts of "ho, ho, ho" that use contrapuntal techniques reminiscent of the "fa-la" refrains found in the earlier works of the English composer Thomas Morley. The first chorus "Harm's our delight" is a lively dance-like song in the major key, but with the unusual procedure of using a five-bar phrase to provide an unbalanced feel to music that traditionally fits into four-bar phrases. Sir Jack Westrup, the eminent musicologist, felt these choruses were flawed "and the choruses are jolly rather than frightening". The witches may sing "Harm's our delight and mischief all our skill" but they might just as well be a crowd of rustic merrymakers for all the music does to help illusion (Westrup, 1980, cited in Price, p.197). I believe that Westrup is wrong to condemn Purcell since I think it extremely likely that he wanted the witches to sound grotesque as a contrast to the Sorceress and to provide some humour in an otherwise desolate situation. Their final chorus "Destruction's our delight" introduces the fore-mentioned "ho, ho, ho" refrains that were also used between the Sorceress' previous recitatives. The witches' echo-chorus "In our deep vaulted cell" provides a stark contrast to the other choruses since it is slower and chorale-like. Musically it acts as an impressive contrast between the previous witches' duet and the following 'Dance of the Furies'.

The prelude to the entry of the Sorceress and witches succeeds in changing the mood from the 'Triumphing Dance' at the end of Act I to a dark 'Cave Scene' at the start of Act II. 'The Witches' Dance' in Act III contains a number of noteworthy features. It has a stage direction "Jack o' Lantern leads the Spaniards out of their way among the Inchantresses" [witches]. In the 1700 edition the dance is referred to as "A Dance of Wizards and Witches", therefore one cannot be sure exactly what was intended. The Spaniards might be taking the same parts as the sailors in which case the witches could be equated with the "nymphs on the shore". However, the nature of the music is not appropriate for this since although marked 'pomposo', the first section contains quite extreme rhythmic irregularities followed by a lively lilting section and a sudden change of time and key for the somewhat chaotic final part. It is likely that the dance was inserted to allow Priest, who was the dancing master at the Dorset Garden theatre, to indulge himself with an exotically choreographed scene.

'The Echo Dance of the Furies' contains echo sections for each main phrase. The music is fast and rhythmically disjointed and allows for grotesque movements from the dancers. This section is concluded with the stage direction "Thunder and lightning, horrid music. The Furies sink down in the cave, the rest fly up." This undoubtedly implies the use of stage machines to allow the witches to fly away and the Furies to be sucked into the ground. Furthermore, sound effects possibly improvised by the orchestra could have been used to suggest the "horrid music".

Purcell has provided the listener with different types of music to accompany his Sorceress, witches and other supernatural characters. The Sorceress' music is imposing, dramatic and controlled. She is not a hag-like character but more of an enchantress with similar characteristics to the Circe of Greek mythology or Morgan La Fay from Celtic traditions. The witches mainly sing or are accompanied by discordant and rhythmically angular melodies that Purcell probably intended to be humorous. They lack the control and grandeur of the Sorceress and are not meant to inspire fear. The exception is their chorus "In our deep vaulted cell" that is open to a humorous rendition and could be interpreted as a parody on Catholic ritual. The music, together with the rest of the opera, takes the listener beyond the banalities of the English masque through Purcell's use of contrasting melody, harmony and rhythm to achieve a tragic masterpiece.

Purcell wrote two other semi-operas that presented witchcraft/ pagan-type activity, namely *King Arthur* and *The Indian Queen*. The former was produced in 1691 at the Queen's Theatre, Dorset Gardens, London, with a libretto by Dryden. Its dances were arranged by Josias Priest, but the story has been described as "a fantastic jumble" (Fortune, sleeve notes to *King Arthur*, Decca Record Company). However, the opening scene consists of "Majestic Heathen Worship" (to Woden, Thor and Freya) and sacred spirits are conjured. "Magic horrors" are said to surround the Saxon fort and Merlin's spells are sought to provide assistance. Other mythological characters that are used in witchcraft rituals (Pan and Venus) are also included in the action and sirens are sent to tempt Arthur into indiscretion: "Come Bath with us an Hour or two, Come naked in, for we are so; What Danger in a Naked foe" (Act IV, Scene ii). As to the music, it is melodic and typically uses echo effects with expertise. The 'Frost scene' is a stunning example of Purcell's capability to express a scene of unusual aspect with consummate skill but overall the work lacks the tragic dimensions of *Dido*. It is stirring and patriotic and only hints at paganism via its mythological sentiments. This is similarly true of *The Indian Queen*, produced in 1695 at Drury Lane with a libretto by Dryden and Sir Robert Howard. There is an invocation in Act III by Ismeron, a conjuror, to the God of Dreams that is reminiscent of witches' spells: "By the croaking of the toad, In their caves that make abode...", but apart from the appearance of some 'aerial spirits' and a 'High Priest' it does not add to the witchcraft music repertoire. In *Dido and Aeneas*, he undoubtedly added personifications that had a major influence on later composers. He did not provide his witches and the Sorceress with attributes of pathos or sensuality but he certainly succeeded in making the latter a powerful figure and one to be feared. The witches are grotesque creatures combining hag-like stereotypical characteristics with the element of parody and humour. In these respects Purcell continues the prevailing images of witches as women who are social outcasts to be both feared and mocked for their beliefs and practices. The social status of witches as outcasts had a double historical significance. On the one hand Western European tradition identified witches as generally female, elderly and poor, people on the economic and social margins of society. On the other, their power of dealing with spirits placed them on a different borderline, between human and the demonic. The Sorceress is portrayed in a way that contributes to an ongoing tradition of a strong quasi-mythological figure, a tradition that continues in subsequent centuries.

The lowly witches found in Purcell's works are not represented in the European examples. These tend to use well-known characters from mythology such as Medea and Circe. Medea, the sorceress in Greek legend who helped Jason to steal the Golden Fleece and then murdered her brother, children and Jason's new wife, was the main character in a number of operas from the period. These included works by F. Cavalli and M. Charpentier. Cavalli's *Giasone* of 1649 is a strange mixture of comedy and serious elements and departs from Euripides' play by providing a happy ending for all the main characters. Apart from this, the work is not outstanding in its portrayal of Medea as a fully developed character. Charpentier's *Médée* (1693) was a grander example that hinted at Lully's later compositions. Lully did not use the story of Medea in his operas but he composed the opera *Armida* (1686) based on the Saracen sorceress that appears in Tasso's *Gerusalemme liberata* of 1581.

The emphasis on stage spectacle within seventeenth century opera did not provide composers with any encouragement to explore detailed personalities. *Dido* came the closest to this, but in the eighteenth century with composers such as Handel and Mozart this situation started to change. In the first half of the eighteenth century, stage spectacle was still of prime importance. Much of the music to J. Galliard's operas has been lost but with the title of 'pantomime' being attached to such works as *Necromancer. Harlequin Dr Faustus* (1723) and *Merlin or the Devil of Stonehenge* (1734) it is not difficult to speculate that there was little genuine attempt to portray any witches' or wizards' deepest emotions and that they were presented as superficial comic characters. His one opera with a sorceress as the main character *Circe* (1719) has been lost apart from three songs. Antonio Vivaldi's *Orlando furioso*, first performed in Venice in 1727, tells the story of the enchantress Alcina with a libretto by Braciolli after the Ariosto epic of Roland against the Moors. It is a complicated plot with magical transformations, monsters, Hecate's temple and underground cavern scenes. The character of Alcina is not expanded on though one begins to see the signs of how future composers would portray the enchantresses with a variety of human emotions, including vengeance at being rejected in love. This coalition of the essentially human with the evil, powerful mythological character continues to develop from this time. The part of Alcina was sung by a mezzo-soprano voice but since women were banned from performing on stage in eighteenth-century Rome, males would have been used for all the parts there.

The famous German composer Handel spent a considerable amount of his life working in London and wrote around fifty operas. He had large venues in which to continue the tradition of stage spectacle and dancers were available to further enhance the overall experience. He wrote five operas that contain characters possessing magical characteristics normally associated with sorcerers and sorceresses, witches and wizards, etc.

- *Rinaldo*
- *Teseo*
- *Amadigi*
- *Orlando*
- *Alcina*

Handel used his finest music for the sorceresses who failed to win over a lover despite the use of spells and supernatural powers. In *Rinaldo* (1711) the sorceress Armida sets out to bewitch the hero Rinaldo. She sings an aria 'furioso' when he does not succumb to her charms and she is finally defeated by his magic wand. Despite the paraphernalia that surround her, including a chariot for a descent into hell and a magic castle guarded by monsters and furies, her character comes to life in a way that previous portrayals had not achieved through the use of contrasting music.

In *Teseo* (1713) Handel contrasts the sorceress Medea with her virtuous rival Agilea. Medea's music is similarly disparate, moving from tender moments of love ('Dolce ripioso') to venomous invocations of the furies. He is not so successful with the opera *Amadigi* (1715) where the sorceress Melissa kills herself when her lover deserts her. The music is monotonous and uninspired, showing little characterisation of the main performers. The quality is restored in *Orlando* (1733) where the librettist Braccioli introduces a magician Zoroastro who does not appear in the original Ariosto story. The character is an obvious forerunner of Mozart's Sarastro in *The Magic Flute* with an operatic bass voice required for the part. He reads the stars, causes fountains to spring up, flies a chariot, commands genii and invokes Jupiter. Magic is an essential part of the opera and even the opening overture contains a dance (gigue) for spirits.

Handel's final 'magic' opera *Alcina* (1735) is similar to *Orlando* and contains many special effects as well as extensive use of the chorus and ballet. His Alcina is similar to Circe, transforming suitors into animals, vegetables and minerals. She has six arias - two in each act - where she displays a range of feelings. When wooing Ruggiero, she is voluptuous but when rejected she turns to sorcery for her vengeful fury. There is a conflict between her grief, love, injured pride and fury. In Act II she stands before a statue of Circe and sings in dramatic recitative an invocation to the spirits of hell to prevent Ruggiero's escape. She is not answered and between her divided emotions of love and revenge the latter prevails. She is finally destroyed by Ruggiero and her magic island disappears. Alcina's music displays for the first time in opera a sorceress who is a fully formed character: "She has the stature of a queen, the passion of a woman in love, the evil glitter of a sorceress, and the pathos of pride brought low" (Dean, p.47). Although she is essentially portrayed as an evil character, the audience is led towards a degree of sympathy because of an ability to relate to her human dilemmas.

It is not generally well known that Haydn wrote approximately twenty operas, some of which have not survived whilst the remainder have been mainly neglected. However, his opera *Armida* (1784) is still played occasionally and he provides the sorceress with a wide range of emotions including seething anger and love-lorn affection. His other works do not contain references to either witchcraft or sorcery and his operas are generally thought to be surpassed by the works of Mozart. In 1768 Mozart wrote *Bastien und Bastienne* K. 46b, a one-act singspiel to a text by F. W. Weiskern after H. de Guerville and C. S. Favart. He scored the work for three voices (soprano, tenor and bass) with a chamber orchestra. The reason for its inclusion here is the character Colas who is a magician, fortune-teller and cunning man. His activities and music are mainly far-removed from those of Purcell's witches or Handel's sorceress. Pastoral strains representing the bagpipes accompany him and it is only when he consults his magic book, in a dramatic 'andante maestoso' with oboes and fast string playing, that anything approaching the supernatural is suggested. Even here the text suggests that this is not to be taken seriously: "Diggi, daggi, schurri, murry, horum, harem, lirum, larum, randi, mandi, giri, gari, posito, besti, basti, Saron froh, fatto, matto, quid pro quo." The work was commissioned by Dr Anton Mesmer, the originator of 'animal magnetism', and it was first performed at his house in Vienna. It can be speculated that the young Mozart (he was twelve years old at the time and undoubtedly precocious) may have been making fun of Mesmer's sometimes outrageous activities in applying his magnetised passes in Colas' pseudo-magical invocation.

In turning to *The Magic Flute*, K. 620 one discovers that the mature Mozart is very capable of setting magic within ritual in a serious setting. There are no witches as such in the opera but the tale is full of magic and the Queen of the Night and Sarastro may be viewed as a sorceress and sorcerer respectively. The librettist E. Schikaneder favoured magical tales and had used a similar story before (*Der Stein der Weisen* with music by B. Schack). The Queen of the Night is the sorceress of the work and her music displays grandeur, pathos and revenge. W. Mann describes the voice needed to sing the difficult role as "...a vulture with the throat of a nightingale' (Mann, 1977, p.611). It has been argued (ibid.) that she represents the 'White Goddess' of Robert Graves in an inspiring and destructive way. Although the High Priest/Magician Sarastro has music that is grand and harmonious, the Queen of the Night's aria 'Der Hölle Rache' provides a fierce and florid outburst for only the most accomplished singer. Here she alternates "pathos with spitting venom" that further develops her "unwavering megalomaniac personality" (Branscombe, pp.127 and 199).

The Magic Flute is usually equated with the Masonic movement since it is immersed in such symbolism. However, a case might be made for the Queen of the Night and her attendant 'Three Veiled Ladies' as representing a more pagan outlook in its imagery. The use of three ladies bears comparison with the 'Three Norns' in *Götterdämmerung* and the three witches in *Macbeth*. Mozart's work differs from previous composers in so far as it emphasises a male dimension through the choice of the character of the cunning man and the inclusion of the High Priest. The male role is no longer simply that of a lover who provokes the female to sorcery, playing instead an active part in magical practices.

Cherubini wrote the three-act opera *Médée* at the end of the century (1797) using a libretto by F. Hoffmann and it displays many of the characteristics that were to arise in the following century's operas. A dramatic overture begins the work and tremolando string playing in the minor key announces Medea's arrival. This string device is used again as she curses the woman that Jason now loves. Her mood changes as she tries to win Jason back to her with gentle major key music for her prayers and loving side. He rejects her and the trembling strings and minor key returns as she curses their forthcoming wedding. Medea's emotions change again as she fears that her children will be brought up to hate her and she melodiously begs the King to be allowed to stay for a day with them. She then plots to kill Jason's new wife with a poisoned robe and diadem. An introduction of minor chords, harsh chromaticism, moments of silence, and the use of bass instruments enhances the atmosphere rising to a hellish fortissimo as she summons the dark forces. Her mood changes again as her children arrive. She finds that she cannot kill them as planned but her hatred for Jason arises within her again and she slaughters them and burns down the temple at the opera's tragic conclusion. The character of Medea as the jilted sorceress has developed further in that the range of emotions and relationships portrayed are far more complex. The conflict in her character and the audience's response to it is finally resolved in her final act. The operatic conventions were now prepared for the dramatic characterisations that would be demanded in the following centuries. It was no longer sufficient to litter the stage with spectacular devices, produce several dances whether they were relevant to the action or not and rely purely on the vocal ability of a few static singers. From henceforth both the music and the drama would be equally important.

The Romantic Movement's spirit had a direct influence on cultural taste in the nineteenth century and it was specifically relevant to perceptions of witchcraft and the supernatural within operas of the period. It can be generally accepted that in literature from the late eighteenth century the characteristics that were later identified as being 'romantic' were expounded. These included an opposition to the rational, the arousal of strong emotions and the strength of the creative imagination. Later in the nineteenth century music received poetic titles and the world of legend and folklore were increasingly popular. One finds the largest number of references to witchcraft and pagan ideals in this section. The century witnessed a resurgence of interest in the supernatural possibly partly caused, ironically enough, by the advances in science that were industrialising rural areas and providing logical answers to problems that had previously only been encountered in superstition and the supernatural - traditional witchcraft realms. It might therefore be said that the Romantic Movement was a reaction against eighteenth century rationalism, thereby exalting the emotional and fantastic. It brought with it nostalgia for a more natural past, again albeit arguably an aspect of witchcraft. For instance, medical science was treating diseases that had formerly been attended to by the village witch or cunning person and psychological afflictions were no longer thought to be the work of the devil but malfunctions in the brain (Foucault, 1993). The power of the churches was further eroded, and the tendency of the educated to blame them for the former trials of witches, and to regard the latter as exemplars of ignorance and bigotry, was proportionately increased. Revolutionary sentiments were interpreted by composers such as Verdi who was directly involved and whose very name was used as a rallying cry. Communications and education had improved, leading to more people in more countries being aware of each other's cultures, and an increased spreading of wealth allowed for more sponsorship of the expensive business of staging an opera.

The great Italian tradition of 'bel canto' reached some of its heights in this century with works by Bellini, Donizetti, Rossini, Puccini and Verdi. Bellini's opera *Norma* (1831) does not contain any parts for witches or sorcerers but the druid high priestess (Norma) is the leading character in the plot and has a particularly moving invocation to the moon goddess in 'Casta diva'. The setting for the action is pagan in so far as it involves druids, but Norma is not personified as an evil woman, as witches previously were, since her actions are governed by the love she feels for the enemy Roman pro-consul. The opera's conclusion sees Norma and her lover dying at the stake. Boito's Mefistofele (1868) represents the Faust legend. The story of the scholar who sells his soul in exchange for power first appeared in the *Spiess Urfaustbuch* in 1587 and it was translated into English in 1592. Goethe finished his first part in 1801 and it is this part that has been put to music the most frequently. It contains two scenes involving witches. The first is referred to as 'The Witch's Kitchen' and it is not usually included in the musical settings despite providing opportunity for dramatic or even humorous interpretation: On a low hearth a large cauldron hangs over the fire. In the fumes that rise up from it are seen several strange figures. "A female monkey is sitting beside the cauldron…" (Goethe, translated Wayne1967, p.110). Mefistofele converses with the animals and the witch curses them before she realises his identity. She casts a circle and prepares a potion that Faust drinks. It is evidently an aphrodisiac since Mefisofele comments: "A dose like that within your guts, my boy, and every other wench is Helen of Troy" (ibid. p.120). The most commonly used part of the story for a musical rendition is the 'Walpurgis Night' gathering: "The Festival of Witches and Spirits upon the Brocken, or Harz-Mountain" (ibid. p.167). Faust and Mefistofele

---

Dr. Melvyn J. Willin

travel by broomstick into the abyss where there is dancing, music and a chorus of witches and warlocks. The 'Lyrical Intermezzo' that follows contains further references to music and dancing, but is from the fairy realm of Oberon, Titania and Ariel. Boito omits the 'Witch's Kitchen' scene but he provides dramatic music for the witches' sabbath and Walpurgis orgy. In some ways this "whirling" music is reminiscent of Mussorgsky's *Night on a bare mountain* where one has returned to the early modern characterisations of witches being hags indulging in satanic practices. Verdi conveyed more elements of witchcraft in his works than any other nineteenth century Italian composers but in some of his works the link is tenuous. For instance, *Atilla* (1846) only contains a hint of paganism in the druids scene in Act II Scene ii, where they mutter darkly of the portents and the priestesses dance and sing. In *Falstaff* (1893) a spoof of witchcraft is presented as Falstaff has a trick played on him whilst waiting for an assignation at the haunted Herne's Oak in Windsor Forest. However, in three other operas, namely *Il Trovatore* (1853), *Un Ballo in Maschera* (1859), and *Macbeth* (1847), witchcraft and sorcery are prominent features.

Il Trovatore concerns the story of a woman who was burned at the stake for witchcraft many years before the early fifteenth century setting for the opera. Her daughter (Azucena) sought a terrible revenge by attempting to throw the heir to the throne into the fire but mistakenly threw her own child into it. She has therefore brought up the heir as if he was her own son. She is accused of spying and once recognised is condemned to the same death as her mother. At the end of the opera the mistaken identities lead to the execution of the heir by his own brother and Azucena's own death. She is at the centre of the action and expresses two opposing passions namely filial love and vengeance. Her 'Strida la vampa' is a fiery invocation of her enemies' destruction using the minor key with strong accents and attack. In *Un Ballo in Maschera,* the fortune-teller Ulrica plays a dark and austere role that balances the other personalities' lightness. From her dwelling, in Act I, Scene i, she is accompanied by low woodwind instruments playing discordant tritones, an increasingly popular harmonic device to indicate evil. She sings the invocation 'Re dell'abisso' and later in 'Della città all'occaso' she tells of a plant that grows in the gallows-field that heals tormented love. In *Macbeth,* Verdi treated the witches with the utmost importance. He specified that there should be three 'covens' of six witches in each and they were particularly prominent in Act III. He

186

wrote to his colleague Escudier: "The witches dominate the drama; everything stems from them – rude and gossipy in Act I, exalted in Act III. They make up a real character, and one of the greatest importance" (Higgins quoting a letter Verdi wrote to Escudier, 1976). Verdi was so determined that their role should be understood that he invited the librettist Maffei to set their text in Act III since he was dissatisfied with Piave's text. The first performance was in Florence in 1847 but it was re-adjusted for Paris in 1865. The first act's music is dramatic using minor keys with the woodwind dark and shrill and the strings fleeting and syncopated. Tritones are used for the prophecies and brass and percussion provide stabbing punctuation. A lively circle dance in the major key contrasts with the 'all hails' that are chorale-like. Act III has a stormy introduction and reintroduces the witches' chorus from the prelude. A lively melody depicts the supernatural with a following three movement bizarre ballet as they dance around the cauldron. The minor key is used with heavy interjections from the brass. Contrast is provided by a flowing melodic tune from the cello with string accompaniment but this is interrupted suddenly by trombones, bass strings and percussion. Hecate is summoned in a richly chromatic movement and a sinister wild waltz follows in the major key. There is no doubt that, from his musical representation of the witches, Verdi has returned to the Purcellian interpretation of evil hags, but using nineteenth century musical forces.

Puccini's two act opera *Le Villi* (1884) also contains a scene entitled 'The Witches' Sabbath'. Somewhat frustratingly the Narrator describes the legend of the Villi unaccompanied by music, but a following instrumental dance contains the musical elements one often encounters in representations of the witches' sabbath in the nineteenth century, namely fast frantic music with brass interjections evoking images of the demonic. The story has similarities with Wagner's *Tannhäuser* in so far as the hero is beguiled into joining a bewitching orgy, thereby leaving his beloved with tragic consequences. Although Puccini provides furious dance music for the Villi he fails at the end of the opera to convey the menacing sounds that one might expect as the Villi close in on the lovers. The music is admittedly fast and fiery but the tonal feel and grand operatic conclusion with full orchestra distracts from either the tragedy or the diabolical aspects of the work.

Apart from the differences of language, there have always been differences between French opera and other countries' works. This has often centred on the French love of rhythmic piquancy, dance and ballet with less emphasis on the pure beauty of singing as can be found in Italian works. The composer Meyerbeer was born in Germany but since he spent a great amount of time in Paris he is usually included in the 'French' sections of books studying nineteenth century operas. His *Robert le Diable* (1831) does not contain scenes or characters pertaining to witchcraft as such, but in Act III an orgy of evil spirits takes place in a cavern that is certainly reminiscent of the alleged witches' sabbath. Furthermore, the main character Robert is said to be the son of the devil though conceived by a mortal woman. Offenbach's *The Tales of Hoffmann* (1881) similarly does not provide witches' scenes but a leading character Dapertutto is described as a sorcerer who uses a magic mirror for supernatural power. It is with the composer Gounod that one returns to scenes of witchcraft in his five-act opera *Faust* (1859). Although the 'Witch's Kitchen' scene is omitted, the final act contains an elaborate ballet for the Walpurgis revels.

Probably the most widely known composer of nineteenth century Russia is Tchaikovsky and of the few operas he wrote, one bears the title *Charodeyka* (*The Sorceress*) (1887). However, it cannot be included in any discussion of operas here because the title is misleading. The story concerns an innkeeper's daughter who is courted by a father and son and she's just an alluring woman, lacking any associations with magical practices. Rimsky-Korsakov composed a three-act opera after Gogol's *Maiskaya Noch* (*A May Night*) (1880) that contains allusions to stories of witches and the appearance of water sprites. The mayor's sister-in-law is almost burned as a witch but the witchcraft connections within the work are weak. This is similarly true of *The Golden Cockerel*, completed in 1909. The main character is an astrologer who displays various magical powers but without a direct link to witchcraft per se. The association with it is more apparent in Glinka's *Russlan and Ludmilla* (1842) since an evil sorceress Naina (sometimes referred to as an 'evil fairy') is feared for her powers and lives in an enchanted palace where sirens seek to entice men. She is opposed by the good magic of the wizard (or 'good fairy') Finn. Since the Orthodox Christian world had no history of large-scale witch trials, images of witches were much more bound up with peasant beliefs than scholarly constructions of a demonic religion. Accordingly, folklore elements are combined with ideas of sorcery that give Eastern European opera different characteristics to Western European specimens.

The nineteenth century German operatic tradition was centred on three composers, Humperdinck, Weber and Wagner. The continuation of a nationalistic German style of opera based on folklore, using the German language and giving prominence to the dramatic aspects of the plot, can be found in the operas of Weber and most notably *Der Freischütz* (1821). Strictly speaking the work should not be included in these discussions since there are no witches in the libretto by F. Kind. However, the plot is so steeped in supernatural elements that are common to works containing witches that its omission would be unforgivable. The 'Wolf Glen' scene in Act II presents Kaspar, who is in league with the devil (Samiel), and Max who has been tempted by Kaspar to procure magic bullets from him. These bullets will allow Max to hit the target at a shooting competition that he has to win to be allowed to marry his beloved Agathe. What he doesn't know is that the final bullet is intended to kill her and claim his soul for the devil in exchange for a further period of life for Kaspar. This exchange of a soul for special powers has obvious Faustian overtones to it. The spell casting takes place in the haunted Wolf's Glen as the moon eclipses. Kaspar places the ingredients for the spell into the cauldron - the glass from a broken church window (easily found, he comments!), quicksilver, three bullets, the right eye of a hoopoe, the left of a lynx. After each invocation a stage event occurs including thunder, lightning, hail, meteors, flames and the dreaded Wild Hunt. Weber wrote about the music he wished for this scene:

> "...it had to be dark, sombre tone colour; thus, the lowest regions of the violins, violas and basses, then, in particular, the lowest notes of the clarinets, which seemed to me especially suitable for depicting the sinister element, furthermore the plaintive tones of the bassoon, the lowest notes of the horns, muffled rolls of the kettle drums or single strokes of the same...the sinister element predominates by far..."

(Conversation between Weber and J. C. Lobe: *Gespräche mit Weber*, in *Fliegende Blätter für Musik*, 1853, Warrack, July 1982.)

Weber's other operas *Oberon* and *Euryanthe* also introduced supernatural elements but neither contained witchcraft scenes. The two operas of Humperdinck *Hänsel und Gretel* (1893) and *Königskinder*

(1894-6) must be considered since a witch plays a very prominent role in both, especially the former. *Hänsel und Gretel* was set to a libretto by Humperdinck's sister A. Wette, after the story in the Grimm brothers' *Kinder – und Hausmärchen* (1812-14). The huge influence of the Grimms' fairy tales on Western readers was to give a continued wide currency to the image of the witch as an evil, child-killing old woman in the modern creative imagination. After domestic unrest two children are sent into the woods for berries where they get lost and fall asleep. After waking up they are drawn to a gingerbread house where they are trapped by an evil witch who wishes to eat them. They trick the witch into entering her own oven and she is duly baked in the form of a gingerbread cake. The Witch's presence is felt in each act. The children's father describes her at the end of Act I. In Act II she rides around her house on a broomstick and in Act III she sings her main solo items. The mezzo-soprano voice is required to sing in a most "acrobatic" way with awkward and large leaps from a low register to a high soprano. The exaggerated character takes on a humorous quality because of its caricaturised qualities. In the 'Hocus pocus' aria she has sudden changes from the quiet, evil and sinister to the loud, violent and vicious. This is often accompanied with wild uncontrollable laughter and she is shown to be thoroughly evil throughout in a pantomime-like sense. *Königskinder* has a similarly unsympathetic witch as the force of evil. The witch's spell traps a goose girl and she is forced to bake a poisonous loaf of bread that eventually causes the death of her and the prince she falls in love with. The witch's part is again sung by a mezzo-soprano voice and often is required to use the new musical device of 'Sprechgesang' i.e. 'speech-song' or combining pitched notes with spoken dialogue. The work was originally billed as a melodrama of incidental music to the play by E. Bernstein-Porges (alias Li. E. Rosmer) but it was reworked as an opera from 1908-10. The witches that Humperdinck produced were very different characters from the sorceresses that Wagner incorporated into some of his music-dramas. They were successful as typical hag-like caricatures but with little or none of the personality development with which the latter excelled.

Wagner's music-dramas have been studied in considerable depth by eminent musicologists many of whom are cited in *The New Grove Dictionary of Music*. Four of these works contain links to the theme of paganism and witchcraft - both directly and indirectly. They are *Tannhäuser* (1845), *Lohengrin* (1850), *Götterdämmerung* (1874), and *Parsifal* (1882). The link with *Tannhäuser* can be surmised in the 'Venusberg' revels that have a 'Bacchic' or orgiastic aspect to them that has often been associated with witches' sabbaths. Wagner's instructions for the work included directions for wild dancing and uninhibited disporting. The location of the Venusberg is the Hörselberg, near Eisenach which, according to the Grimm brothers, is where witches make pilgrimages and is the haunt of devils. The music for the Venusberg scene changes according to the part of the landscape focussed upon. Feverish violas suggest the wild aspects but the music becomes seductive for the sirens and Venus' own attempts to keep Tannhäuser with her. When he insists on leaving, her music becomes agitated to display her anger. However, the work does not provide any characters that can be directly equated with witchcraft or sorcery. This is also true of *Götterdämmerung* that is mentioned here because of the opening scene with the three 'Norns'. They spin the web of destiny and have powers of divination similar to the witches in *Macbeth* and the 'Moirai' in Greek mythology. Unlike Shakespeare's witches they are not evil or scheming but majestic and wise. Their music is slow and subdued and uses leitmotifs (musical themes representing thoughts, characters, ideals or even physical objects that appear throughout complete works). In *Lohengrin,* one is introduced to Ortrud who worships pagan gods (she refers to herself as the daughter of Odin) and practices sorcery unlike the rest of the Christian cast. The motifs for her evil are power and, like Lady Macbeth in some ways, she schemes for her husband to gain a dukedom through murder and sorcery. Her role is a complete contrast to that of the heroine Elsa who is naïve, tender and loving, and Ortrud's music reflects this. It is unconventional and startling, using the cor anglais and bass clarinet in minor keys for effect. She has the power of second sight and uses it to trap Elsa into forcing her enemy Lohengrin to depart. In the prelude to Act II, a sinister syncopated cello melody uncoils like the psychological poison she is placing into Elsa's mind. When invoking Wotan and Freia she can become frenzied, as her desire for vengeance is unleashed. She is not a character to be pitied, unlike the sorceress Kundry, in *Parsifal*, who is one of Wagner's most impressive characters. *Parsifal* is a three-act music-drama with the libretto by the composer after Wolfram von Eschenbach's poem *Parzifal* from the early thirteenth century. Briefly the story tells of Amfortas who guards the spear that was said to have pierced Christ's side at the crucifixion. The magician Klingsor, embittered at having been rejected as a knight of the Grail, has created a garden of temptation to lure the knights into sin and deprivation. His servant is Kundry who has been cursed for laughing at Christ as he bore his cross to the crucifixion. She is under his domination and successfully seduces Amfortas, thus allowing Klingsor to steal the spear and wound him in the process. Klingsor is aware that only the "perfect fool" will defeat him and win back the spear, and he is therefore very suspicious when such a person arrives (Parsifal). He commands Kundry to seduce him after Parsifal has defeated his retainers and she almost succeeds, but Parsifal resists at the last moment. Klingsor hurls the spear at him but Parsifal catches it, thereby transferring its power to himself and destroying Klingsor. In the final act Parsifal returns after many years of travel. He reveals the Grail, heals Amfortas and baptises Kundry who is therefore forgiven and dies. Klingsor's role is essentially that of an evil magician but it can be argued that his malevolence is prompted by his rejection. This equates to the frequently portrayed motivation of the sorceress that lies in rejection by a loved one. Kundry is a leading player in the drama and possesses a very complex character. Despite the music drama's underlying themes of baptism and forgiveness, her attempts to seduce Parsifal and her being in league with Klingsor ensure her identity as a sorceress. The musicologist E. Newman quoted Wagne speaking of her "as the greatest of his female creations" (Newman, p.713) for her first entry in Act I, Scene i:

> "Her skirts are tucked up with a snake-skin girdle with long hanging cords, her black hair hangs loose and dishevelled, her complexion is deep ruddy brown with piercing black eyes which at times flash wildly, and yet often seem lifeless, staring blankly."

> (Lewsey, 1997, p.118)

In Act II, Scene ii, she is transformed into a beautiful woman to seduce Parsifal but when he finally pulls away she knows that she has met her nemesis as a sorceress and seductress. In the final act, she has become a penitent and her wildness has gone. She is a servant to Gurnemanz (an old retainer to the Grail knights) and she bathes Parsifal's feet and dries them with her hair in an obvious reference to the biblical Mary Magdalene and Jesus episode. Kundry's music reflects her varying emotions and feelings. For her opening entry, hurrying discords and stabbing accentuation intensifies her wild appearance. She is connected to Klingsor through Wagner's use of leitmotifs to highlight their attachment. In Act II the music is centred on Kundry and Parsifal and her link is with sorcery, the music being wild and demonic, distorting the Grail motif, but also combined with Parsifal's own motif. When Klingsor wishes to summon her, the brooding pianissimo music changes to a sudden fortissimo as she awakens. Her sensual music for the seduction scene has a magic motif woven into it that reminds the listener that evil is intended. She is possibly the most complex sorceress to be personified in operatic terms and musically the most stimulating - and the character differs in that although she meets a tragic end the possibility of salvation is introduced before her death.

It was not until the twentieth century that serious English opera was to produce examples that could rank with Handel's domination of the eighteenth century or Purcell's *Dido*. However, in light opera one composer produced very fine examples, namely Arthur Sullivan in conjunction with his librettist W. S. Gilbert. Two of these works have themes that are connected to witchcraft and sorcery albeit from a jocular aspect. The works in question are *The Sorcerer or The Elixir of Love* (1877) and *Ruddigore or The Witch's Curse* (1887). *The Sorcerer* was Sullivan's third comic opera and the plot, in typically Gilbertian terms, is centred upon the confusion caused by misunderstandings within affairs of the heart. The sorcerer of the title is a shop-owner, J. Wellington Wells, who is asked to prepare a potion that forces people to fall in love with the first person they see after half an hour. Chaos ensues and the only way that nullification of the philtre can be achieved is by either the sorcerer or the person ordering the philtre (Alexis) giving himself up to the evil demon Ahrimanes. The former is coerced into accepting this fate and the work ends in general rejoicing. The 'patter song' performed by J. Wellington Wells in Act I reveals a great deal about how middle class Victorian society viewed magic and witchcraft. To be caricatured demands an understanding of the matters concerned and either a disbelief in their efficacy or the use of humour as a distraction from a genuine fear. Act I, no.12 is reproduced below in an edited version:

"...I'm a dealer in magic and spells, in blessings and curses, in prophecies, witches, and knells. If you want a proud foe to 'make tracks'. If you'd melt a rich uncle in wax. You've but to look in on the resident Djinn, number seventy, Simmery Axe. We've a first rate assortment of magic; and for raising a posthumous shade...Love philtres, we've quantities of it! And for knowledge if anyone burns, we're keeping a very small prophet...for he can prophecy with a wink of his eye, peep with security into futurity, sum up your history, clear up a mystery, humour proclivity, for a nativity...he has answers oracular, bogies spectacular, tetrapods tragical, mirrors so magical, facts astronomical...He can raise you hosts of ghosts. And that, without reflectors; and creepy things with wings, and gaunt and grisly spectres...he can rack your brains with chains, and gibberings grim and ghastly...driving your foes to the verge of insanity...in demonology, lectrobiology [!], mystic nosology, spirit philology, high-class astrology..."

(From the score)

For the following invocation (Act I, no.13) similarly exaggerated language is used that reminds one of the witches' scene in *Macbeth*:

"Sprites of earth and air. Fiends of flame and fire! Demon-souls, come here in shoals, this fearful deed inspire! Appear! Appear! Appear!...Noisome hags of night! Imps of deadly shade! Pallid ghosts, arise in hosts, and lend me all your aid! Appear! Appear! Appear! Now, shrivelled hags, with poison bags discharge your loathsome loads! Spit flame and fire, unholy choir! Belch forth your venom toads! Ye demons fell, with yelp and yell, shed curses far afield! Ye fiends of night, your filthy blight in noisome plenty yield!"

(Ibid.)

The idea of treating sorcery as a spoof is further refined in *Ruddigore* where a witch's curse at being burned at the stake is passed on to all the baronets of Ruddigore who are forced to commit a crime every day to avoid death. The 'Haunted picture gallery' scene contains suitably 'spooky' music (tremolando strings, minor keys, sudden interjections etc.) and a mad, witch-like woman (Margaret). Love interests dominate the plot that ends happily with the lifting of the curse.

The inclusion of these works as the only nineteenth century examples of British opera to make any reference to witchcraft lends credence to how poor the state of opera was at the time compared to Italy, France and Germany. This could be similarly upheld with other operatic themes but it was to change in the twentieth century. The latter part of the twentieth century saw a decline in the number of operas being composed partly because of the huge costs involved to stage such productions and also since many composers reacted against the large orchestras of the nineteenth century by writing music for chamber groups. However, at the start of the century this was not the case and mainstream composers were still writing large-scale works for off and on the stage. The Danish composer Nielsen included a mezzo-soprano part for the 'Witch of Endor' in his opera *Saul and David* (1902). However, the caricatured witch has largely been replaced by a nature-based pagan ethos that is particularly apparent in, for instance, Tippett's *The Midsummer Marriage*. Exceptions to this have been when an image has been disseminated in popular literature for instance J. McCabe's *The Lion, the Witch and the Wardrobe* based on C. S. Lewis' popular book of the same name. In these modern politically correct times composers have avoided portraying women as evil hags and a far greater sympathy for witches and their kind has been portrayed. In the USA regret has been expressed concerning the Salem witch trials and an opera was composed on the subject – *A Witch of Salem* (1926) – by C. Cadman.

The Czech composer Dvorak wrote two operas at the start of the twentieth century, namely *Rusalka* (1901) and *Armida* (1904). The former consists of a folk tale about a water nymph (Rusalka) who wants to become human to enable her to be with a prince whom she has fallen in love with. The theme of love needing the help of sorcery is a recurring theme in many operas. She is tricked by an evil witch (Jezibaba) and the opera ends in tragedy. Jezibaba is often accompanied by tremolando strings and discordant interpolations. For the spell scene in her cottage the bass instruments are prominent with brass playing fortissimo. She does not appear in Act II but returns in Act III with awkward leaping music and discordant tritonal intervals in the minor key. Dvorak's last opera *Armida* tells the story of the enchantress of the opera's title and accordingly contains various scenes of magic and sorcery.

The Russian composer Prokofiev also wrote two operas containing witchcraft issues, namely *The love for three oranges* (1921) and *The Fiery Angel* (1927). The former has a curious plot that includes a witch (Fata Morgana), a magician (Tchelio), a devil (Farfarello) and a servant to Fata Morgana who also possesses supernatural powers (Smeraldina). It is set in the style of the *commedia dell'arte* with farcical events throughout, including the curse by Fata Morgana that the Prince will fall in love with three oranges - hence the opera's title. An orchestral suite is marked 'Scène infernale' and there is a scene of transformation where Smeraldina transforms the Princess Ninetta into a rat. The work is an entertaining spoof on relationships and supernatural powers. It is a complete contrast to Prokfiev's other opera mentioned that is a very serious work. *The Fiery Angel* is set in the 1520s in Cologne and tells the story of Renata who is obsessed by what she believes to be an angel called Mabiel who appeared to her and then left her at puberty. A mercenary soldier (Ruprecht) is besotted with her but she marries a count (Heinrich) initially believing him to be the angel. Ruprecht meets with Faust and the sorcerer Mephistopheles who show him an orgiastic scene of black magic, devils and wild exorcism in a convent. The Inquisition arrives there and Renata is executed as a follower of Satan. The work stemmed from Prokofiev's interest in the supernatural elements in Rimsky-Korsakov's operas and he based the libretto on a novel by V. Bryusov involving magic, alchemy and possession. Four of the five acts contain scenes using supernatural themes:

Act I: A fortune teller contacts the spirit world.
Act II: The casting of a magic circle, spirits/devils, and the sorcerer Agrippa.
Act IV: Introduction of Faust and Mephistopheles.
Act V   Possession and exorcism at the convent.

The music contains many contrasts in accordance with Renata's moods. There are gentle expressive moments as well as times of violent, frenzied activity with discordant sounds from the large orchestra employed. In this respect her character bears comparison with that of Medea. The overall effect is one of tragedy at the heroine's unstable state, false accusation and final execution.

The German tradition of opera continued in the twentieth century with Wagner's son Siegfried who wrote *Schwarzschwanenreich* in 1910. He was influenced by a visit to a Canton prison where female prisoners guilty of child murder or killing their husbands were held prior to their execution. He was further intrigued by the injustices of the German witch trials, that he had read about, and even included a reference to J. S. Bach's *O sacred head sore wounded* in the opera's prison scene. This might be thought to be making a link between the scapegoat aspects of Christ's and many witches' treatment. In *Schwarzschwanenreich* Linda has killed and buried her illegitimate child. She visits the grave of her child in the forest but is spied upon and arrested. Under torture she confesses her guilt and is burned at the stake. The music is dramatic but lacks the emotional strength and power that the composer's father possessed in its harmony and melodic development.

There are references to sorcery in Richard Strauss' opera *Die Frau ohne Schatten* (1919) where a nurse is a minion of Keikobad, a ruler of spirits, who invokes air spirits and conjures visions and also in *Die Aegyptische Helena* where a sorceress Aithra conjures up visions and mixes potions. The only other German work worth perhaps a brief mention is H. Henze's *König Hirsch* which includes a magician Cigolotti who transforms people into animals. However, it is a speaking part only and devoid of music.

There was an increase in the importance of British opera during the twentieth Century, mainly through the works of Benjamin Britten and Michael Tippett. In the early part of the century some works were popular but did not increase Britain's reputation as an opera-producing nation. R. Boughton's *The Immortal Hour* (1914) contained parts for druids and was acclaimed by Elgar as the work of a genius and Vaughan Williams' *The Poisoned Kiss* (1936) was a three-act extravaganza with forty-six numbers that satirised it. A bizarre work in one act by H. Birtwistle, *Punch and Judy*, contains a character, Pretty Polly, who is later represented as a witch, and Havergal Brian's opera *Faust* (1956) was unfinished and unpublished. In *Merrie England* (1902) by E. German, the character Jill-All-Alone is accused of witchcraft and her execution by burning is planned. But after an appearance by a forester impersonating Herne the Hunter, all the problems are resolved and the work ends happily. An altogether more serious situation is presented in Delius' *Koanga* (1904) which contains scenes of voodoo chanting, magic working, sacrifice and wild dancing. It is set in Mississippi in the latter half of the eighteenth century and borrows a prelude from his opera *The Magic Fountain*. In turning to the works of Britten there is a deep understanding of emotional evolution but a lack of witchcraft or pagan orientated material. Fortunately another major British composer of the century had a deep interest and insight into paganism and mysticism. Tippett's opera *The Midsummer Marriage* was the outcome of this study.

He wrote the three-act work between 1946 and 1952 and it bears a Greek motto and translation: "You shall say: I am a child of earth and of starry heaven" (from the Petelia Tablet in the British Museum, of the Orphic Tablets of the late fourth century B.C.E., cited in Kemp, 1984, p.215). He originally referred to it as a masque but it expanded as the work progressed. He found that particular rituals described by Frazer in *The Golden Bough* had "taken root in his imagination" (ibid. p.224) and he combined these with Greek mythological aspects (Harrison, 1912) into a ritual rite of passage. Another literary influence was *The White Goddess* by R. Graves and Shakespeare's *A Midsummer Night's Dream* provided its dream-like characteristics. Tippett took as his setting a hillside with a Greek temple, dancing with flutes, a 'He-Ancient' and later appearance of Strephon, all of which can be found in G. B. Shaw's *Back to Methuselah*. Musical influences included Mozart's *The Magic Flute* with its balance of theology and nature, and the natural and supernatural worlds in *Don Giovanni*. Although the influence of Wagner is not discernible in the opera, Tippett nevertheless praised Wagner's ability to "fill an empty stage with nature" (Elfyn Jones, 1985, p.59). He referred to his music as a "magic musical veil to clothe my strange libretto" (Tippett, 1959, p.49). Tippett wrote of the influence of Jungian archetypes within his soft rhapsodic man and harsh coloratura woman. (Whittall, 1982). In essence one observes a Midsummer's Day ritual in a magical pagan setting with a union of male, female and nature. The action moves between temporal and spiritual reality and therefore instigates a concept that has not been encountered in other operas using pagan or witchcraft themes. The plot takes place in a clearing in a wood with a sanctuary and Greek temple with spiral staircases leading up and down. A pair of lovers, Mark and Jenifer, and their friends meet there. 'Ancients' (priests and priestesses) and dancers emerge from the temple. Jenifer decides to ascend the staircase and Mark, hearing her father in the distance, descends the other. Her father, King Fisher, is a pompous business man and he presumes that the couple have eloped together and are hiding in the temple. Three ritual dances are performed that are significant in highlighting the polarity of the sexes in the opera and together with the fourth, in Act III, speak of birth, death and renewal in the natural world:

1. 'Earth in Autumn': a hound (girl) chases a hare (boy)
2. 'Waters in Winter': an otter (girl) chases a fish (boy)
3. 'Air in Spring': a bird with a broken wing (boy) is swooped down on by a hawk (girl)

In the final act, King Fisher attempts to 'out-magic' the Ancients with his clairvoyant Madame Sosostris. She speaks of the dream world and reveals beneath her veils an incandescent bud the petals of which open to reveal Mark and Jenifer. King Fisher is threatening but he is vanquished and a funeral march follows: "It is not only the funeral march of an archetypal villain but of a Priest-King, who must die that life can be re-born" (Kobbé, 1987,1 p.144). This is followed by the fourth ritual dance that is subtitled 'The voluntary human sacrifice':

4. 'Fire in Summer': a celebration of carnal love

Jenifer and Mark are drawn into the bud that closes around them and darkness falls. When the light returns it is to reveal the temple in an early morning mist and Jenifer and Mark are together. They proclaim that they have found "the truth" and the opera ends with the feeling that all the action could have been a dream or a playback from a different time plane. The music of *The Midsummer Marriage* is tonal and often in major keys. The diatonic and lyrical melodies emphasise the positive energies and his use of flutes, bells and the celeste, similarly to Mozart in *The Magic Flute*, suggest magical qualities and the world of the imagination. Muted horns, sustained violins and the gong add to the mystery, for instance, when Jenifer descends the staircase. The ritual dances are an integral part of the opera and their instrumentation and melodies portray the animals and their movements. It is generally agreed that *The Midsummer Marriage* is a masterpiece of British opera in evoking a magical pagan world that is worthy of serious scrutiny.

I have traced the changing themes of witchcraft through operas from the earliest examples in the seventeenth century up to the present time and shown that the theme has been seen to be a popular one with opera composers. Quite distinct types of witches have been portrayed in these works with varying degrees of characterisation. They have tended to be female since male witches have been referred to as wizards or astrologers, for instance the Astrologer in *The Golden Cockerel* (Rimsky-Korsakov). When appearing in groups they have tended towards Shakespeare's concept in *Macbeth* (Verdi and many others) appearing as old hags with divinatory powers. If one accepts the three Norns in Wagner's music-drama *Götterdämmerung* as possessing witch-like qualities, then they are exceptional in being wise and prophetic without evil undertones. Individual witches have sometimes been nameless and similarly conforming to the evil old woman, as can be seen in *Hänsel und Gretel* (Humperdinck). However, the addition of a name to a character has brought with it an identity that has been developed to varying degrees. These women have often been given greater powers and a greater role within an opera, even to the extent of playing the leading part as in the many examples of *Medea* and *Circe*. Medea has often been shown to have a conflicting nature torn between the love of Jason and her children, the hurt and then anger of rejection, and finally the revenge and use of supernatural powers. One can even feel considerable sympathy for witches such as Kundry in *Parsifal*, where she is forced to undertake evil tasks against her wishes, and Linda, in *Schwarzschwanenereich* where she is executed for what one might call the mercy-killing of her own child. Sorceresses are often given sexually alluring roles where they use their powers of seduction to try to achieve their intentions. These can be for evil purposes, in Kundry's case, or to win back a lover as Armida tried in several operas of the same name. Neither should one forget the humorous aspects of witchcraft and sorcery as displayed in Gilbert and Sullivan's works and, by implication in the exaggerated music, the broom-stick riding episodes in *Hänsel und Gretel*.

I now wish to explore works where the voice or voices are the dominant feature of the music. The examples are accompanied by a variety of instruments and varying sizes of orchestra but these are generally thought to be subservient to the voices. Genres will include cantatas for chorus and soloists as well as solo songs.

Using the Bible as a source of reference one can find numerous musical works (known as 'biblical dialogues') using the story of the 'Witch of Endor' (1 Samuel 28 vv. 8-20). During the seventeenth century the English composers Robert Ramsey, John Hilton, Nicholas Lanier, Benjamin Lamb and Henry Purcell produced 'dialogues' entitled *In guilty night* based on the biblical reference (Chan, 1980, pp.205-214). In these works the witch is not a comic character but more of a medium being consulted for her powers of divination. Purcell's setting is to be found in John Playford's second book of *Harmonia Sacra* (1693) that contains five 'devotional songs'. The story consists of Saul in disguise visiting a witch to learn of his fate in an ensuing battle against the Philistines. She is fearful to conjure up a spirit for him since he had previously ordered the death of all witches. She agrees but on being asked to contact Samuel from the dead she realises that it is Saul himself that has commanded her. Samuel duly arrives and tells Saul that he, his son and his army will all perish. Purcell's music for the witch is some of his most poignant and he combines a soaring melodic line with minor key harmony of breathtaking beauty. The chamber accompaniment of viols, lute and harpsichord further enhance the drama of the melodies. This is a total contrast to his treatment of the witches and the Sorceress in *Dido*. A somewhat different effect is achieved by Thomas Linley in his *Lyric Ode on the Fairies, Aerial Beings and Witches of Shakespeare* (1776). The ode is a supernatural evocation of Shakespeare and includes a bass soloist and chorus questioning the deeds of witches. Bass strings are used and the minor key to set the gloomy scene in a dark cave and there are sudden musical interjections by the wind instruments. The witches' music is unusual, in places being almost chorale-like and in the major key, but he nevertheless manages to hint at the orchestral devices that were to be used in the following century to accompany scenes of the supernatural, namely fast string passages, minor keys, discords, etc. The music suggests the dark, mysterious and unpredictable nature of witches

In the nineteenth century the musical and literary traditions that had applied to opera could also be recognised in vocal and choral music that was not for the stage. Examples were composed by some of the leading composers of the period. A strange scene is included in Berlioz' *L' Enfance du Christ* (1854) when the "soothsayers and prophets of Judaea" are commanded by Herod to explain his nightmare. They conjure up the spirits of earth, air, fire and water in a weird cabalistic rite written in 7/8 time and they dance frenziedly as they tell Herod he must kill all new born babies to avoid his downfall. Apart from the all-male chorus required for this scene and Jews being the participants it could easily be viewed as the conventional witches' coven conjuring up their demons. This suggests that it is the Jews, another group traditionally treated with suspicion by the established Church, who are indulging in occult practices. The other work by Berlioz that introduces indirect references to witches is *La Damnation de Faust* (1846). It is a 'dramatic legend' in four parts with words by A. Gandonniere and Berlioz after G. de Nervals' translation of Goethe's *Faust*. Strictly speaking there are not witches present but the 'Ride to the Abyss' and references to the legions of hell to begin their revels have all the hallmarks of the wild witches' sabbath. The music reflects this with crescendos and accelerandos from the stringed instruments punctuated with very deep trombone notes and other brass and percussion.

Mussorgsky wrote four versions of the *Night on a bare mountain* of which two have been lost, but a choral version *St John's night on the bare mountain* (1866-7) has survived. It uses the more famous orchestral music quite extensively and noticeably for the black mass scene of demons and witches centred on the arch-demon of Slavonic mythology, Chernobog. The vocal version is associated with N. Gogol's story *The Sorochintsy Fair* and tells of a youth who dreams of the revels of the witches' sabbath and its dispersal as the church bell sounds. The words are mainly sung by witches and demons and intentionally do not make sense to provide further alienation: "Sagana! Sagana! Pegemot! Astarot!…Aksafat! Sabatan! Tenemos! Tenemos! [a sacred space in Greek?!] Allegremos! etc."

The German composers Mendelssohn, Schumann and Brahms are represented in this section. Mendelssohn's *Die Erste Walpurgisnacht* (1832) was written for solo voices, choir and orchestra and taken from Goethe's *Faust*. Its plot is somewhat different to the popular Walpurgis night demonic activity. A druid group disguise themselves as demons to scare away Christians to enable them to hold a ceremony to praise their nature gods and the seasons. The music avoids the dissonance associated with the black sabbath and "articulates both Goethe's critical reservations about Christianity and medieval-ecclesiastical superstition and the poet's sympathies for a mythical pantheism of nature" (E. Kroher, Sleevenotes to *Die Erste Walpurgisnacht* (RCA Victor, 09026 625132, 1994). Schumann's *Scenes from Goethe's Faust*, scored for soloists, choir and orchestra, does not include the Walpurgis, but a section with 'Grey Women' who emerge at midnight to music in the minor key with fast string playing and ominous chromaticisms interjected is appropriate for the witches' scenes in all but name.

Both these works used large choral and orchestral forces in contrast to the final German work to be mentioned - a song for two sopranos and piano by Brahms - *Walpurgis Nacht* op.75 no. 4. It is a brief (less than two minutes) piece with a sustained melody over piano arpeggios in the minor key and is included here simply to provide an example of German song involved with the subject. Further songs were written by the British composer J. L. Hatton, *The Hag* for baritone and piano, and by the Irish composer C. V. Stanford *Witches' Charms* for tenor and piano. The first is a Victorian 'parlour song' that is melodramatic in the same way as some scenes in Sullivan's *Ruddigore* and the latter, using words by Ben Jonson, is a humorous caricature about charms being used.

There have been enormous changes in society, culture and music throughout the twentieth century. Various songs have been composed with a very harsh example by Busoni – *Hexenlied* (1925) for baritone and piano. It consists of a frantic repeated figure on the piano with a declamatory voice above with awkward leaps, jagged rhythms, sotto voce (whispering) passages and even Sprechgesang-like moments. The hag-like *Witch* by Armstrong Gibbs is similarly jagged and discordant but provides a humorous interpretation from the viewpoint of the witch's pets. The American composer Corigliano decided upon a more thoughtful interpretation for his *Song to the Witch of the Cloisters* (1967) for tenor and piano. It is based on a woman who used to roam about the Fort Tryon Park Gardens in Upper Manhattan who was thought to be unstable and insane rather than directly malevolent. The music is at times discordant and jagged but also contains sustained melodious music for mentions of the moonlight and the cloisters themselves. A curious work is Max von Schilling's *Das Hexenlied,* Melodram op. 15 (1902/3) for speaker and orchestra, following the tradition of G. Benda's melodramas. It is based on a ballad by E. von Wildenbruch and tells of the deathbed confession of a priest Medardus who admits that for his whole life he has regretted not eloping with and helping to escape a condemned witch whose confession he once took. The music and narration together paint a picture of great poignancy as one shares with the priest's guilt and bewails the witch's false imprisonment and eventual death. It is unusual for a witch to be represented in this way and the music highlights the anguish with minor keys, laments and a love song as Medardus rejoices at his death that he will soon be re-united with her.

One returns to the more typical representations of witches in Heward's *The Witches' Sabbath* (1919) consisting of a choir of SSATB and tenor solo but without accompaniment. The text is from Jonson's *The Masque of the Queens* (1609) and the music attempts to treat the theme seriously but is rather embroiled in the English choral tradition, thus maintaining a somewhat mild use of dissonance and 'cosiness' that is so characteristic of this style. Havergal Brian composed an altogether larger-scaled work, *The Hag* (1911), for double female choir and orchestra based on Herrick's *The Witch*. M. Nyman uses three voices (two female and one male) for his dramatic *This damned witch Sycorax* (1993) that is taken from the music to the film *Prospero's Books* which was in turn inspired by Shakespeare's *The Tempest*. It is harsh and discordant using a style known as the 'neo-baroque' using fragmentation and repeated notes. Sycorax is represented as an evil and dangerous woman who does not appear in the play but whose presence is felt. Arthur Bliss' *The Enchantress* (1951) for solo voice and orchestra is a lesser-known work about a jilted woman Simaetha who uses sorcery to charm her lover back. She prays to Circe and Medea, and Hecate arrives to grant her wishes. The music is dissonant and chromatic for her scenes of anger but languid as she laments their separation. Bliss' sorceress is different to any of the witches that have been characterised in other songs and cantatas since she displays numerous contrasting moods.

It can be seen once more that a variety of representations are used for witches in the twentieth century. The evil hags are still present, a sorceress still has charms to trap a lover with, humour is present in the stereotypical witches and lastly, and possibly most importantly, a genuine figure of pathos emerged in the von Schillings' work. This suggests that a broader definition of the concept of witchcraft was being evolved throughout the music composed about it. A variety of written sources have been used and a similar variety of musical forces have expressed them. The varying interpretations of witches, sorceresses and witchcraft have maintained their popularity with some of the most highly regarded composers of Western music.

The final section investigating references to witchcraft in instrumental music has obvious problems attached to it. For instance, titles such as 'Faust' or 'Macbeth' may or may not include the appropriate witches' scenes and unless the composer has written about the work or has included some sort of programme one is forced to speculate. As has been the practice in the previous sections, the works included only represent a selection of works either mentioning sections portraying witches or titles indicating them that are either generally available for further study or are felt to be worthy of mention for any number of possible reasons.

The instrumental works that have survived from the seventeenth century with clear references to witches are very few in number and the links are often tenuous. Anonymous dances, referred to as *Witches' Dances,* have appeared on disc but the source of the music is often unidentified (Delos DE 1003). A lute solo by Holborne called *The Fairy Round* consists of a galliard in a lively major key with no further details provided (SK 60767). In the eighteenth century Samuel Arnold wrote *Eight Entr'actes* (1778) to *Macbeth* as orchestral pieces based on Scottish folksongs but most of his works have not survived and his works' musical content has been described as "often abysmal" (Fiske, 1980, p.617). The other eighteenth century example is by the well-respected composer Haydn but its title is hardly appropriate. His *String Quartet in D minor, op. 76, no. 2, Hob. III: 76. 'The Fifths'* contains a minuet that is traditionally referred to as the *Hexenmenuett.* The quartet is referred to as the 'fifths' because of a descending motif of the first violin in fifths but one has to use considerable artistic license to explain why the minuet should receive its title of 'witch'. Possible clues might be the use of the minor key and relatively low pitches being used but it lacks dissonance, awkward leaps or angular rhythms that have been prevalent in other works. One can surmise that either a publisher wanted to attract a memorable title to sell further copies of the work or that Haydn himself, who was known for his joyful sense of humour, attached the title as a joke!

Purely instrumental music representing witchcraft was almost entirely absent from the seventeenth and eighteenth centuries. This might be explained by the domination of stage works and that orchestral music was only just starting to appear in the public domain. The nineteenth century was the time when the orchestra was expanded both in size and the types of music written for it. It was the symphonic age and new instruments were devised and new harmony was created for them. The spirit of revolution was not only found in political activities but also in musical performances. In particular, composers in France and Eastern Europe wrote orchestral music that highlighted witchcraft and sorcery.

One of the most famous works that introduces one to the world of the witches' sabbath is Berlioz' *Symphonie Fantastique* (1830), the fifth movement of which is the *Songe d'une nuit du Sabbat*. It was probably originally written for a *Faust* ballet but he finally produced his programme for the work encompassing an opium-inspired dream. This in itself was a bold move since composers did not provide pictorial indications to their musical material. His programme was originally simply going to consist of a night of revelry but Berlioz' infatuation and jealousy at the activities of his beloved Harriet Smithson caused him to turn her into a witch at the centre of a demonic orgy:

> "He sees himself at a Witches' Sabbath surrounded by a fearful crowd of spectres, sorcerers, and monsters of every kind, united for his burial. Unearthly sounds, groans, shrieks of laughter, distant cries, to which others seem to respond. The melody of his beloved is heard, but it has lost its character of nobility and reserve. Instead, it is now an ignoble dance tune, trivial and grotesque. It is She who comes to the Sabbath! A shout of joy greets her arrival. She joins the diabolical orgy. The funeral knell, burlesque of the Dies Irae. Dance of the Witches. The dance and the Dies Irae combined."

(Berlioz translated in Hopkins, 1984, p.116)

The opening has shimmering strings in eight parts and ominous bass instruments. The flapping of wings are suggested as if the witches are flying to the ceremony. The main motif of the whole symphony (referred to as the *idée fixe*) that suggests his beloved is distorted on a shrill clarinet and by orchestral interruptions of the phrasing. Mayhem breaks out in the orchestral music as the witch (referred to as a whore) arrives. A sudden hush allows the bass instruments to prepare the listener for bells and the Gregorian 'Dies irae' chant that is debased by bass brass instruments, woodwind and pizzicato strings. A wild fugal dance starts up with violent syncopation in the strings that use the wood of the bow and trills that are combined with the 'Dies irae' in the wind instruments. A massive final cadence completes the work. The music inspires associations of the orgiastic and demonic activities that were alleged in the mainly Continental illustrations of the sixteenth and seventeenth centuries.

This movement and Mussorgsky's *Night on a bare mountain* are the two works probably more than many others that have painted in people's minds the imagined pictures of the witches' sabbaths. However, for somewhat different interpretations of sorcery and the supernatural one might mention the French composer Dukas. He wrote *The Sorcerer's Apprentice* (1897) in a humorous vein that has been expressed visually in the Walt Disney film *Fantasia*. It is not meant to be interpreted as a serious representation of sorcery but it shares some musical devices with serious works from the period. The opening of repeated tremolo strings, chromaticism, frantic activity, sudden silences and loud chords for brass and percussion remind one of the witches' sabbaths of Berlioz and others.

Two works that are often cited as epitomising the witches' sabbath and the evil hag are Mussorgsky's *Night on a bare mountain* (1867) and *The Hut on fowl's legs (Baba Yaga)* from *Pictures from an exhibition* (1874). *Pictures from an exhibition* was originally written for piano but orchestrated by Ravel in 1922. Mussorgsky wrote at length about the various interpretations that he investigated for the *Night on a bare mountain* and he envisaged subterranean sounds and spirits with the demonic Chernobog being glorified in a black mass, the orgy only being disrupted by the sound of a far off bell heralding a new day and the dispersal of the witches and demons. It is the Korsakov revised version that is usually heard in the concert hall and it portrays a sense of infernal pandemonium with swooping strings, manic crescendos and brass discords, serenity only returning as the church bell is heard.

Mussorgsky's other portrait of witchcraft is based on T. Hartmann's picture of a clock representing a witch's hut on fowl's legs. He imagined her flying through the air seated on a mortar and grinding up human bones with a pestle. The work was originally written for piano as part of a collection of ten pictures plus a connecting 'promenade'. The music is ferocious and chromatic with jagged rhythms and an explosive melody made all the more effective by a relatively quieter middle section. The orchestration by Ravel makes effective use of the orchestra, notably strings with brass interjections.

Mussorgsky's fellow citizen Tchaikovsky treated the theme in some ways differently with his *Manfred Symphony* (1876). It is based on four tableaux from Byron and because it is the only symphony not to be referred to by number it is often thought of as a symphonic poem. A programme was attached to the work that includes a supernatural entity appearing referred to as the 'Fairy of the Alps' that was often referred to as 'The Witch of the Mountain' as well as Bacchanal activity and the evocation of the ghost of Astarte. The music, like the main character Manfred himself, is taken through many moods. For the orgy scene there are frantic strings and loud brass interjections and the use of a large-scale orchestra and organ. The music lacks the dissonance of some composers in treating the supernatural elements and even contains chorale-like passages for Manfred's death at the end of the work.

The Czech composer Dvorak explored the subject with two contrasting works in terms of interpretation and orchestration. *The noon day witch* (1896) is a symphonic poem that tells the story of a mother who threatens her child with a witch who only works between eleven and twelve noon. The witch is summoned by the mother's idle remark and demands the child. When the father arrives home for his lunch he finds his wife unconscious with the dead child in her arms. Despite a gentle pastoral opening, firstly the wind instruments and then the punctuation of dark sounds from the bass strings suggest that sinister events are to be witnessed. Sudden brass accents and the use of silence leads to the death of the child and a rather strange conclusion with loud cadences more appropriate for a 'Romantic' symphony than to express the father's despair. Dvorak's other work about a witch is the piano piece, *The Witches' Sabbath*, for four hands (1884). The third *tableau* of the group is called *The Witches' Sabbath* and it is very unlike any other similarly entitled work. It consists of a lively dance in the major key that is almost waltz-like in its overall feel. A middle section changes to the more traditional minor key but the major key heralds the return of the opening music. The work ends contemplatively but still sprightly.

Considering the strength of German orchestral music in the nineteenth century, one might have expected a larger number of works presenting the witchcraft theme, but this is not the case. Apart from a *Faust* overture (1855) by Wagner that was originally the first movement of a symphony in 1839-40, I could find only one other purely instrumental work, namely Mendelssohn's *Hexenlied* for violin and piano. It opens with repeated notes in a similar style to Schubert's song the *Erl König* prior to the entry of the violin in the minor key.

There are crescendos and further repeated notes from the piano but the work is otherwise uneventful.

Twentieth century orchestral and instrumental music, similarly to the other twentieth century sections, has seen a great deal of change from the 'Romantic' start to its present situation. The start of the century produced impressionistic works such as Debussy's *Danse sacrée et profane* (1904) for harp and strings, that contains a 'profane' dance that is concordant and unlike any witches' dances previously encountered. However, the Russian composer Lyadov's *Baba Yaga,* subtitled *Picture from a Russian folk-tale,* from the same year, uses the more characteristic effects from a full orchestra with tremolando strings, jagged rhythms and brass interjections to portray the witch's propulsion around her yard on a magic mortar, pestle and broomstick. A somewhat different image is achieved by Scriabin using the solo piano for his sonata *Messe noir* (1913) that was conceived as a diabolical counterpart to his seventh sonata *Messe blanche*. It uses discordant harmony and repeated notes leading to a savage march.

The final work to be mentioned by a Russian composer projected the spirit of paganism in ways that might be said to transcend the narrow and biased confines of stereotypical witchcraft. The ballet *The Rite of Spring* by Stravinsky received its first performance at the Théâtre de Champs Elysées in Paris in 1913 and it caused an uproar. It consists of a vision of pagan Russian fertility rites concluding with the victim's sacrificial dance to death to propitiate Nature. The work is in two parts: 'The Adoration of the Earth' and 'The Sacrifice'. The latter section contains such episodes as 'The Evocation of the Ancestors', 'The Rites of the Ancestors' and 'The Sacrificial Dance'. Stravinsky felt he was the vessel through which the music manifested itself and he has provided his own thought processes concerning the ballet:

> "I had a fleeting vision which came to me as a complete surprise. I saw in imagination a solemn pagan rite: sage elders, seated in a circle, watched a young girl dance herself to death. They were sacrificing her to propitiate the god of spring.

> (Druskin quoting Stravinsky, trans. Cooper, 1983, p.39)

Musically, the large orchestra uses most of the devices and harmonic, melodic and rhythmic elements that have been discovered in many previous works. Harsh discords combining chords a semitone apart often disguise some of the Lithuanian folksong origins of the work. The specified dances, including a round dance ('Horovod'), provide the most commonly encountered features of jagged rhythms, sudden brass interjections, bass punctuation and the use of silence balanced with heavily scored fortissimo chords. The raw power of Nature is dramatically displayed in this important work and its influence can be seen in works such as *Carmina Burana* by Carl Orff and composers of twentieth century film music in particular.

A German tradition of interpreting scenes of witchcraft and paganism has not been well represented in the twentieth century despite the importance of such composers as Gustav Mahler. The nearest he came to depicting a witches' sabbath is the D minor 'scherzo' that is marked 'Schattenhaft' and lies between two 'Nachtmusik' movements in his seventh symphony. The music is discordant and uses large melodic intervals and shrill orchestration to convey exaggerated movement. This is further achieved by combining a waltz and ländler together with violent pizzicato strings, glissandi and further melodic fragmentation. The only other German work to be mentioned is the fourth sketch called *The Witches' Sabbath* from *Goyana. Four Sketches* (1960) for solo piano, percussion and string orchestra by F. Waxman. It strives to paint a musical picture of a group of witches seated around a giant demon-goat. The piano begins with slow arpeggios in the bass, followed by repeated xylophone notes. The strings enter with frantic *Dance-macabre* and *Rite of Spring*-like music after a chromatic bass run in the piano that has more than a hint of parody about it. This can also be sensed in some of the following British orchestral works.

The composer Bantok was very interested in paganism and witchcraft material but many of his compositions have not been published. His *Pagan Symphony* (1928) is more influenced by classical Arcadia and Victorian concepts of idealistic pagan times than on witchcraft. Bantok's *The Witch of Atlas* (1902), a tone poem, contains lines from Shelley's poem of the same name. It concentrates on the witch's seductive beauty and sensuousness and is directly related to the poem via identification marks in the musical score. John Ireland's tone poem *The Forgotten Rite* (1913) displays similar preferences to some of Bantok's pagan ideals using evocative slow and mysterious horn to hint at the occult forces of nature. Malcolm Arnold takes an altogether more robust interpretation in his overture *Tam o' Shanter* (1955) following Burns' story. After a pastoral opening one is presented with a great array of orchestral devices to interpret the stormy night, coven of witches and devil's appearance. Wailing trumpets, tremolando strings, sudden interjections, prominent percussion and bass strings, a parody of a Highland fling with bagpipe-like drone accompaniment all add up to produce an exciting experience that is truly in the ironic vein of the original melodramatic poem. This could not be in greater contrast to the extremely serious work by the Scottish composer James MacMillan, *The Confession of Isobel Gowdie* (1990). It is a unique example of a trial being represented in orchestral music and reflects the changing attitudes towards the activities and fates of the many women who were executed for witchcraft activities. The work concerns the trial and death of the Scottish witch Isobel Gowdie and he uses the orchestra, starting with a nebulous woodwind sound after which a dense texture of string writing unfolds. He incorporates a number of melodic quotes into the music, including the Scottish ballad *The Cruel Mother*, Gregorian chant and Gaelic psalmody. Influences can be discerned from Stravinsky for some of the violent writing and Barber or Gorecki for the use of sustained strings. The work is very powerful in directing the listener's thoughts towards the brutality of the witch trials especially in Scotland:

> "This orchestral work makes a powerful and emotional statement out of the brutalities and prejudices that were part and parcel of the witch-hunt, hammering out its central repeated chords with uncompromising musical assurance, and evoking an explosive response at its première."
>
> (Purser, 1992, p.274)

A final work to be mentioned before leaving the British composers is *Walpurgis Night* (1998) by I. Ballamy. It is a modern chamber work scored for piano and saxophone and contrasts quiet moments with frenzied activity using dissonance and chromaticism.

An American tradition of orchestral and instrumental music was relatively late in starting and the initial influences came from Europe. MacDowell was praised by Liszt and wrote *Hexentanz, opus 17* using many of his techniques, namely very fast scales and trills contrasted with more contemplative music. More expansive techniques were used by Charles Ives in *Hallowe'en* (1906) for string quartet and piano.

However, the leading composer Samuel Barber, albeit using mainly 'Romantic' techniques and orchestration, wrote the ballet music to *Medea* and notably followed this up with a separate orchestral work *Medea's meditation and Dance of vengeance* (1948). The work traces Medea's emotions through the music from her mysterious aspects and anguish into eventual frenzy. The orchestra and prominent piano use mainly diatonic harmony with resolved discords and the influence of *The Rite of Spring* can be heard in the rhythmic angularities.

The Spanish composer Manuel de Falla composed the ballet *El amor brujo* (*The Love of the Wizard*) (1915) that has also been called *Wedded by Witchcraft* and *The Demon Lover*. The work does not contain witchcraft as such but an evil spirit that haunts a gypsy girl. The thirteen sections contain such titles as 'The Magic Circle', 'Midnight Witchcraft' and 'Ritual Fire Dance'. The music is very heavily influenced by national idioms of Spanish dance with lavish orchestration but very little terror is evoked.

Within the confines of the stylistic characteristics of each period of music there have been notable features that have arisen that would seem to be particularly appropriate for the orchestral and instrumental portrayal of paganism and witchcraft. Of course, this cannot be applied all of the time to all of the pieces, but several examples have been given to provide evidence of a prevalence of dissonant harmony, jagged rhythms, sudden brass interjections, moments of silence, tremolando strings, minor keys and fast tempos. There have been fewer examples of the sensuous sorceress in orchestral and instrumental music than was found in opera. On the other hand the hag-like witches have been exceptionally well represented in works by Berlioz and Mussorgsky; the power of Nature can be felt in Stravinsky's *The Rite of Spring*; and the brutality of the witch trials in MacMillan's *The Confession of Isobel Gowdie*. The absence of words has not proved counter-productive in inspiring composers to write some of their finest music for this theme.

It may seem to be a strange place in this essay to consider *The Wicker Man* but I am placing it here for musicological reasons in so far as its music embraces the categories of classical music previously investigated, notably vocal and instrumental genres. It contains music that is associated with pagan and Wiccan ideals, and further to this it was quoted as being used in at least one coven at certain celebrations (see later notes). The film was originally released by British Lion in 1973 and is available in three slightly different versions according to the director's cuts. The plot and notably the music are mainly the same. The film was written by Anthony Shaffer and directed by Robin Hardy and starred Edward Woodward (Howie), Christopher Lee (Lord Summerisle) and Britt Ekland (Willow) in leading roles. The full version released in the USA is referred to in this study since it contains most of the footage obtainable.

The story consists of a devout Christian policeman (Howie) being tricked into investigating the bogus disappearance of a young girl (Rowan) on an island off the coast of Scotland that is governed by a local lord. The inhabitants of the island practise a pagan religion and, unknown to the policeman, require him as a human sacrifice for the return of the fruitfulness of their harvest. He witnesses many pagan practices and becomes convinced that the girl has been murdered or is about to be. He resists the sexual temptations offered him by the innkeeper's daughter (Willow) and therefore retains his virginity, a further necessity for his eventual demise. In the final scenes, disguised as Punch the perfect fool, he is trapped on the coastline where there is no escape. Under the direction of the lord of the island (Lord Summerisle) he is washed and baptised before being burnt to death in a giant wicker effigy of a man.

The American composer and arranger Paul Giovanni, who died in the late 1970s, wrote the music, and it was his only film score. The press material prepared by the American distributors in 1977 described the music as follows:

> "The music for *The Wicker Man* is based heavily on actual songs and music that are part of the folk tradition of Scotland. Giovanni attempted to prepare music that would sound like a small, town band might have orchestrated for themselves, and thus, be able to play. There was an attempt on his part not to write traditional film mood music. Some of the songs are re-writings of existing songs, to make them more specific to the subject matter, in one instance combining three old lyrics into one with some editing. The title song 'Cornrigs and Barleyrigs' is a piece of Gaelic mouth music, on one of Robert Burn's [sic] 'songs' set to music. ['The Rigs of Barley', Burns, 256]."

> (Brown, 2000, pp.34-35)

The original soundtrack music and effects was released on CD in the 1970s. It was originally recorded at Shepperton studios but some tracks had to be re-recorded because of poor quality. Giovanni states that this actually enhanced the wind band scene at the May Day procession since a polished performance by members of the London Symphony Orchestra would not have been in keeping with the amateur nature of the supposed village band. For the public house scenes involving music, students from the Royal College of Music were hired and given authentic folk instruments to play.

The film opens as a seaplane flown by the police sergeant prepares to land beside the mainland close to his station and there is a brief music fragment of a drone with reed pipe. He is informed that a letter has been received concerning a missing girl. On board his plane again he approaches an island to a Celtic sounding drone and sung duo that enhances the visual scenery. As the plane lands, the music changes to 'Corn Rigs and Barley Rigs', a lively folksong. After a brief conversation with the harbourmaster and some local men, Howie sets off for the post office to interview the missing girl's mother, to the accompaniment of the same music. Apart from the sexual innuendo in the words to the song there is no hint from the music that Howie is going to face so much adversity during his time on the island. In the pub (The Green Man) the music is of a very different nature, consisting of the re-working of an eighteenth century Public Harlot ballad 'The Landlord's Daughter'. It is a jolly, waltzing song with lewd words referring to the sexual act and is sung by various men in varying states of intoxication and accompanied on acoustic instruments (concertina, violin, guitar, recorder and small drum). Howie breaks up the activity and shows a photograph of the allegedly missing girl whereupon the music changes back to 'Corn Rigs', but at a slower tempo. For both his walk outside where couples are openly copulating and back in the pub where the landlord's daughter (Willow) is helping a teenage boy to lose his virginity, the music played is 'Gently Johnny'. This languorous ballad is heard in the background played on a solo clarinet with flutes and recorders providing an arpeggiated accompaniment. Back in the bar it is sung by the composer (Paul Giovanni) and accompanied by a small chorus of voices and solo guitar. This helps to encourage the listener to view sex within the film as both a pleasurable and almost mystical act, in contrast to Howie's belief that it should be saved for after marriage and according to the dictates of the Church. The next day sees a group of young boys dancing around a maypole. They sing a lively song 'In the woods there grew a tree' that describes the reproduction system in a natural manner. They are accompanied by Jew's harp, guitar, violin and recorders and in the nearby school house the girls beat on their desks to add the percussion. There is a very innocent and joyful feel to the scene that Howie finds unacceptable, especially after his visit to the school. His visit to a graveyard is accompanied by descending scales, flutes, trumpet, recorders and harp to suggest a 'spooky' scenario. However, the mood changes once again as he visits the Lord of Summerisle. He passes by a group of naked girls leaping and dancing to a lively folksong 'Make the baby grow' that is accompanied by recorders and flutes and returns the mood to one of joy at the growth of life in pregnancy. After Howie exhumes what he believes to be the grave of the missing girl only to find a dead hare in it, he returns to the castle, but finds the Lord and the school mistress drunk and singing a bawdy song accompanied by the Lord himself at the piano. After breaking into the chemist's to find further evidence, he returns to the Green Man and goes to bed. This is the setting for one of the most famous scenes in the film where Willow, who is naked, tries to seduce him from the adjacent room by singing a sensuous song and beating in time on the walls and other parts of the room in a hypnotic manner. Guitar, tremolo strings and drum set the pulse as Willow dances around her room singing what is usually referred to as the 'Say how do' song (or 'Willow's song'), since it does not have a name as such. It is the longest single musical track in the film, being just over four minutes in duration. Its slow tempo and delightful sustained melody are enhanced with gentle syncopations and modulations from major to minor keys that produce an effect of seductiveness but also innocence. For the May Day celebrations, various types of music and effects are used. A brass band is heard when Howie is in the library and metal strings are plucked slowly and electronically distorted to produce a menacing sound as some animal-masked people appear at the quayside. As the festivities are prepared and during his search for Rowan, there are jigs and lively music accompanied by violin, bassoon and recorders as well as tremolo strings and guitar. A jig version of 'Baa, Baa Black Sheep' is given a humorous rendition and in contrast a slow eerie tune is played on strings and recorders when a magical 'hand of glory' is placed beside Howie's bed. The procession takes the form of a pavane based on the traditional song *Willy o' Winsbury* with a slow drum beat and accompanied by a wind band. At a moment of halt, six swords form a six-pointed star and each member of the procession has to place their head within it and risk being beheaded. Ironically the music performed is *Oranges and Lemons* played on bagpipes and strings. Howie's demise is fast approaching as he attempts to flee with Rowan through some caves to the rather incongruous sounds of the electric guitar. His preparation for sacrifice consists of a motif of descending scales on a zither and surreal voice effects that lead to his final incarceration in the giant wicker man. As Howie sings 'The Lord's my shepherd' (new version) the group gather around the burning effigy singing the canon 'Summer is icumen in' to the accompaniment of wind band and bass drum. A heraldic voluntary for trumpets concludes the film.

Taken as a whole, the musical score consists of mainly quite brief extracts. However, it is an integral part of the film, binding parts of it together and highlighting the overall pagan theme. With the exception of the inappropriate electric guitar music for the cave chase scene, the music fits quite naturally into the plot. One can easily imagine both the bawdy music of the pub as well as the contemplative 'Gently Johnny' being performed in the locations suggested. There is great exuberance in the lively folk music around the maypole and for the fertility dance and the amateurish feel of a village band is perfectly presented in the *Willy o' Winsbury* performance. Willow's song of seduction has already been praised. The final combination of 'The Lord's my shepherd' sung by the heroic Howie and the chanting of 'Summer is icumen in' by the assembled population is particularly striking. Many pagans believe that music is inseparable from their lives and rituals and *The Wicker Man* would similarly be greatly impoverished without its musical score.

Conclusion

A large number of works were omitted from this study because they were deemed to be unsuitable because of genre, i.e. not defined as classical music, or because the association with witchcraft or paganism in the broader sense was somewhat tenuous. The criteria by which I chose the works as suitable included titles that included direct references to witchcraft or sorcery and works that contained scenes of that nature not specified in the titles. The dividing of the genres into operatic, vocal/choral, and orchestral/instrumental examples facilitated the discovery of musical ideas and characteristics applying to the aspects of witchcraft included. Furthermore, the personalities and powers of the witches, sorceresses, etc., were also discovered through the words and music that they performed. Obviously some aspects changed throughout the four hundred-year period studied. For instance, the lavish stage spectacles and importance of dance was gradually replaced in the operatic examples with far more personality development and in the instrumental examples the greatly expanded orchestras of the nineteenth century allowed a greater variety of timbres and effects to be achieved.

There were many examples taken from the operatic repertoire that developed the theme of witchcraft and paganism. Two distinct types appeared on the stage from the start of the operatic tradition in the seventeenth century, namely the hag-like witches and the more developed sorceresses who were usually given specific names such as Medea or Circe. The witches of Purcell followed Shakespeare's tradition but with a certain amount of humour included. Dance music was very important for their roles and the music was discordant and rhythmically angular by the standards of the day. This type of group representation of witches was notably encountered again in Verdi's *Macbeth*. He used minor keys, tritones, brass interjections and a wild waltz for their music and this combination was not typical of his other works or characters. Wagner's representation of the three Norns is in complete contrast since he provides them with majestic music and does not trivialise them. The other times when witches were brought together was for the purpose of the black sabbath that usually took place on Walpurgis night. The many examples of operas on the 'Faust' theme often included such a scene as in Gounod's opera of the same name that used the ballet to provide the spectacle and there was also a Walpurgis scene in Puccini's *Le Villi*. Similar orgiastic revels take place in Wagner's *Tannhäuser* but the music is considerably more sensuous than frantic and diabolical in accordance with Venus' alluring charms. The solitary witch was often represented as an evil hag who did not demand any sympathy, although Fata Morgana in Prokofiev's *Love for three oranges* is a farcical character. The witch was not named in Humperdinck's works, but appeared as Nairna in Glinka's *Russlan and Ludmilla* and Jezibaba in Dvorak's *Rusalka*. In these works the witches' music is awkward and unpredictable. Jezibaba in particular is accompanied by tremolando strings, sudden interjections, tritones, awkward leaps, use of the minor key, loud brass passages and an importance of the bass instruments. This music is very characteristic of the portrayal of witches in opera and is not usually found to represent other concepts unless there is a supernatural element to it.

It is difficult in some examples to differentiate between the classification of witches and sorceresses but some traits can provide guidance. For instance, the sorceresses tend to be named in the text and often have a central role to play. Sometimes the score's list of personae actually specifies them as such or their mythological definitions are known. Purcell's 'Sorceress' was contrasted with the witches by her powerful music and place in the plot. Mozart's 'Queen of the Night' is another powerful sorceress with dramatic music. Medea and Circe were popular choices from the seventeenth century onwards and the former displayed a wide range of emotions and mood changes in the music to Cherubini's *Médée*. Handel introduced the enchantresses Armida and Alcina, the latter as a fully developed character with varied music according to her emotional state. Verdi also found inspiration with the characters Azucena and especially Ulrica whose music contained tritones and prominent bass instruments for her plotting. Although Wagner's Ortrud uses startling bass music and minor keys for her sorcery, his finest creation was Kundry who appeals to one's sense of pity as well as being at different times in the opera both evil and sexually alluring. This is similarly revealed in her accompanying music.

A few characters from opera do not fit neatly into any of these categories. For instance, Linda in S. Wagner's *Schwarzschwanenreich* is accused of witchcraft and murder and dies at the stake, but she commits no spells or sorcery and demands one's sympathy throughout. This is also true of the male wizards who are not usually as important as their female counterparts. The cunning man Colas in Mozart's *Bastien und Bastienne* is a comical character whose spell-casting is not meant to be taken seriously in much the same way as J. Wellington Wells' in Sullivan's *The Sorcerer*. Zoroastro in Handel's *Orlando* and Dapertutto in Offenbach's *The Tales of Hoffmann* receive relatively little importance in their musical representations and even Mozart's Sarastro in *The Magic Flute* is mainly grand and majestic rather than displaying supernatural powers. Klingsor, in Wagner's *Parsifal,* is an exceptional role being an evil sorcerer who is integral to the plot and has musically significant music. Further exceptions were included that did not contain witches or sorceresses but were steeped in similar alleged activities. Hence, the importance of druids in, for instance,

Bellini's *Norma,* voodoo in Delius' *Koanga* and the spell-casting scene in Weber's *Der Freischütz.* For a modern interpretation of paganism I felt it necessary to draw attention to Tippett's *The Midsummer Marriage* because of its insight into the mysteries of Nature and the film *The Wicker Man* was similarly highlighted as an example from the world of cinema.

Having scrutinised the music from many different works there are musical characteristics that have become evident throughout the repertoire and relative to the musical traditions of the periods concerned. This takes into account stylistic changes such as the lessening of the impact of dissonance in twentieth century music and other features such as orchestration, colour and texture. These might be summarised as below:

Witchcraft and sorcery

Melodic content: awkward interval leaps, chromaticism
Harmonic content: discords, especially the tritone, minor keys
Rhythmic content: syncopated, dance music (witches only), use of silence
Instrumentation: bass, brass interjections, tremolando strings, percussion

Obviously these characteristics are not heard all the time for all the examples discussed - and indeed when the sorceresses in particular are displaying their loving, gentle side, most of the listed features are absent. The composers then use their varied powers of lyrical writing to achieve the effects desired. This is similarly true of the music in *The Midsummer Marriage* and *The Wicker Man* where the power of Nature is expressed in its many faceted ways.

The operas investigated provide evidence of the changing and contrasting images of women portrayed throughout the period researched. Increasingly they have shown depths of emotion that have removed them from the stereotypical evil hags to become 'real' women who have often been abused by a male-dominated society, especially when they have fallen in love. This can be seen, in particular, with the development of the character Medea who has, in operas increasingly throughout the centuries, been shown to have been a victim of her over zealous love for Jason. One can identify a depth of characterisation that reflects more concern with the explanation or understanding of women's feelings and motivation. This is particularly evident when it is portrayed through their relationships with others. In contrast, the male sorcerers and wizards continue to receive scant attention with little or no character development and they have remained as aloof eccentrics sometimes involved with evil and on other occasions with the supernatural.

Although the attitudes to witchcraft have not changed dramatically in the works researched, nevertheless the images of paganism that emerge in *The Midsummer Marriage* and *The Wicker Man* provides a startling contrast to the typical scenes of witchcraft previously encountered. A positive modern interpretation of paganism is presented without the evil overtones. Tippett uses themes of Jungian archetypes in his opera to stress not only the importance of Nature, but also the blending of male and female sexuality and emotion. *The Wicker Man* stresses the role of Nature as a pervading force that has to be propitiated at times by sacrifice.

There was a relative lack of representations of witchcraft in vocal/ choral music to scrutinise. One fine exception was Purcell's *The Witch of Endor* that provided a sympathetic and lyrical character as the witch's role. Further examples maintained the use of fast strings, minor keys, discords and interjections that have become commonplace in representing scenes of witchcraft. The nineteenth century was more productive with several mainstream composers writing suitable works. These included Berlioz' *L'Enfance du Christ* with a frenzied dance scene for male soothsayers and traditional brass interjections and swooping strings in his *Faust* cantata. Mendelssohn's *Die Erste Walpurgisnacht* mainly avoided harshness, but his contemporary Schumann maintained the minor key, fast string playing and chromaticism in *Scenes from Goethe's Faust*. Songs by Brahms, Hatton and Stamford were somewhat unsubstantial and even caricatured the witch. In the twentieth century Busoni continued the tradition of jagged rhythms and repeated notes in a declamatory style in *Hexenlied* but other composers treated the theme in different ways. Gibbs chose to parody in *The Witch*, Corigliano's *Song to the witch of the cloisters* was thoughtful and von Schilling's *Das Hexenlied* was full of pathos. Overall there were varying interpretations evident with the frequently referred to attributes still prevailing. Thus, there are similar trends to be found in vocal music to those in the operas, but with fewer examples overall. The word 'witchcraft' still has a negative connotation but the witches are increasingly treated positively and with increased emotional depth. Once again men are almost totally excluded, apart from minor appearances and the enduring character Mephistopheles. Images of paganism tended towards the idealised realm of Arcadia without expanding its contemporary representations.

In representations of witchcraft in orchestral and instrumental music, the problem of identifying witchcraft or paganism in works without a text was encountered. Apart from instrumental items included in stage works, there were very few examples from the seventeenth century and Haydn's *Hexenmenuett* could barely be included from the following century. The expansion of orchestral music and the spirit of revolution that was felt in the nineteenth century allowed composers to follow the dictates of their imaginations. The works by Berlioz and Mussorgsky have been used as examples for witchcraft, and in particular the black sabbath, ever since and have reinforced the use of tremolando strings, dissonance and interjecting brass instruments, etc., as the instruments and devices to convey such activity. Other composers such as Dvorak and Tchaikovsky followed these ideas to varying extents. In the twentieth century, the tradition continued in Lyadov and Scriabin's works. However, a contrast was found in the works of the British composers Bantok and Ireland who demonstrated the more idealistic and sensuous sides of paganism and witchcraft. Arnold's *Tam o'Shanter* uses the common orchestral devices but in a parodying style. However, this in turn can be contrasted with MacMillan's serious and powerful work *The Confession of Isobel Gowdie*. A similar diversity can be found in other twentieth century works including American examples such as *Medea's Meditation and Dance of Vengeance* by Barber and the only Spanish example discovered *El amor brujo*. However, there is one work that has probably had a greater effect on twentieth century orchestral writing than any other, namely Stravinsky's *The Rite of Spring*. Although it does not concern witchcraft per se, it nevertheless portrays the pagan sense of nature in orchestral terms in a way that might be compared to Tippett's overview of the theme operatically in *The Midsummer Marriage*. The portrayals of women and men in orchestral music are less precisely defined through the lack of texts. However, composers' own writings and the nature of the music itself allows one to realise that similarly to operas, vocal and choral works, the works encountered have continued the trends discovered before. As previously stated, *The Rite of Spring* encourages a nature-based interpretation of paganism that is far removed from stereotypical witchcraft.

The place of musical representations of witchcraft and paganism in music within the genres chosen has not been balanced in either historical or musical ways. The fact that an increasing number of examples have been found the closer to the present time one has come is not altogether surprising since a greater number of works would have survived and become accessible to study. However, a far greater number of interpretations have also been given to the theme in more modern times thus allowing composers a variety of definitions to be inspired by. The word 'witch' itself in the twenty-first century can still convey the idea of an evil old hag complete with broomstick attending a demonic black sabbath, but this idea can be treated both seriously and, more commonly, humorously. Furthermore, the pathos of the victims of the 'burning times' is now musically represented as an issue to demand our sorrow. The use of 'sorceress' can evoke from composers many interpretations, including power and majesty as well as sensuality and sexual allure. Women like Medea have inspired composers to reveal the many complicated traits of her character as she feels rejection by her lover, anguish, anger and vengeance. Many psychological issues can be raised concerning the origin of her final evil acts and the composers seek to present these in musical terms. Paganism can still be viewed as a pre-Christian religion and some composers have chosen the druids to represent this concept, but other interpretations are presented. Some composers have written idealistic works imagining that the times of ancient Greece, and Athens in particular, were particularly peaceful and inspiring. In the twentieth century, paganism has been re-investigated and its affinity with nature and polytheism has generally been stressed. This concept has been echoed in the music surrounding it, thus placing it quite firmly in the context of the prevailing culture.

The balance within musical genres has been weighed on the side of opera despite, I would maintain for financial reasons, there being fewer operas written in contemporary times than previously. Opera appeals to both the visual and auditory senses and it better represents character. It is therefore more appealing to the general populace. Composers have been able to convey their feelings more directly with opera than with other forms. When suitable resources are available it is possible to stage works with considerable spectacle that enhances the power of the music. The stylised music curiously bears little relationship to the music that was either allegedly used in previous times for witchcraft activity or is used in contemporary witchcraft and paganism that will be discussed in the next essay. However, there have been four fairly distinct types of woman that have been personified within the music presented. These may be identified as participants of misrule in society, seductresses, victims demanding some sympathy and nature-worshipping pagans. The concept of negativity and the reversal of good in society and religion as displayed by witches can be seen in masques and at the alleged sabbaths. These introduce women who have either been thought to have fornicated with the devil or have committed crimes against individuals with their spells and poisons. These characteristics have not been maintained in twenty-first century western culture. However, the seductress, or at least the idea of a witch being sexually attractive, has survived in the media with such people as 'Elvira' in the films of the same name, 'Morticia' in *The Addams Family* and a host of teenage personifications. A combination of twentieth century political correctness, the rise of feminism and the American apologetic feelings for the Salem witch trials has drawn attention to the aspects of the witches being victims of persecution, notably in the seventeenth century. The continued decline of the established Church and cynicism concerning some of their exploits, for instance wars and the accumulation of vast wealth at the expense of the poor, has further encouraged society to view such women with sympathy and feel regret at their inhumane treatment. There are even comparisons made between the treatment of the Jews by the Nazis in the Second World War and the witchcraft trials in Europe (Trevor Roper, 1984). Finally, the neo-paganism and Wicca of the twentieth and twenty-first century has provided a link with the bygone pagan ideals as they are interpreted contemporarily. The modern pagan women and witches are portrayed very positively with an emphasis on their affinity with nature and, if one accepts the previously mentioned works of Tippett and Giovanni, they have to be respected as at least the equal to their male counterparts.

Finally, it could be argued that throughout the classical music repertoire, enduring trends and changes mirror developments in the nature of the western society that provides its context. The concept of witchcraft has maintained a negative inference but it has been largely replaced in the twentieth century by nature-based paganism that is similarly reflected in modern Wicca. For example, the ideas of satanic orgies have not been maintained except when referring back to distant times. The portrayal of the sorceress has become increasingly more complex. There are also examples of witches who have been treated with more depth and emotional substance. In contrast the men have been increasingly neglected as their role has been, and largely still is, subservient to the woman's role in witchcraft and paganism. Undertaking evil for evil's sake has been largely replaced by revenge for unrequited love or previous abuses and in the twenty-first century positive images have secured one's support and sympathy. Love and sexual feelings play a very important role in the repertoire since they form a fundamental core of the human experience. They are also at the heart of modern paganism and Wiccan practices. Composers have also used humour either to diffuse emotions in over-dramatic scenes or to satirise the witches' actions. This could be viewed as providing evidence for the enduring conflict of emotional response to the awareness of practices in witchcraft. On the one hand there is fear of the potential power of the supernatural as expressed in witchcraft, whilst on the other an uncomfortable respect for it. These mixed reactions and portrayals are indicative of the diversity of views of witchcraft and paganism in all its representations.

Music and Paganism at the Start of the 21ˢᵗ Century

Few academics have written on this subject and none in quantity but Joscelyn Godwin and Karen Ralls-Macleod can be included as having made some contributions. Joscelyn Godwin (Professor of Music at Colgate University in New York State) has written several books exploring music in both magical and spiritual terms within the Church and folklore. Although he does not study paganism and music as such, he nevertheless provides incites into music's place within ritual. Karen Ralls-Macleod has written in some detail about Celtic music in what she calls the "Otherworld" and her work embraces paganism generally. Further to these academics, there are several well-read and erudite writers who deserve to be treated as possessing some authority on the subject in varying degrees of quantity. These include David Tame, Stewart and Janet Farrar, and Robert J. Stewart. These authors and others have contributed to the data that I have investigated for this study.

I wanted to obtain contemporary information about the use of music in pagan/Wiccan ritual and culture so I devised a questionnaire that I sent to over two hundred practising pagans throughout the UK. People were contacted through the magazine *Pagan Dawn* and local newsletters throughout England. Furthermore, I also contacted my own friends and acquaintances within the religion. The questionnaire attempted to find any common themes throughout pagan use of music and the effects it was claimed to have on participants before, during and after rituals. A majority of the replies came from women which is in accordance with the numbers that follow paganism and especially Wicca. Eighty-eight people returned the questionnaires in varying amounts of detail. Many of the answers provided information that had obviously been well thought-out and, in the examples of group replies, indicated that the issues raised had indeed been discussed by the members of covens concerned.

(For reasons of confidentiality throughout the respondents quoted will not be identified):

> "Music is psychologically important to our wellbeing. It also connects to the psyche and triggers raised levels of consciousness. Music is integral to magick because it weaves spells on the soul. The use of music is both complex and vital. It has different effects on individuals. I also use it for individual rituals, but it is much more energising when used to link an individual into group consciousness."

A question was asked to see if there were any differences between solitary practitioners and coven/group members in their use of music, and this was not apparent. There was a considerable amount of overlap in the answers since some coven members also held individual ceremonies and some hedgewitches joined covens for occasional major celebrations. If one takes into account the views of coven members being expressed when an individual high priest or priestess actually filled in the form, then over one hundred pagans can be said to have commented on their music via the questionnaires. Some contrasts were found in the terminology people used to describe their groups. Most used 'coven' or 'group' but a few references were also made to each of a 'meditation group', a 'hearth' and 'groves'. The latter two referring to 'Northern' tradition paganism and 'Druidism' respectively.

One question asked whether music was used before, during and/ or after rituals to which replies were often very detailed concerning what types of music were used and exactly when they were used. The percentage of replies stating that they used music in one form or another were:

- Music used before ritual: 60 per cent
- Music used during ritual: 89 per cent
- Music used after ritual: 64 per cent
- No music used at all: 3 per cent

The reasons given for music not being used were that it might act as a distraction from concentrating on the ritual being undertaken and in one instance because no one played an instrument. For outdoor rituals, complications were mentioned of not having a power source and the problem of inclement weather damaging instruments. Intoning spoken words does not seem to have been included as a "musical" experience whereas chanting songs was classed as "music". The music used before a ritual was mainly recorded and was used exclusively to "set the mood" and "enhance the atmosphere".

During the ritual many more factors were mentioned to justify and confirm the importance of using music, for example, the "mood" or the "atmosphere" was enhanced was mentioned in many of the replies. In some cases help was provided by the music being identified but at other times the word "appropriate" was used to describe music to improve the ritual. When music was played or listened to after the ritual all the replies that used music mentioned its role as providing "fun", "relaxation" or entertainment. Dance music was also quoted in this category as well as during rituals. Numerous examples from recently published literature also commented on music being used at pagan gatherings and rituals. For instance:

> "The most important use of song is in ritual, the predominant Pagan form of worship and the central art-form of the movement...Some covens have songs or chants for opening and closing the circle, for calling the quarters [invoking the 'spirits' of the four cardinal points of a circle representing the so-called elements earth, air, fire and water], or for invoking the deities...Pagans also use songs as raw materials for spells and rituals."
>
> (Magliocco and Tannen, 1998, pp.175-201)

> "If you have musicians in your coven, live musical backing to rituals, including spell-working, can be very helpful in setting and maintaining the atmosphere. But every group should build up a collection of recorded music for Circle work...For the concentrated building-up of power required in spell-working, strongly rhythmic music can be effective – particularly if the music itself builds up as it develops (as with Ravel's *Bolero*, for example)."
>
> (Farrar and Farrar, 1990, p.35)

It would seem from the information gathered that music is frequently used before, during and after pagan rituals. Many of the replies were precise about their use of live or recorded music and gave details about which were used at different parts of the meetings. Every possible combination of live and recorded music being used before, during or after rituals was encountered. Several groups and individuals also mentioned using only recorded music throughout their meetings and slightly fewer only used it during rituals. A similar number of replies spoke of only using live music. The overall results for groups and individuals were:

- People using live music at some stage of their meetings: 73 per cent
- People using recorded music at some stage of their meetings: 68 per cent

Information about covens' musical activities that has been published also provided data about the use of music. For instance: "…while most Circle music these days is from tape or disc, this is certainly one of the occasions for using a musician if you have one…who can play the *bodhram*" (the Irish hand-drum, ideal for this Conga-type dance) (Farrar and Farrar, 1984, pp.55-6). Of particular interest was an extended conversation (in Colchester, June 4th 2001) with a member of Gerald Gardner's coven and high priestess Patricia Crowther concerning the use of live and recorded music. She informed me that they did not use any recorded music since it was not readily available in the 1960s, but they certainly chanted songs and played the tambourine and sistrum during dances and rituals. During our meeting she sang to me a new chant which she was hoping to incorporate into her coven in Sheffield. It consisted of a very simple tune that was sequential in pattern and easily learned.

The question concerning who actually chose the music was the most straightforward to answer. When individuals were replying it was obviously their own choice and in non-hierarchical groups everyone passed an opinion concerning the selection. Quite often the high priest or priestess was mentioned but only when he or she was leading the proceedings. If someone else was directing a session then it was that person's choice of music but taking the group's wishes into account - "the group must relate to the music". Similarly, if a person wrote the ritual then she might well have indicated suitable music. It was obvious from the replies that considerable care was taken by people choosing music that it should not be too obtrusive or have any known negative emotional effects on any of the attendees. When live music was used it was always the choice of the musicians concerned according to their level of expertise, knowledge of repertoire and improvisational capabilities. One reply stated that the 'spirits' chose the music but the remainder of responses specified human sources!

The types of music chosen varied extensively but an obvious method of systemisation is to split the music into the two categories of live and recorded. When the informants told me that both types of music were used in a ceremony it was usually played at different times and the types were not merged together. Because of the nature of the instruments used in live music, i.e. acoustic, percussion and voice, and because of a general scarcity of professional musicians at meetings, differences were apparent.

Live music has two contrasting places in rituals, namely as a passive element to enhance the surroundings or more formally to direct the proceedings as an integral part of the ceremony. This has similarities within Christianity where musicians have often been condemned by the Church for composing music that distracted the congregation and took its mind away from the worship: "...the Church mistrusted all music that was unsanctified by a sacred text - a fact which held up for centuries the development of instrumental music" (Godwin, 1987, p.51). Some of the reasons for the Church's hostility towards music has stemmed from its connection with the worship of pagan deities together with exotic and sexual connotations. This is expanded upon:

> "Under the Roman Empire music was associated with all the things the Christians shunned...The Church Fathers allowed the singing of hymns, but could not conceive of anyone actually listening to music except for mere sensual enjoyment. Not for many centuries did the organ, the instrument of the circus, become a fixture in Christian churches, and other instruments were never completely at home there. The fears of the Fathers were justified in post-Reformation times, when the High Mass and major Offices

tended to degenerate into concerts, the congregation into
an audience…"

(ibid. p. 62)

The links between paganism, dancing, music and the Church
have often caused problems for Christianity and this controversy is
still present. However, music is inexorably linked to ritual in most
religions:

> "There are few religions in which music has played no part
> at all…music is being used to help express and heighten
> the content of ritual action…Music is part of the universal
> language of ritual, and without it ritual must always be
> impoverished…Music is one of the several elements in
> cult or ritual, for it is in the context of ritual that 'religious
> music' has found, and still finds, its main area of expression.
> First there is purely physical movement and action, with
> the dance as its most important aspect…"

> "In ancient times, therefore, there seem to have been
> two potentially distinct ways in which music was used
> in the context or religion. The first of these was emotive
> and magical, and is seen most clearly in the link between
> music and the dance. The second was more conceptual and
> intellectual…and depended on the link between music and
> the holy word…"

(Sharpe, 'Music', Man, Myth and Magic, 5, 1910-12)

It is to the amateur that one looks to in providing live music at pagan
meetings - and the enthusiasm that amateurs often bring to their music
is admirable - but sometimes they can annoy other members of a group
if their standard of performing is poor or obtrusive:

> "A word on drums: Fantastic if people can really play
> them, especially if outdoors, but otherwise they're from
> Hell! People assume they're easy to play and anyone can
> therefore pick one up and bang it – big mistake! Strong
> rhythms can, however, be an extremely good method of
> attaining a trance state, but should be part of recorded
> music unless a really excellent drummer is present!"

After a ritual the social element is paramount and a degree of humour is welcome as attendees release any energy they may have built up by spontaneous music making. Songs are performed with pagan themes such as *John Barleycorn* (specified four times in the survey), *Summer is icumen in* etc. Rounds and part-songs are also sung. Pagans, similarly to other cultures and religions, often use existing melodies and add different words to them. This has been commented upon, for instance:

> "All kinds of tunes were pressed into service…There was a fashion for parodies, for adding pagan words to well-known tunes such as Christmas carols. The justification was that 'everybody knows the tune'…Then drawing on the revival of traditional British folk song, a rather small number of songs with a good pagan feel to them were drawn out of the treasury…Most notable here is *John Barleycorn*."

> (Wybold, March 1995, p.23)

> "Finding the lyrics of folk music with their pagan meanings still intact is an exciting pastime for many pagan people… For many centuries the farmers and rural folk continued to live by and with the cycles of the sacred seasons, and it was they who preserved folk songs for us through their oral traditions."

> (McCoy, 1996, p.133)

One reply to the questionnaire confirmed this with a specific example:

> "Dancing and singing after are a regular event. Modern pop, blues, and joke songs are common e.g. 'Let's talk of Aphrodite looks great in a nightie. Tends to be flighty, that's good enough for me'. We have had army chants, madrigals, elemental drumming…folk in all forms…Most of my group will improvise words to trad. songs… "

There is an important tradition of live music within paganism that has its roots in traditional and composed folk music. It is not designated as pagan or Wiccan as such, but the words often hint at its origin. Some Christmas carols contain intriguing hints of pagan associations:

"Music for Yule: Music is another important part of Yule, and Christmas carols are yet another idea taken from paganism. Many common Christmas carols contain pagan images that are not so subtle. 'Carols'…were also the name of round dances celebrating the rebirth of the Frankish pagan gods…The English Christmas Carol *Deck the Halls with Boughs of Holly* contains not one Christian religious image."

(McCoy, 1996, pp.85-6)

Some pagans feel it is unfortunate that the mantle of group commercial pagan music has moved away from folk bands such as Steeleye Span, at least as known in its early days, and more towards rock groups like Inkubus Sukkubus. However, more traditional music is still being produced in an attempt to re-define a contemporary pagan repertoire of easily performed music and "Traditional ballads…find their way into a number of Pagan musical contexts" (Magliocco and Tannen, 1998, p.178). However, a warning must be sounded about the belief that such songs contain direct references to ancient customs: "The idea that traditional folksongs contain pre-Christian imagery has been propounded…a perspective that has long since been discarded by academic folklorists…" (ibid. pp.183-4). Songs and chants are particularly popular in after-ritual gatherings and people that have access to Starhawk and Buckland's works have readily available music provided in an easy-to-read format. (For instance, Starhawk, 1997 and Buckland, 1999.)

The responses to the questionnaires named many instruments as being used at pagan meetings, including gongs, singing bowls, guitars, bodhráns, general percussion, sistrums, flutes, rattles, whistles, chimes, bells, a didgeridoo, violins and a mouth organ. (Singing was mentioned in twenty-six per cent of the answers and chanting forty per cent.) However, the 'drums' were identified in fifty-nine per cent of the replies compared to only two or three mentions for the other instruments. There are many possible reasons as to why this number of appearances was much higher than for any other instrument. The drum is portable and can be purchased without great cost. It is not difficult to play basic rhythms and can allow the least musical of performers the chance to participate in the group working. Drums have an historical association with pagan religions from different countries and continents. The shaman's drum is an important tool of his craft and voodoo, American Indian and African drummers all use these instruments in their rituals. With the revival of Celtic music, the bodhrán has become popular in pagan ceremonies and folk music, arguably from the 1950s (Baines, 1992). It is not only believed by members of religions and cults that drums have powers beyond their purely musical attributes, but also some ethnomusicologists have studied their ability to induce trance. Gilbert Rouget, a well-respected academic in this field, devotes many pages to the subject in his book *Music and Trance* (1985) and one complete section 'A Neurophysiological Theory of the Effects of Drumming'. He believes that drumming can act as a "triggering" effect upon trance thus producing a "conditioned reflex" but only in so far as it is a part of the overall experience. He cites the *candomblé* drumming as an example of this and accepts throughout the text the role that drumming plays within rituals. This is corroborated elsewhere:

"Man's use of drums for a wide variety of practical and magical purposes seems universal and of the greatest antiquity. They have been employed...in religious ceremonies of all sorts...and to drive away demons and evil spirits...They are sometimes linked with initiation rites...

The drum is probably most famous, however, for its ability to induce strange states of mind, conditions of trance and ecstasy and weird powers...the drum...has been used as the chief instrument of divination..."

(Man, Myth and Magic, vol. II, 1970, p.725)

Many pagans use drumming as part of their ceremonies:

"...generally a rapid, rather hypnotic drum beat [is chosen]. The belief is that this rapid rattling and drumming, which can be accompanied by dancing as well, helps one achieve a light trance state that can induce what Jung would call active imagining, visionary experiences etc.

Spontaneous live music - especially rhythmic drumming and chanting can induce trance states in which spirits are seen and communicated with."

It is clear that the drum is given the highest place of importance within a pagan's collection of instruments and many of the other instruments listed are from within the percussion family - rattles, singing bowls, etc. (For an interesting article see Tickill, *Gippeswic*, *vi* pp.14-16.) The relative lack of orchestral instruments (only the flute and violin were mentioned) may be attributed to the difficulty of playing them without practice and training. It has been alleged that in antiquity "music at the time of the offering of incense to the gods was prevalent" (Ralls-MacLeod, 2000, p.163) and that flute players were present on these occasions in ancient Rome. *O'cean* [sic] the flute music of the New Age musician P. Larkin has also been strongly recommended by Farrar "as Circle music for a Water occasion" (Farrar and Farrar, 1990, 37).

The guitar's cult place in Western music has ensured that many people can play a few chords to accompany themselves and these of course include pagans and witches. Plucked-stringed instruments have often been associated with non-Christian activities and it has been written that "...enchanting music of the fairy harp is referred to by St Patrick as having a suspicious 'twang of the fairy spell'" (Ralls-MacLeod, 2000). Gerald Gardner, the founder of modern witchcraft, believed that the history of plucked-stringed instruments stretched back into 'Stone Age' times:

> "They probably had crude drums and there is a cave painting in France of a man dressed in a bull's hide with horns, dancing and twanging the string of a small bow. It is probable that by a number of people twanging bow-strings they could produce a harp-like effect."

> (Gardner, 1982, p.47)

Singing and chanting were frequently referred to as being important in pagan gatherings and, once again, one can suggest many reasons for this. Concerning chanting: "Repetition has the effect of sedating the conscious mind and allowing the subconscious mind to readily accept unfiltered stimulation" (Grimassi, 2000, p.71). Many of the chants and songs are very simple - even part songs often take the form of rounds and canons - thus allowing trouble-free learning. They are "typically sung in unison... often with improvised harmonies, to accompany circle, spiral or individual dancing" (Magliocco and Tannen, 1998, p.182). Some people find the chanting of words easier to learn than speaking them and psychological studies have given evidence of the benefits of chanting whilst employed in various tasks (Horden, 2000).

The voice is believed to have similar trance-triggering abilities as drumming in some cultures and its therapeutic benefit is well documented:

> Music heals: "When I sing I use vocables [sic] and words in my native language. Lines of power exist all around us. What I try to do is tap into that power through sound and vibration using my voice and a drum… When the lines of power are met, it is said a healing can occur" (Howard, 2000).

It would seem that modern pagans and witches mainly use their voices in song and chanting to give praise to and connect with their deities and to bind themselves within their group. They would also seem to use their voices purely for the joy of singing. Some statements received were:

> "We as a couple have been immersed in singing for many years. We also meditate and have explored our own spiritual and religious lives… The hymns and chants we create have their origin in our love of nature, the coming together of male and female, the deep sense of religious devotion and love for the earth and heavens… The melodies and harmonies are strongly rooted in the folk tradition we both love, and our words are our own or from the mystical poets of many spiritual traditions.
>
> …we always have [live] music whenever we meet together, whether for rehearsal, ritual or socialising. We have music during our led meditations, always as a focal point of our rituals…and afterwards on an informal basis. The intonation of the Awen [an inspirational chant that calls creative power into the being of the person and used by druids] is performed at every ritual. The key is chosen by the person who starts the chant, but individual notes are chosen by each singer for themselves, to blend in…[The music is] absolutely anything at all that can be performed solo a cappella in the open air…[The purpose is] to add

a deeper dimension to the ritual being performed, the meditation being entered into to or the social event being enjoyed."

I visited the pagan choir *Vox Magica* and they provided me with a list of their repertoire and some reasons for the pieces being chosen. There were obvious practical reasons why some works could not be performed since the choir only numbers about a dozen and is of an amateur standard, but many of the items reflected a pagan theme including: *Deck the Hall with Boughs of Holly, John Barleycorn*, and *Welcum Yule*. A spokeswoman told me:

> "We are a Pagan choir and sensitive to the fact that there are few Pagan choirs around. We therefore don't want our repertoire too much diluted by non-Pagan stuff. Equally, our membership requires people to be at least sympathetic to Paganism, and we would not sing music which actively promotes anti-Pagan religion, though like early Christians, we are not above lifting a good tune and Paganising the words."

Some members informed me that they did not tend to perform at rituals but enjoyed singing pagan songs together socially and at appropriate functions. As individuals they used singing and chanting in private rituals the importance of which was often commented upon:

> " ...chants and tunes that have deep meaning and power in them, and that can transport us into altered states of consciousness. Songs sung in praise of a Goddess or God, chants used as invocations, to cast circle, or for other ritual uses, are all clearly Pagan songs. Many Pagan songwriters have ballads about the Craft, or concerning the lives of Pagans..."

(Hill, cited in Magliocco and Tannen, 1998, p.176)

It would appear from the above comments about live music that it plays a very important part in pagan activities. It is used for a variety of reasons, including binding people together, healing, blocking out external noises, contacting or praising what informants termed the 'spirits', giving a focus to a ritual and simple enjoyment. In addition to the voice being used, relatively easy to play instruments are chosen such as a range of percussion instruments and most notably the drum. Other instruments are used according to the capability of group members. Spontaneity is important but care in the choice and execution of music is also vital.

The use of recorded music allows pieces that are technically and musically beyond the capabilities of the groups to be incorporated in the rituals and activities of pagans and witches. It considerably widens the number of experiences available by its discriminate use but it is certainly not to everyone's taste. The scholar Tina Luhrmann wrote of a ritual she attended where: "We lit a fire in the cauldron and danced around it to the cassette, the taped music feeble and incongruent" (Luhrmann, 1989, p.76). Statements such as: "There is a certain kind of music that is evocative of the Middle Kingdoms…Mendelssohn's incidental music *A Midsummer Night's Dream*, or Stravinsky's *The Fire Bird* and *The Rite of Spring*" (Hope, 1987, p.44) were not conducive to a greater understanding of the reasons why the music was selected. Elsewhere, even less information was forthcoming: "Many respondents also mentioned well-known groups and performers such as Jethro Tull (especially the albums *Songs from the Wood* and *Heavy Horses*) and Loreena McKennitt…" (Magliocco and Tannen, 1998, p.177) but no further details were given. An intriguing example was the music *Sinfonia Antarctica* being used for a 'Drawing Down the Moon' ceremony at Midsummer! (Farrar and Farrar, 1984, p.186). Other works such as *The Night on a Bare Mountain* (Mussorgsky) and *The Danse Macabre* (Saint-Saëns) were linked to the Wiccan festival Samhain (McCoy, 1996, p.52). Suggestions for music to represent sun imagery at Midsummer Solstice included *Morning has Broken, Here comes the Sun* and *You are the sunshine of my* life (ibid. p.171).

An article entitled 'Music for the Elements' (Green, 1970, p.23) details suitable music for each of the elements as follows:

Earth	-	*Hall of the Mountain King*	Grieg
		Symphony no. 1 op. 1	Shostakovitch
Water	-	*Fingal's Cave*	Mendelssohn
		Theme from *The Last Rhapsody*	Wreford
Air	-	*Pas de deux The Nutcracker Suite*	Tchaikovsky
		The *Classical* Symphony	Prokofiev

Fire	-	*The Magic Fire Music* from	Wagner
		Die Walkure	
		Act III prelude from *Lohengrin*	

The New Age composer Chris Gosselin also provided a list including the elements as well as the sun and moon (Gosselin, 1998, pp.5-6):

Sun	-	*Also Spracht Zarathustra*	Strauss
		Daphnis and Chloe (Dawn section)	Ravel
Moon	-	*Ys: Renaissance of the Celtic Harp*	Stivell
		Clair de Lune	Debussy
		Gymnopédies or *Gnossiennes*	Satie
Air	-	*The Lark Ascending*	Vaughan Williams
		Birth of Liquid Pleiades: Zeit	Tangerine Dream
Fire or Earth		*Rite of Spring* ('different bits')	Stravinsky
Water	-	*Danse Sacrée et Danse Profane*	Debussy

Interesting though these choices may be, one might speculate how much the titles influence their association with the elements concerned and how much the music actually conjures up thoughts or feelings about the elements. If the titles were unknown would a listener associate, for instance, *The Hall of the Mountain King* with earth and *The Magic Fire Music* with fire? *Also Spracht Zarathustra* might well be associated with space or the element of air since it was used effectively in the film *2001 Space Odyssey*.

It was clear from the answers received in the questionnaires that recorded music is used as mood-enhancing material before indoor rituals and as support and sometimes an integral part of the rituals themselves. Afterwards it tends to be used as background sound and is therefore of less importance. One informant told me:

> "As part of our rituals I create pathworkings that use music to set the scene/change the mood etc. The music must be chosen well to enhance the pathworking and not detract from it. Sometimes I put the word/pathworking to the music and sometimes vice versa. The length of a recorded piece of music is important in ritual too."

Several replies provided lists of music that were used in meetings and in many cases titles of composers and titles were given. Generally the recorded music that was used was not necessarily the same as which might be listened to in everyday life except when private meditation or other individual pagan activities were happening. There were several different types of music presented which might be categorised as follows:

- Classical
- Folk
- New Age
- Rock and Pop
- Miscellaneous or unknown

Twenty-eight per cent of the replies wrote of classical music being used at some parts of the meetings. The works mentioned in the questionnaires were mainly taken from the better-known repertoire of popular composers. For instance, J. S. Bach's *Toccata and fugue in D minor* and (surprisingly considering the Christian nature of the work) *Jesu joy of man's desiring* were both mentioned and Beethoven's *Moonlight Sonata* and *Pastoral* Symphony were both cited. Handel's *Water Music* was quoted in connection with the element of water. This rather misses the actual meaning of the title that was applied to the music because it was played at a procession along the Thames and did not seek to represent water. The *Seasons* by Vivaldi was mentioned once as being used as background music at the appropriate time of the year. The *Planets Suite* by Holst was listed five times and *Mars* once specifically. The planets' named associations with gods and goddesses as well as their further links in the music with emotions – Venus with love, Jupiter with jollity, etc - were cited as the music's reason for inclusion at pagan gatherings, sometimes humorously:

> "She - and hence we - sometimes use specific pieces of Holst's Planet Suite when we are doing invocations to relevant gods. Sometimes this blows back in my face, as in when she didn't know that Uranus in Holst's book was not only the magician but in astrological terms is the ruler of unexpected collapses. The result she wanted was only partially achieved. She also invoked Mercury via the music to bring wealth for a mutual friend. She seemed to forget that Mercury is also the trickster god: literally at the moment that the ceremony finished and I said, 'The temple is now closed', my trousers (from which I had taken my

belt to hold my robe together) fell down to my ankles. I kid you not."

Mozart's music was only mentioned twice - the *Requiem* and one unspecified work. This relative lack of popularity may be arguably explained by the fact that his works with pagan ideas are not well known and many people find difficulty in listening to opera because of its length and use of foreign languages. Some of Mozart's pagan themes are to be found in works such as *The Magic Flute*, with pagan and Masonic rituals, and *Bastien und Bastienne* that contains magic spells and a leading role for the village cunning-man.

Four different groups/individuals quoted *Carmina Burana* (1937) by Carl Orff and the section on spring was also written about. The texts originated from thirteenth century manuscripts in Latin and medieval German from which the composer selected poems the contents of which celebrate spring and nature; wine and drinking; love and lovemaking. The work is popular in many different western cultures not only for its pagan concepts but also through the use of powerful harmony and orchestration to drive these points home. Wagner was the only other popular composer to be mentioned several times. His music was always used in connection with Odinic tradition rites where pagan gods and goddesses were being praised: "As an Odinist, I prefer Wagner, *The Ring*, *The Ride of the Valkyries* and *The Entrance of the Gods into Valhalla*." A case has been made (Tessa P.,1973) that Wagner's music is particularly appropriate for pagan use since it contains so many references to nature throughout the operas – the Rhine, the flames of Valhalla, Mother Earth (Erda in *Siegfried)*, etc. A few works by other composers were referred to, including *From the New World* Symphony (Dvorak), *In the Hall of the Mountain King* (Grieg) and *The Rite of Spring* (Stravinsky) and there were unspecified works by Reich, Glass, Sibelius and Hildegard von Bingen listed. Other classical themes were illustrated with such descriptions as "early church choral music", "classical music", "Gregorian chants" (mentioned several times), and "medieval music". *Summer is icumen in*, *Now is the month of Maying* and the *Music from Richard III* by the *York Waits* were named.

Most of the choices seem to reflect personal enjoyment or mood enhancement qualities regardless of the absence or presence of pagan characteristics.

Obviously with large-scale works the whole piece would not be played (for instance, *The Ring* cycle takes more than twelve hours to complete) and the music was edited accordingly in some instances. One respondent wrote: "...I have a habit of chopping up classical music to get the bits which work, and drop the others - I know its sacrilege to the music!" An interesting observation is the pagan use of overtly Christian music in rites - something that one cannot imagine being reciprocated intentionally. Gregorian chant was popular and Hildegard von Bingen's music was mentioned twice: "...using Hildegard von Bingen in a pathworking. I don't think it matters that this is christian [sic], music is music and after all the Virgin is the Goddess in another form." The calming effects of plainsong (often referred to as Gregorian Chant) have been written about at length (for instance Le Mée, 1994 and Goldman, 1996). It is generally not disputed that the effect of listening to or performing such chants slows the pulse and allows the brain waves to enter a slower mode of operation. Some pagans insist that this further enhances communication with elementals, spirits, or the Gods and Goddesses.

One viewpoint was that there is very little religious music being written currently:

> "...I have noticed that there is pathetically little good religious music of any sort - pagan - Christian or whatever - being written these days. John Tavener, yes, for the Christians: Harrison Birtwhistle, occasionally for pagans: Duruflé, Satie, Debussy, Tippett, somewhat in the past..."
>
> (Gosselin, 1998, p.5)

This may not be altogether surprising because of the decline in belief in orthodox religion and the huge commercial interest in popular as opposed to classical music. It would seem from the information received that pagans use classical music in their meetings for a combination of reasons which include feeling that appropriate titles suggest appropriate music, mood enhancing qualities and, above all, personal taste. Only one reply spoke of not using classical music because of its "snooty" connotations with concert halls and the opera.

Defining 'folk' music precisely is a difficult task. The term folk music is generally used to describe music of an oral tradition performed by amateurs to distinguish it from the classical or commercial music of a particular country or culture. This definition, however, makes it only relevant to cultures that have a classical, art music tradition, such as Europe and North America, and other countries tend not to recognise the distinction. The influence of western music around the world, and in particular western popular music, has produced differences with the traditional music of many countries and this non-western music has been categorised as world music. In Europe at the end of the nineteenth century there was a resurgence of interest in folk music. This may have been because of a fear that it might be lost to posterity in the face of increasing urbanisation. There was also a wider interest in music of other cultures, which led to the establishment of the new discipline of ethnomusicology. A popular view suggests that folk music is always the genuine music of a nation but when one discusses folk music with references to the people there is a generally-held belief that these are of the less educated sections of society. However, the music is often connected to the nation as a whole. Because folk music is often modal, it resisted assimilation into the well-established formulas of major-minor tonality and thereby challenged composers to adopt unusual harmonies. When folk music was exploited for nationalistic purposes it was often only heard by so-called educated people and not the population as a whole. In England, the efforts of Cecil Sharp and Ralph Vaughan Williams continued this work into the twentieth century. Their work was not without controversy since it encouraged an interpretation of folk music as being totally rural and from mainly South West England. It encouraged the concept of 'Merrie England' in an idealised village setting (Boyes, 1993, p.63 passim). In the twentieth century ardent nationalist composers like the Hungarian Bela Bartok and Zoltan Kodaly also sought authentic national musical elements by recording and transcribing folk music throughout the countryside. R. J. Stewart comments:

> "Folk songs and music retain the roots of primitive magic and religion…The theory suggests that certain basic *images* found in traditional poetry, and certain musical phrases linked inseparably with the songs, are those common to Celtic and pre-Celtic worship, later absorbed by Christian development…The songs should never be separated from their music, or their true effect and meaning is shattered."

> (Stewart, 1988, p.2)

He even provides a possible origin of plainsong from ancient folk songs:

> "One might begin to suspect that some of these [folk] songs *are* liturgical chants or ritual music, no matter how corrupt or altered the form. The similarity discovered is *not* with the hymn-singing or congregational music of the present day or even recent centuries, but with much earlier forms. It cannot be seriously argued that folksong is derived from the influence of early Church music. There is, however, a mass of evidence that plainsong modes were naturally developed from the types of scale and song used by the common people"

(ibid. p.18).

Traditional folk music has received investigation of its pagan associations which has been approved of by pagans generally:

> "There are two broad categories of pagan material in traditional song. The first is obviously ritual material found in songs connected with folk-dramas and seasonal ceremonies, songs that portray a clear ritual action such as *The Cutty Wren* and various May songs. Secondly, there are many 'ancient' ballads, which use established mythological images either directly or indirectly in their plots. Additionally, there is subsidiary action and superstition which runs through a far wider body of songs, such as herb-lore, popular superstition regarding death and haunting, the influence of Other-worldly beings on humans, and general material related to luck, love, and death, which lives on un-noticed in traditional plots.
>
> These basic images are timeless in that they exist out of historical time or context or religion and cult, and are 'true' in two ways. Firstly, they represent ingredients of human consciousness related directly to men and women living with each other and with their fellow creatures in their native environment. Secondly, they act as cosmic symbols, or representations of apparent natural laws, which were

eventually realised to exist through and beyond individual
awareness and to be part of the basic pattern of existence"

(ibid. p.44).

Further complications arise in terminology since categorising
is always an artificial and difficult exercise in this field. So-called
'New Age' music often incorporates folk music into its own modes
and practices but with a greater emphasis on 'high-technological'
music (Blake, 1997, p. 88). I have decided, with some trepidation, to
classify music as 'folk' when it follows the majority of the following
characteristics:

- It is described as such by its performers or composers.
- It is largely unaccompanied.
- It does not rely on synthesisers and special effects to any great
  extent.
- It refers to mythical or ancient traditions.
- It possesses nationalistic traits.

There are obvious problems in using these guidelines since some
performers could truly be included in more than one category. I
have included Clannad and Loreena McKennitt in this section as
folk performers since they seemed out of place in any other section
and because of their Celtic influences being more an extension of,
for instance, the 1960s Irish duo 'Tir Na Nog' rather than the Celtic
influences to be heard in Elgar or Bax. Thirty-eight per cent of
the questionnaires cited recorded folk music being used in pagan
gatherings. Countries mentioned included North America (Native
American chants), Afro-Caribbean, Egypt (belly-dancing and 'zaar'
instrumental music for energy raising), Capoeira (Brazilian martial-art
dance music), Irish traditional, Finnish and unspecified 'World Music'.
Morris dancing music was only referred to in one reply, however this
may be explained by its need for prior practice whereas most dancing
in rituals would appear to be fairly spontaneous and of a circle or spiral
nature:

"Magic involves the use of energy and a change in
consciousness. In a Wiccan circle, the first step is usually
for the group to perform a circle dance and chant in order

to release etheric energy or *raise the power*...Dance is one
of the eight ways of raising magical power..."

(Crowley, 1996, p.82)

This viewpoint was confirmed in several replies, for instance:
"Music, particularly when linked with dance/movement, provides
a very powerful working tool to assist with Craft work. It has the
power to provide both an individual and collective stimulus to those
present."

The music of the British group Steeleye Span was popular and
their arrangement of *John Barleycorn* was often used at the harvest
festival of Lughnasadh: "Where this is the time of the main grain
harvest, the God is in his guise as John Barleycorn, the Grain God"
(Tuitéan and Daniels, 1999, p.59). The words of the song are typical
of fertility myths and it can also double as a rowdy drinking song.
The voice of the lead female vocalist for many years (Maddy Prior)
had a strength and timbre that was very different from the polished
sounds of classical singers. When specific tracks were mentioned in
the replies they were usually taken from Steeleye Span's earlier albums
(for instance, *Below the Salt*). Maddy Prior was also cited in her own
right with her recording of *The Raven* being used by one group for their
Samhain ritual. Other groups and individual performers were listed
only occasionally, which implies that personal taste was responsible
for the choice. (For instance, Donovan, Fairport Convention, the
Chieftains and the Waterboys received isolated mentions.) A magical
quality is believed to be present in the Fairport Convention song *Come
all you rolling minstrels,* the aim of which is to "rouse the spirit of the
earth and move the rolling sky...An eerie traditional, shape-shifting
ballad..." (Gale, 1997). What was even more surprising was the
absence of any reference to the British folk group Pentangle since their
"name and logo inevitably conjure up pagan associations, although this
element was only infrequently demonstrated in their work...but the
'Pents' were, in reality, positively pagan" (John Renbourn) (ibid.). One
can only guess as to why this came about other than speculating that
their appearance on the folk music scene was prior to the expansion of
pagan-orientated music. In short, they were too early!

Celtic literature contains many references to music in a "spiritual
or supernatural Dimension" and there are many descriptions of its
"powerful effect on the listener". It is portrayed as "one of the most

potent forces of the Celtic imagination" (Ralls-MacLeod, 2000, p.1-2). Celtic music was mentioned five times in the questionnaires and Celtic performers such as McKennitt, Enya and Clannad a further four, nine and thirteen times respectively. Almost half of music users favoured what could be described as 'Neo-Celtic' music. This is very much in accordance with what might be described as the 'Celtic revival':

> "The Celts have undoubtedly made a comeback. The renewed interest in and honouring of the Celts among pagans is part of a broader social trend, in which Celts have re-emerged as noble savages."
>
> (Bowman, 2000, p.250)

This is explored further by Magliocco and Tannen:

> "The prevalence of Celtic music is just one part of the predominance of Celtic cultural elements...Instead, it is likely that early Witchcraft revivalists, among them Gerald B. Gardner, grafted the names of Celtic deities onto an existing practice during the 1930's,...in order to bring it into syntony with Margaret Murray's interpretation of medieval Scottish witchcraft as based on pre-Christian religion... they were the first victims of British colonial expansion. They were romanticised by early folklorists as the 'noble savages' of Europe, and in fact were often compared with Native Americans by 19th century ethnologists."
>
> (Magliocco and Tannen, 1998, p.196)

A romanticised view of Celtic culture and music, about which very little is known, promotes the idea that the world was a better place to live in during those halcyon days and this is reflected in the use of modern pseudo-Celtic music. There are further issues to be mentioned before discussing the music itself. The use of Clannad's music for the television series *Robin of Sherwood* linked it with a pagan theme from antiquity - living at one with nature and outside of conventional society. The facts that Clannad traditionally dress in black and perform in dark or misty settings might be seen as resonating well with the association of Wicca with nocturnal mysteries. They have given several of their albums and songs pagan-friendly titles such as *The Magical Ring* and *The Fairy Queen*. The tendency for Irish folk music to be a prominent folk musical genre within the UK might also enhance its reputation. The music is melodic and often uses modal passages and harmonies as opposed to the classical tradition of diatonic-based major and minor scales. Apart from extensive use of reverberation in the recordings and performances, synthesised effects are kept to a minimum. The instrumentation has an acoustic 'feel' to it that is achieved by careful mixing and editing of the instruments played. These include the harp, guitar, mandolin, flute, recorder, whistle etc. In an interview about the group the lead female vocalist Máire Brennan spoke about people talking about "…the etherial [sic] sound and your haunting voice". She continues:

> "Our music would be leaning towards the spiritual side of the aura of it. I'd say it's very earthy, where we get our sounds. Maybe it's because Donegal having such valleys and cliffs and mountains and everything. I really do think that Donegal has an awful lot to do with the sound we get."

(Brennan, 1995)

It is perhaps ironic considering pagans wish to "harm none" that Clannad's "leap to fame" was with the background music to *Harry's Game* (1982), a film about subterfuge and violence in Northern Ireland. However, the music's 'haunting' sound, using Brennan's clear voice without vibrato and the close harmony of the rest of the group, intangibly takes the listener beyond the film's violence and emphasises the pathos of the situation. The Scottish group Capercaille was mentioned once (*Waiting for the Wheel to turn*) and the music of Enya was also popular. One reply quoted Clannad and Enya recordings being used despite the group avoiding music with lyrics in their rituals: "And we avoid vocals, unless they're Enya/Clannad type vocals that 'sound instrumentalish' and moodyambient." Loreena McKennitt's music seemed to have a quality that was particularly in harmony with pagan concepts and her music was mentioned four times in the survey and many times in conversation with non-pagans about the music they like. She describes the music herself as "eclectic Celtic" in her company's publicity material (*Quinlan Road*) and certainly her early material is strongly influenced by Neo-Celtic ideas. It is understandable from the titles of some of the tracks on her albums alone why pagans find her work attractive. These include *The Seasons* (from *To Drive the Cold Winter Away*), *Samhain Night, Standing Stones* and *Huron 'Beltane' Fire Dance* (from *Parallel Dreams*), *All Souls Night* and *The Old Ways* (from *The Visit*). Her video releases include a series of three films devoted to "women's spirituality, goddess worship, and the environment" (publicity flyer) issues that are of importance to most pagans. One of these ('The Burning Times') provides a potted history of witchcraft that is attractive to pagans because it embodies many of their own views of the witch trials. However, her publicity officer stressed, in private conversation, that she does not hold pagan beliefs as such and wishes her music to appeal to all people whatever their convictions. McKennitt's music appeals to a wide range of people following different religions but pagans can certainly be included amongst her most enthusiastic followers.

Folk music is popular within pagan and Wiccan rituals and meetings. It is used for its nature-based and seasonal words as well as to give an authentic 'feel' to proceedings, i.e. to lend support to the notion of an ancient tradition being continued. In reality the actual oral tradition is almost extinct and therefore the information received is somewhat distorted. Stewart has commented: "The main body of songs from the people are no earlier than the nineteenth, though some are traceable to the previous century either directly or through oral metamorphosis" (Stewart, 1988, p.57). Most of the music referred to in the questionnaire replies was composed during the last thirty years by such groups as Clannad and is therefore very much part of a Neo-Folk or Neo-Celtic repertoire.

In *The Triumph of the Moon,* Ronald Hutton discusses whether pagan witchcraft is an integral part of the New Age movement. He mentions their differing beginnings in the USA and Britain, respectively, and other contrasts but reminds us that the two movements "have some points of similarity and overlap" including the importance of personal development and self-expression. Pagans use New Age music where it enhances their rituals and the often seamless, minimalistic effects of such music can help in the altered states of consciousness that are sometimes desired. Furthermore, the New Age movement's inclusion of music from different traditions such as Native American Indian encourages a broadening of listening that is not necessarily found in other types of music. One searches in vain for a precise definition of New Age music that can be agreed upon by a majority of composers, listeners and critics (Werkhoven 1998). In *The Secret Power of Music* David Tame (1984) is somewhat dismissive of such music but without expanding upon of what it actually consists.

> "Does it impel us to awaken to the challenges of the hour in the world at large, as, directly or indirectly, any genuine New Age music must? Not when it is an impulsive chaos of jazz. Not when it is over-electronic and divorced from human feelings. Not when, as it so often is, it is a synthetic mist of psychedelic miasma"

(p.126).

Watson and Drury devote a chapter to such music which they describe as being based "on the idea that we can create music to alter our moods and expand our levels of awareness" (Watson and Drury, 1987, p.79). They trace its origin to the late 1960s and claim its origins to come from "cosmic rock music, Indian ragas, meditative folk music…". It is also affirmed that currently the music has become more "mellow" since it is often used for meditation and relaxation. The problem with these ideas is that New Age music has changed considerably over the last fifteen years and has branched out to include many more nature-based sounds and concepts. Ethnomusicological research and commercial marketing has brought the music of distant lands within reach of European understanding and performance. A possible origin of the term 'New Age' is provided by Kay Gardner (1997) suggesting its first appearance in the 1968 musical *Hair*. She elaborates on the music's content:

> "…extremely broad ranges of musical styles and forms within this new category - jazz, folk, compositional, improvisational, ethnic, fusion, and various combinations of styles. Even breaking new age music down into two parts, calling the electronic music 'space music' and the acoustic music 'Earth music', doesn't express its variety. It is the *intent* of this music which ties together the category's diverse styles, the intention of expressing the concerns of the new age - spirituality, communication among all ethnic

groups, and the celebration of Earth and all Her living beings."

(Gardner, 1997, p.208)

The composers and performers of current New Age music tend to be of a younger generation, born after 1960, with a skilled knowledge of the technical effects that modern sound equipment can provide them. Many of them also possess a high degree of artistry in vocal and instrumental techniques and possess knowledge of medieval material and music of other cultures. The music reflects their own belief system that are often pagan or nature-based and exotic mythological subjects are often chosen for musical interpretation. Carolyn Hillyer and Nigel Shaw are particularly forthright in this respect believing that nature (in their case specifically Dartmoor in Devon) directly influences their music in a spiritual way. New Age music, in contrast to most other types of music, has also been said to have healing qualities in other than purely therapeutic ways. The work of Peter Guy Manners, Steve Halpern and others make various claims for its efficacy. Halpern believes his music is "an anti-frantic alternative to the noise pollution and stress-producing music". However, this has been disputed by a leading music therapist stating that "...the vast majority of New Age music healing philosophy is fatally flawed by the oversimplification of complex psychological, physiological, acoustical, and musical phenomena" (Summer and Summer, 1996, p.9).

Unspecified New Age music was claimed to be used by individuals and groups in twenty-three per cent of the questionnaires returned but this figure is increased to forty-three per cent if specified New Age performers are included such as Philip Thornton, Medwyn Goodall and Lisa Gerrard. New Age music received a higher number of representations than any other type of music and a selection of these will therefore be scrutinised in more detail when composers were mentioned by more than one group or individual. These included:

- Dead Can Dance
- Lisa Gerrard
- Enigma
- Mediaeval Baebes
- Medwyn Goodall
- Chris Gosselin

- Carolyn Hillyer and Nigel Shaw
- Gabrielle Roth
- Philip Thornton

Dead Can Dance consists of two musicians Brendan Perry and Lisa Gerrard. They named their first album, released in 1984, *Dead Can Dance*. The official web site informs one:

> "The album artwork, a ritual mask from New Guinea, attempted to provide a visual reinterpretation of the meaning of the name 'Dead an Dance'. The mask, though once a living part of a tree is dead; nevertheless it has, through the artistry of its maker, been imbued with a life force of its own. To understand why we chose the name, think of the transformation of inanimacy to animacy... Think of the processes concerning life from death into live [sic]..."

(www.dcdwithin.com)

Lisa Gerrard was the lead female singer and joint leader of the group (together with Brendan Perry) as well as performing as a solo musician. The pair joined forces in the early 1980s and produced eight recordings with other musicians before moving apart in the late 1990s to pursue solo careers. Gerrard released a successful album in 1995 (*Mirror Pool*) and won an award in 2001 for her music (with Hans Zimmer) to the epic film *Gladiator*. Tracks from their recordings have been given evocative titles such as *Chant of the Paladin* (from *The Serpent's Egg*) and *The Wind that Shakes the Barley* (from *Into the Labyrinth*). This helps to focus a listener's mind prior to hearing the music. According to Perry, the music is born of "a love for natural, primitive music of the world, and a love of very natural sounding things..." (press kit). This frequent pagan evocation of the power of the natural world and of a spiritual link with remote, pre-Christian ancestors resonates well with pagans and the music is very suitable for both raising energy and enhancing meditation. Despite making substantial use of synthesised sounds, the music displays a remarkable range of different influences, notably from medieval music and ethnic music of the Middle East, Africa, Australasia and South America. Numerous reproduction medieval and Renaissance instruments are used as well as traditional instruments from many other countries. Gerrard's voice combines exceptional technical skill with a clarity and strength that is reminiscent of the best of Middle Eastern chanting. The music can be deeply moving (*Song of the Sibyl* from *Aion*); immensely exciting (*Saltarello* from *Aion*); or mentally stimulating (*How Fortunate the Man with None* from *Into the Labyrinth*). Although the group and Gerrard only received six mentions in the replies to the questionnaires, it has come to my notice that their music is often used at gatherings but without people being aware of the performers or titles used. At a recent well-attended Cambridge pagan moot, everyone asked stressed the spiritual quality of the music to the film *Gladiator* but nobody knew who had composed the music to it. It is therefore possible to speculate that the music of Dead Can Dance is used in pagan gatherings more than the total number of mentions indicated in the forms circulated.

Enigma (Greek for 'mystery') was the brainchild of Michael Cretu who was later joined by his wife Sandra who provides the vocals. The 'project' was started in late 1990 when Cretu "wanted to make music that he liked himself and return to the mysticism" (http://www.enigma-archives.org.uk). The first album, *MCMXC a. D.,* features Gregorian chants, flowing strings, flutes and female vocals. The words highlight the conflict between the Church and sexuality. One track, *Principles of Lust* incorporates the musings of the infamous Marquis de Sade whereas another, *The Voice & the Snake*, is based on the book of *Revelation* from the Bible. The album *Cross of Changes* is based on numerology and contains pictures in the accompanying booklet of witchcraft symbols and the Hindu god Shiva. *Le roi est mort, Vive le Roi* makes use of Mongolian vocals and instrumentals and most recently, *The Screen behind the Mirror* (2000), incorporates the opening section (*O fortuna*) from *Carmina Burana* by Carl Orff. In *Silent Warrior* he takes a stand against the forced colonisation of Native American Indians and in *The Dream of the Dolphin* he pursues shamanic ideas. Although none of the four replies from the questionnaires specified which albums or tracks were listened to, it is clear that Enigma's combination of spirituality and sexuality; awareness of environmental issues; and use of a wide range of instruments and synthesised effects, explains the appeal to a pagan audience manifested in responses to the questionnaires.

The Mediaeval Baebes were formed in 1996 when a medieval music enthusiast, Dorothy Carter, inspired Katherine Blake, a professional singer with the group Miranda Sex Garden, with her performance on medieval instruments. Blake founded a number of singers who were interested in forming a twelve-strong all girl group who would perform medieval music in a modern way and make use of their allure and charm in the process. The result was the release of a very successful album, *Salva Nos,* followed by *Worldes Blysse* and extensive tours in 1997. At the *Pagan Federation* Conference in 1998 they reported: "There was a great feeling and a good energy there. We felt we were more appreciated, but there was a concern about some of the Christian-based songs. Having said that, when we sing about Mary, we know we are really singing about the Goddess" (Randall, 2000, p.17). Their third album, *Undrentide,* released in 2000 extended their medieval material by including such songs as the *Maypole Song* from the film *The Wicker Man.* The music is mainly composed by the director, making use of medieval idioms, and the words are often adapted from original sources that are indicated in the sleeve notes. Instrumentation is for effect rather than authenticity – guitars, saxophones, rhythm samplers, synthesised effects and 'pieces of metal' are all used according to the tastes of the arrangers. In conversation pagans have mentioned that overall they quite like their music but would not use it in rituals because it is too obtrusive and the rock music element in some of the arrangements would not be suitable. The sleeve notes confirm this somewhat: "…Mediaeval Baebes have played in such diverse venues as castles and S & M clubs, as well as some of the biggest rock festivals in the world including Glastonbury and Lilith Fair."

Medwyn Goodall's twenty-four albums have sold over a million copies and *Earth Healer* was voted the best *New World* album of 1992. Although he claims on a web site (http:www.gardenofbadthings.co./ medwyn.htm) that the guitar is his main instrument, this is not apparent from the recordings that sound entirely synthesiser-based. He admits to possessing many samplers that can reproduce electronically virtually any instrument desired. His music was named eight times in the replies to the questionnaires, which comprised the highest number of mentions of any individual composer in the survey. On six occasions the albums were unspecified and the remaining times examples included *Druid* (twice), *Excalibur* (twice), *Merlin* and *Feet in the Soil.* However, no one wrote about the music in anything but general terms, for instance: "Medwyn Goodall for summer use." The titles of his works are certainly appropriate to pagan interests (for example, *Pagan Dawn, Moon Goddess*, etc.) and this may be a part reason for their popularity.

The music itself is bland and repetitive and its unobtrusive quality might be found to be particularly useful where background sound is required that does not disturb the function of a ritual.

Chris Gosselin has produced a number of privately-distributed compact discs and tapes. He defined his music as "New Age crossed with classical" and claimed that his music holds "magickal energy within it...and might even mean that it is effective". He cited Bachoven's *Myth, Religion and Mother Right* in paraphrase as conveying similar beliefs to his own about music:

> "Human language is too limited to deploy the concepts that can be employed in the magic-working state. Music awakens intimations: speech is better at explaining. Music plucks all the strings of the human spirit at once: speech is compelled to take one thought at a time. Music strikes roots into the depths of the soul; language skims over the surface of the understanding like a soft breeze. Music aims inwards, language outward. Music can combine the most disparate elements into a single impression. Language deals in successive particulars: it expresses bit by bit what must be brought home to the soul at a single glance if it is to affect us profoundly. Words make the infinite finite, music carries the spirit beyond the finite world of becoming into the realm of infinite being."
>
> (Gosselin, 1998, p.6)

His music displays its classical influences with traditional, mainly concordant harmony and a full orchestral sound created on a synthesiser. An occasional direct quote can be heard from standard repertoire, for instance, a few bars of *In the Hall of the Mountain King* (Grieg) make an appearance and one of the main chants sung was used in Elizabethan times as a drinking round. In some ways Gosselin's work personifies the English tradition of amateur music without any derogatory implications of the term.

Carolyn Hillyer and Nigel Shaw can be linked together since they work as married partners but often publish under separate names. The extent of their popularity can be seen in the number of recordings that they have produced and that in conversation about pagan music their names are often mentioned. At the Conference of 'Music and Song in Contemporary and New Age Religion' held at the Open University in May 2001, their music was cited by two of the speakers as being particularly appropriate for use in pagan ceremonies. Shaw is described as:

> "...a composer, musician and flute maker...Originally a keyboard player, Nigel has developed his work into a unique combination of electronic technology, sound recordings gathered from nature, and a broad range of ancient instruments including wooden and clay flutes, traditional whistles, drums and percussion."

Hillyer is described as:

> "...a musician, a composer of strong beautiful songs and raw inspiring chants...She is an artist, a painter of goddess images of deep-woman archetypes, of sacred landscape in the human form. She is a writer, with an unusual perspective on woman's mystery."

> (Publicity flyer)

At an interview they granted me at their farmhouse in Dartmoor on April 17th 2001, they provided further information about themselves. Shaw previously worked as a music producer and keyboard player in London and Hillyer was a successful cartoonist and illustrator working for a US company. They came together to combine their talents about ten years before. Their inspiration for this stemmed from Dartmoor itself and the surrounding area. Hillyer initially felt the need to paint the landscape and Shaw to produce music inspired by it. As they began to feel at one with the scenery, their artistic talents intermingled, with Hillyer producing songs in addition to her paintings and Shaw carving wooden sculptures as well as making his own flutes.

Musical influences on their work have come from a variety of sources including Classical and medieval music, folk and traditional songs and dance music. Specific influences have been Lisa Gerrard and Brendan Perry (Dead Can Dance) and the Icelandic popular singer Björk. Shaw mentioned a dislike for opera that is shared by many of his pagan contemporaries! Hillyer explained that the words she uses often "emerge from the paintings" and are not consciously worked out - a sort of "sound language" that conveys ideas and emotions without demanding explicit images. (She jokingly mentioned that on a tour in Estonia the audience thought the words resembled their own language but that they couldn't understand it!) Although they tend to work together, when one name appears on an album then that person has had the major input. The expressed intention of the music is to stir ancient memories, to allow performers and listeners to share a mystical journey together and enter an altered state of consciousness. They informed me their goal was to continue to develop both musically and artistically and to be able to maintain their current relatively peaceful lifestyle. They disapproved of my categorising their work as New Age but could not provide a suitable alternative for retail display. They have released twenty-four albums to date (2004) (two of which they have now deleted) including *Songs of the Forgotten People*, *Echoes of the Ancient Forest*, *Requiem: Well of Souls* and *Riven Inside*.

Songs of the Forgotten People (compact disc number SWMCD09) was produced jointly in 1996. Hillyer has produced a series of eight life size paintings that are intrinsic to the music. Publicity details inform one that: "This work explores our indigenous pre-Celtic ancestry, describing a circle of life and of season; ancient foremothers of flesh and of spirit who walked through this land, creating our oldest, deepest Woman Mystery." This applies to the paintings rather than the album itself. The instrumentation includes a variety of flutes and whistles, percussion, synthesised keyboard and Hillyer's voice, which is sometimes double or triple-tracked to achieve descants or harmony. Some special effects are used, namely sounds from nature and bird songs. The textures here tend to be simple and reinforced with a typical instrumentation of sustained synthesised sound as a background punctuated by flutes and drums. Some of the tracks remind one of Native American Indian music (for instance *Lau Hê Kehpê* and *Lau Hê Duhtan*). Hillyer's voice is clear and effective in this context, typically using an alto or mezzo soprano register. Her use of vibrato is minimal, allowing the clarity and richness of her voice to be heard. She uses unobtrusive ornamentation on some of the notes to enhance their emotional appeal. She sings in English and also uses the 'made-up' language. The music is mainly modal, favouring the Aeolian and Dorian modes, but sometimes omitting the sixth note of the mode to disguise its tonality. *Lau Hê Raumi* is a good example of Hillyer and Shaw's style of composing and performing. The synthesised keyboard produces a harp-like accompaniment with sustained bass notes. Flutes and percussion are added by Shaw whilst

Hillyer sings a melody in three parts using triple tracking. Repetition is used to produce an almost mantra-like effect. The album takes one on a journey through the conjunction of the circle of life and the seasons, concepts very dear to the heart of pagans.

Echoes of the Ancient Forest (compact disc number SWMCD10) was composed jointly in 1996 and consists of four tracks: *Willow*, *Birch*, *Oak* and *Holly*. In the sleeve notes, each of the trees is described in poetic ways that the music seeks to compliment and enhance. The music is fairly similar throughout all the tracks with various blends of different flutes, synthesised string sounds, wordless chanting, jingling and bell-like percussive sounds, and "natural recordings of forest sounds and birdsong from surviving ancient woodland on Dartmoor". The pulse is very slow, even dreamy, throughout and the harmony remains mainly in a minor tonality. The music is different from the other albums in so far as it does not draw so much attention to itself and, in this respect, it was mentioned in some questionnaires as being very appropriate for ritual usage. Indeed, one witch admitted to receiving his second-degree initiation with this album as the background music. He, and the rest of his coven, believed that the music provided a calm and ambient background allowing full concentration on the rite being undertaken whilst simultaneously enhancing the feeling of being at one with Nature.

Riven Inside (compact disc number SWMCD12) was composed jointly in 2000 and is intended as the first part of a two CD compilation - the other part being *Riven Outside*. The publicity material explains that this album "encompasses much of the softer dynamic of their music, ranging from Nigel's delicate flute pieces to Carolyn's graceful and shadowy songs through to the strong tribal acoustic rhythms and unusual chants..." The instrumentation is similar to the other albums but extra musicians are employed for some of the pieces. Acknowledgements are made for using the traditional Irish melodies *The Lonesome Boatman* and *Spring Blessing*; the sixteenth-century English ballad *The Three Ravens*; and a fourteenth century Italian *Trotto-Satterello* [sic]. There are three instrumental tracks (5, 11 and 14) that are subdued and gentle, the latter using synthesised sounds of the sea together with soaring flute melodies. One of the most successful tracks (*Be Wary of Lovers who Come from the Greenwood*) starts atmospherically with flutes, synthesised harps and jingling bells. A lyrical melody is sung over this that eventually leads into a lively trotto (medieval dance) played on synthesised violin with flutes, drums and percussion - very rousing. The dulcimer is also used for a lively accompaniment in the oriental sounding *The Mead Bench*. However, the most noteworthy tracks are the vocal orientated items. Hillyer uses her voice in a variety of ways to acquire quite different sounds. For instance, in track 10 (*The Ragged Megs*) she produces a fast patter-song style which includes whispering and a voice-over effect, whereas in track 8 (*The Wisdom of You*) she uses a stark declamatory style to obtain a dramatic outcome. She sings the beautiful melody of track 13 (*Winter Blessing*) using a clear voice but enhanced with an individual breathing technique that adds considerably to the attractiveness of the song. By exhaling audibly on certain words, she achieves a style of legato that adds considerably to the texture of the music, notably in this track but also elsewhere. The music uses modern techniques and effects but is nevertheless devoted to maintaining a focus upon nature-based and earth-based issues. Using ambient background sounds together with Shaw's considerable ability on a wide variety of flutes and, possibly above all, Hillyer's clear, evocative voice, they have produced a sound that has very clear appeal to many pagans.

Gabrielle Roth's music was mentioned five times in the replies to the questionnaires but with none of the pieces identified. Her accompanying group The Mirrors, that she refers to as a "dance/theatre/music company", was not named in any of the correspondences. Typically the use of her music was not specified and statements like "we use Gabrielle Roth's music" were common. Her music is built on percussion and rhythm as its main focus and she says it seeks to give the listener the feelings that a shaman might feel in a trance state. Roth has released eleven albums which include *Zone Unknown* ("dance your heart out and your ass off into the zone") and *Refuge* (ravenrec@panix.com).

Philip Thornton's music was referred to six times in the questionnaires. On two occasions the music was unspecified but four albums were named: *Eternal Egypt, Pharaoh, Fire Queen* and *Shaman*. The first two albums were felt to be particularly useful during an 'Egyptian' ritual. The publicity material states:

"Two of the world's most highly acclaimed musicians [Hossam Ramzy and Phil Thornton] have joined souls to create a tremendously majestic album that evokes all the splendour of this ancient land. Exotic, stirring rhythms interweave with visionary music to provide an outstanding, hypnotic, and wholly captivating recording."

Thornton has released twelve albums which, in addition to the fore-mentioned, include *Initiation*, *Solstice* and *Sorcerer*. His music makes considerable use of the synthesiser to achieve the effects required which are particularly atmospheric in his 'Egyptian' works. Some of the sounds can become repetitive when similar synthesised instrumentation is used.

A broad spectrum of music has been discovered that might be called New Age. It includes vocal music, acoustic instrumentals, natural sounds and notably synthesised effects. It uses ancient modes and Western key structures as well as Eastern instruments and techniques. When words are used they draw attention to ancient and mythological concepts as well as 'Nature' as a vital focus within such music. The music is used to prepare for ritual, to block extraneous sounds or to enhance altered states of mind. To aid the latter, the music is often repetitive and trance inducing. The quality of the music varies quite considerably from the banal to the inspiring and this will probably remain so as commercial interests attract an increasingly large number of professional and far from professional musicians to produce recordings for a similarly increasing audience.

It has been stated before that rock and pop music will not be investigated in any depth because of its connection with the commercial and entertainment industry that seems to militate against its inclusion in pagan and Wiccan rites. This situation is further exacerbated by the connection between Satanism and rock music. The Rolling Stones' song *Sympathy for the Devil* may have been influenced by the film maker Kenneth Anger, a Church of Satan member, who went on to make the film *Lucifer Rising* starring Marianne Faithfull as Lilith. The occult and Dennis Wheatley-style Satanism was continued in the music and stage shows of Led Zeppelin and Black Sabbath. In 1970, the group Black Widow launched a stage show described as a Satanic rock opera complete with a naked girl as the altar. Even in the 1990s some Scandinavian rock music has been associated with racism, arson, murder and Satanism. The one possible exception to this heavy metal and satanic link is the group Inkubus Sukkubus which was formed in 1989. The original musicians Tony McCormack and Candia found that the words they were setting had a strong pagan bias. They are both Wiccans and share pagans' feelings of tolerance towards other religions and people. They have admitted themselves that not all their songs are overtly pagan and that their followers are also numbered from the 'goth' movement as well as paganism. Albums have included *Belladonna and Aconite*, *Wytches* and *Heartbeat of the Earth* (Johnson, 1995).

Pop and rock music received fewer mentions than any of the other types of music listed. It would have been incredible if the Beatles had not been included in the replies, bearing in mind their huge popularity over such a relatively long period. However, they only received two mentions and both for the same track *Here Comes the Sun*, in connection with the arrival of the Sun God in ritual. As large numbers of young people began to enter paganism only in the 1970s, it is possible that popular music before then would not have therefore featured in pagan or Wiccan ritual. Other groups, such as Inkubus Sukkubus, Runestones and Druidspear were named as being overtly pagan. The Black Sabbath track *My name is Lucifer* was mentioned as having a somewhat different use: "The Black Sabbath tape works really well if you are doing an outdoor ritual, and straight people walk by nosing at what you are doing - they tend to leg it when they hear that!" I would maintain that pagans enjoy pop and rock music as much as anyone else but it would seem from the answers received to the questionnaires that they do not tend to use it as part of their rituals.

Sometimes respondents either did not know the title of the music or who the composer was. This provided me with a list of sometimes intriguingly named pieces but with no other information available from the respondents. It required a certain amount of detective work to discover further details. Into this category I placed the following: *Purple Electric Violin Concerto*, *Chaco Canyon Rusty Crutcher*, Oingo Boingo, Putumayo: *Best of the World*, and Sungura: *Echoes of Africa*. Several respondents referred to "natural" sounds and listed tapes of bird song and sounds of the sea as useful in their rites and Tibetan bowls and Buddhist music was mentioned. Magliocco and Tannen make useful comments about pagan music in their article that my own research bears out:

"What is Pagan music?...Songs and lyrics that reach inside you and touch the inner depths of your soul...allows us to touch our past, hear some of the beauty heard by our ancestors...Music was ever an essential element in ancient worship...Pagans are inspired by songs from mainstream sources: pop, classical, and traditional and popular folk music."

(Magliocco and Tannen, 1998, pp.177-8)

I would expand this description to include instrumental music, both acoustic and electronic, that serves inspirational or practical purposes.

The question was asked what the reasons were for the choice of music. The most common reason cited was that the music should support or enhance the ritual. A typical answer was: "To provide a supportive and complimentary backdrop to a ritual, or it may be an intrinsic part of the ritual." Some of the replies were quite precise about what they used during the rituals and why they used the chosen pieces:

"During the ritual the purpose of our music is to raise energy so most of the time we're chanting. We like to fall back on chants we know, so we can focus on the sound/ harmony/ counterpoint and energy rather than trying to learn new words. Our favourites are:
'We all come from the Goddess, and to her we shall return...'
'Everything she touches she changes...'
'I circle around, circle around, the boundaries of the earth...' "

Another common purpose of the music was to provide "atmosphere" or "mood" enhancement:

Mood/Mind Set: "The music I choose sets the scene for my work. It tends to be instrumental to avoid the distraction of words, with a heavy rhythmic beat for ritual and soothing 'pleasing' music before and after. I vary music prior to ritual, but tend to stick to the same music during ritual. The variation is purely according to my mood."

It was believed that music would help raise energy levels that would contribute to greater empowerment and facilitate stronger magic, probably during an altered state of consciousness. With the mind suitably relaxed its focus on such activities as path working and meditation would be enhanced. More mundane reasons for the use of music also included its use to block out external noises and also simply for fun or celebration after "coven work". Some respondents stated that their choice was dependent on nothing more than simply liking a type of music. Almost half the replies stressed that the season was an important factor in the choice of music. The amount of detail provided varied from simple statements such as "seasons followed" to pieces being suggested for specific seasons: "Music at the main festivals usually follows a seasonal theme; e.g. *John Barleycorn* for Lugnassadh, or *Drinking Down the Moon* (Steeleye Span) for Beltane." Another reply stated that all the songs used were seasonally based:

> "They vary according to the season for the most part. All of our songs are seasonally based, though there are a few songs, which can be sung during any season. For the opening ritual we start with one of the 'all-season songs', and then the subsequent songs are seasonal."

In addition to the seasons being important was the nature of the event or ritual itself. For instance, moon rituals, handfastings and other rites of passage were all mentioned as requiring different types of music:

> "The music…is frequently improvised…the majority is acustic [sic] based…our musicians will try to provide music based entertainment to suit the seasons or particular events i.e. happy music for a handfasting and sad music for a return to the Summerlands [a realm visited after physical death], etc."

> "We choose different types of music for ritual, meditation, pathworking, etc. according to what we have found works best. There are certain pieces/types of music we associate with different festivals."

Practicalities of the choices and their duration were also mentioned especially whether the rites were indoors or out; robed or skyclad (naked):

"The length of a recorded piece of music is important in ritual too. To this end we now have a hi-fi that takes 2 tapes and 3 CDs allowing 4-5 hours of music to be used without 'faffing about in the dark'. (A remote control helps too.) With live music I feel simple instruments like drums and shakers are best as other instruments such as guitars are rather cumbersome in the circle and feel a bit strange to play when working skyclad."

Several replies also drew attention to the importance of the people present in influencing the choice of music according to their "fluctuating tastes" as well as, with live music, their level of competence in performing. Overall it would seem that pagans give considerable thought to the music chosen at their gatherings and they seem to combine the hope for stimulation of the mind with appropriateness to the seasons and events and practicalities of performance.

A question asked what effects either the group or individuals believed music had upon them at their meetings and covens. The effects of music on living organisms have been studied in numerous books on the psychology of music and can be tested by using computerised electronic apparatus, (including Critchley and Henson, 1977). Ralls-MacLeod states concisely that "...many cultures have believed music to have a profound effect on humans...from Pythagoras to the Romantics, music was perceived to have a role which far surpassed its modern status as mere 'entertainment' or art form" (Ralls-MacLeod, 2000, p.3). Mentions of "altered states of consciousness", "trance inducement", "meditation" and accessing the right-brain (questionably thought to contain the psychic and emotional side of the human character) were encountered in many of the replies and this is clearly an important part of the pagan ritual that music is thought to benefit. One reply said: "...during the ritual power raising can induce a trance effect or affect the psyche of the individual; can open doorways and bond us with the ancestors. I feel that, whilst music is not essential, in many cases it enhances the ritual." Music was stated as being "very important" for the making of magic and spell-casting. Several of the replies commented upon this and even more alluded to "energy" being released and enhanced by music within a ritual. People spoke of their pathworking being considerably enhanced by its use and even gave music direct healing powers:

> "...a final use for music has been for healing. A group of folks build a 'tone cone' and focus on an individual in the middle. In other words, everyone sings a vowel and varies the tone and the vowel improvisationally. The blend shifts and takes form, usually specific to the intent of the group."

Some replies went further in stating that music was "indispensable" for the ritual and that more music was needed for the pagan tradition to progress. It was said to be an "integral" part of the ceremony and only when it is absent is the void it leaves noticed.

Music was also quoted as having a binding effect on the group as a whole and others felt it focussed the mind of the individual. For instance, one high priestess commented: "It [music] serves to unite the people present plus it gives a single focus for everyone present." This unifying effect was also extended to spirits and other entities variously referred to as "gods", "ancestor", etc. Spirit contact was said to be enhanced by the use of music and it was also said to be "a gift from the gods" and a "gift for the gods".

The role of music in ritual was also given rather more mundane characteristics. Several people said what mattered was their own personal taste as to how they felt at that specific time and stated that the emotional content of music was of prime importance to them. Allied to this, in some ways, were the feelings that a calm and relaxed situation should be sought in most rituals which music could help achieve. It had an obvious role to play as the accompaniment to dance and, as mentioned before, as a very practical blocking device for the external sounds of traffic and neighbour's hi-fi systems.

Physiological effects were mentioned by respondents in both this section of the questionnaire as well as the following 'paranormal' part. One reply expanded quite considerably on the effects music produced in their rituals:

> "Having been physiologically affected when something has 'gone wrong' with beat etc., and having seen various

results on others, I am highly aware of problems that may occur - therefore, we take all possible precautions to prevent mishaps - and to monitor the responses of individuals/ groups when using music and magic/sound ...one person to my knowledge ended up with a heart problem due to a catch in the cassette while she was with another group. The heart had settled into the rhythm - then the glitch and it gave her heart a jolt...she now has a weakness there. I've been almost shot through plate glass windows when my WP [Working Priest] stopped drumming once (he was most impressed)...It feels like those effects you see on tv when someone shoots backwards when they've been hit with a rifle shot. It physically pulls you back - and you can feel it in the solar plexus...Also a case of 2nd degree burns with a lad that went so far into trance that he burned himself against a radiator...It can be used as hypnosis - and with the same anaesthetic effect."

None of the replies drew attention to the 'placebo effect' whereby the music might be having outcomes on people because they believe it will produce certain consequences (Gouk, 2000). In Egyptian rituals that I have attended, some people present have believed that they have been 'taken over' by various Egyptian deities. The music used has added considerably to this belief. In the examples I have witnessed the music was *Eternal Egypt* by Philip Thornton.

Because of the care that was taken in choosing the music, especially if it had words, it was usually appropriate to the occasion. One reply felt that when the music was removed "the experience was quite different to normal":

"When at times one doesn't use music its place in ritual can really be felt - the old not knowing what you've got till it's gone. E.g. at Samhain for a few minutes we enter total darkness and silence when all the candles are extinguished - you really notice when the music stops and starts again. We've also done whole circles in silence, with no words or music, to see what it was like. The experience was quite different to normal esbats. And in hermetic circles too, we

didn't always use music which can be quite strange if one
is not used to it."

Thus, the effect of music may be said to be mainly beneficial to
pagan gatherings for a number of reasons including its capability to
alter states of consciousness, relax and focus the mind, and conceal
background noises.

One question asked whether any paranormal effects were witnessed
in pagan and Wiccan gatherings. Most people believed altered states of
consciousness were perfectly normal and even though they mentioned
them in this section they commented that the music often helped
them to achieve these states to quite high degrees. A few people did
not answer the question at all and a further twenty-five denied any
such activity happened in their rituals, but twenty-four answered
affirmatively. Several people did not, and in some examples would
not, give details concerning their paranormal experiences. However,
several others provided information and the power of music to heal
was remarked on in an almost 'matter-of-fact' manner: "We once had
a powerful healing effect on a previous choir member who was quite
sick." Another reply expanded on this example: "We have also used
music in healing and have found that different notes and sounds are
'experienced' in different parts of the body/charkas."

Cyril Scott, the composer and writer on occult matters, believed that
music would also be used to heal diseases directly and this was also
mentioned by some of the informants: "Before very long music will be
used in a specific manner to heal diseases through special combinations
of sounds…At present, the majority of composers are working entirely
in the dark and are even unaware that their music produces any occult
effects at all…" (Scott, 1935, p.159). The alleged ability of music
to physically move matter, other than through the agency of direct
vibration, has been discussed in various parapsychological sources
(Playfair and Hill, 1978). It was therefore interesting to have this
brought to my notice in a reply concerning the power of the *Awen*
(Druid empowering chant):

> "The sound produced can be used to augment a person's
> physical strength and spiritual power. For instance, a
> stone circle was raised by the power of the AWEN. Stones

weighing more than we should have been able to lift were set in place while chanting."

Several mentioned spirits, ghosts, the 'Watchers', ancestors, etc. contacted them during rituals: "The single drumming can cause disturbance in the surrounding air. At times when I have been at a low I have had a visitation from my dead sister or father." Another reply spoke of "possession": "Yes...astral projection/out of body experiences/meditative feelings...also esp. Loreena McKennitt - *The Visit* which has invoked experience of "possession type" visit by spirit." The connection with spirit contact was also linked with spell-work in one reply: "I do believe it has helped me in my spell-work predominantly with fire and has produced out of body and trance-like states, and to invoke spirits." Another reply spoke of music helping a clairvoyant gift and a self-styled shaman claimed that his astral journeys using drumming were normal for him, but perhaps paranormal for most people. Other replies that linked activity with paranormal manifestations may have had natural or coincidental causes. For instance, one person found the cat was particularly alert when music was being used in a ritual and another believed that as she chanted a spell her neighbour's distracting music stopped. A possible instance of communion with nature was detailed: "I have found the vocal music to be effective in connecting me to animals/birds (real ones). It has led me to discover wells hidden in woods." The contemporary literature is insubstantial for music's place in paranormal situations although some information can be found (Rogo, 1970; *NAD 2*, 1972, Willin, 1999, and Tame, 1984). It is almost totally absent for its place in current pagan and Wiccan rituals but it is hinted at by Magliocco and Tannen:

> "...Then the lights were dimmed and a woman began to sing the traditional ballad *Tam Lin*. The crowd quieted down immediately and began to prepare for the ritual. The combination of the darkness and the a cappella performance created a sense of separation from the ordinary world; because the song itself concerns enchantments and transformations, it created an expectation of the magical and transformative nature of what was to follow..."

> (Magliocco and Tannen, 1998, p.180)

Other sources intriguingly mention the magical qualities of music, but without expansion, for instance:

> "...But for many people interested in magic and religion, the chief significance of sound is mystical...The effect of music on the emotions is so mysterious as to seem magical...it can release powers of the mind of which many people are unaware."
>
> (Parker and Parker, 1992, p.51)

The final inquiry on the questionnaire allowed respondents to add anything that they wanted to bring attention to concerning their use of music. Several people stressed how important dance was to them, with an obvious need for accompanying music. Some of the statements consisted of just a few words: "One of the important parts of ritual is to take part in the great dance." Another raised a practical issue: "To save my neighbour's eardrums I have a set of headphones that work by short wave radio. They allow me to dance and move around unhindered." Others expanded at length:

> "Also when I was working through the Bardic grade, I would put on her [Gabrielle Roth] music which is very rhythmic and driven by various sorts of drums, and dance each element through her five rhythms. For example, I would dance the flow of earth, the staccato of earth, the chaos of earth, the lyricalness [sic] of earth, and finally to the stillness of earth..."

> "I also often get imagery as I do dance improvs to music, especially if I open myself to doing so - that when I dance with an intent to understand something, receive information about something, seek healing etc..."

Conclusion

A wide variety of music is used by pagans and witches throughout their meetings and rituals. The most popular category of recorded music would seem to be what is generally called New Age but folk and classical music is also played. The Neo-Celtic music of Clannad, Loreena McKennitt, etc., is also enjoyed. Rock and pop music is only rarely used for rituals, but it is occasionally listened to before and after ceremonies. Jazz and avant-garde music of any category is almost totally absent from such gatherings. The music tends to have either titles or words that are favourable to pagan concepts. Accordingly, themes from nature, the cosmos, mythology, magic, mystery and the occult are popular. The New Age and folk titles and tracks make particular use of these attributes. One coven sent me a cassette tape of the music the members use at their meetings. The composers are unknown but the titles alone are representative of the themes encountered in music throughout the religion. These included: *Burning Times, Lady Moonlight, Jack in the Green, Ring out the Solstice Bells, Twelve Witches, Songs from the Wood, Return of Pan, Herne, Hooded Pan, Ancient Forest, Woodlands of England* and *Mother Earth*.

The lyrics to such songs can also refer to pagan subjects, for instance *The Cutty Wren* contains symbolism which is closely allied to "mythological, religious and mystical modes of thought" and further pagan connections can be found in the folksongs *The Two Brothers, Edward* and *The Padstow May Song* (Stewart, 1988, p.18). Hillyer's *Winter Blessing* contains lyrics which express deep feelings about nature (*Riven Inside* SWMCD12). The significance of the words in pagan songs are further explored in Magliocco and Tannen and although their examples are taken from questionnaires distributed in the USA there are similar images referred to, namely nature and earth-based concerns, magical elements, astrology, Eastern mysticism and mythology.

Classical music is not generally listened to for its lyrics by pagans. A few exceptions of choral pieces mentioned, for instance, *Carmina Burana* and Duruflé's Requiem, were chosen more because of the music than the lyrics. The classical works that contain specific pagan or Wiccan orientated words were not mentioned in any of the questionnaires. The music to be used in rituals was thought to be 'special' and whether it was live or recorded, classical, New Age or from whatever category, it had a special part to play.

Music is sometimes only really appreciated when it is taken away, whereupon its absence is really felt. Music was also chosen because of the quality of its sound and the effects it had on the assembled people or individuals. Its trance and altered states of consciousness inducing qualities were often stressed and, to this end, rhythmically repetitive instrumental music was popular. It was often described as New Age or composers from that category were selected. Music was selected for its power to relax, to heal, to raise energy, as a mood setting aid before rituals and to provide fun and enjoyment in the post-ritual social gathering. It was particularly necessary as the background to dance. It was believed by some pagans to encourage easier contact with the gods and goddesses or their own spirituality. In a few instances it was believed that music could help summon spirits and ghosts from supernatural realms, but a somewhat more mundane use was its ability to block out external sounds or extraneous noises such as traffic or noisy neighbours.

It was interesting to note that although pagans do not tend to condemn mainstream popular music, neither do they particularly listen to it. There are several possible reasons for this. Pagans are interested in, and in some cases devoted to, issues that effect nature and wo/mankind in its broadest sense. The obvious commerciality of pop music is in opposition to this belief. The music is often aimed at young and impressionable people and it has a 'disposable' quality that titillates briefly but without producing any attempt at deeper insights. It is highly visual and requires appropriate special effects, videos, etc., to be successful. Since pagans are generally more thoughtful they are less likely to be tempted into buying such music by blatant advertising. Being part of a minority religion encourages pagans to seek out music that caters for their own needs, be they practical or spiritual. Pagans frequently draw comparisons from their ancient traditional roots to their contemporary forms of worship – erroneously if one believes Hutton in *The Triumph of the Moon*. It is therefore not surprising that they enjoy medieval and traditional sounding music to enhance this perception and attempt to give credence to their historical tradition.

Ethnic races that are perceived to have deep-rooted traditions, such as the Native American Indians, are also musically represented. Obviously what might be referred to as pagan religions or ways of life - witchcraft, druidism, shamanism, etc. - are included in such works. Pagans often seek to link their traditions with the past, and therefore early music (medieval and renaissance) is popular. Dance music is used for raising energy and literally dancing to. Live music is mainly in the form of chants or percussion, particularly drumming, during rituals and other instruments are only used when suitable performers are available. The words of the chants reflect the nature of the event and may be taken from existing examples or be composed/improvised by the leader of the ceremony. Dance music is usually performed using the same method. Before and especially after the ritual, live music is dependent upon the ability and preferences of the musicians present and is accordingly very varied. There are obvious differences between the recorded music and live music since a greater degree of professionalism and instrumentation is available from the former. However, there are similar characteristics to be found in some of the melodies and harmonies used. In both the live and recorded music presented, discordant harmony is mainly shunned by pagans. There would seem to be a preference for the use of modes together with major/minor tonality. This viewpoint is corroborated by Magliocco and Tannen:

"...most Neo-Pagan tunes are in what could be called the "Dorian/ Aeolian hexatonic" mode, based on the notes D-E-F-G-A-C-D...When Pagans do fill the gap, it is usually with B, rather than Bb, which makes the scale Dorian rather than Aeolian."

(Magliocco and Tannen, 1998, p.182)

This produces music that has an underlying feel of melancholy to it, especially in combination with appropriate tempi and dynamics. Furthermore, Neo-Celtic and much folk music use similar modes and modal harmony. Many of the chants' harmonisations are very plain, often in 4ths and 5ths, suggesting an antique style (the 'organum' of early medieval music) that pre-dates Western key-based tonality. Pagans may find this significant since they often stress the early origin of their religion. The main difficulty of assessing the effect of such harmony within music is the obvious imagery that words or descriptive titles can produce. In some ways the pagan approach to music is similar to that of Christianity. Before a ritual (service) background music is played to set the scene and this will be appropriate to the occasion, e.g. Christmas/Yule or Marriage/Handfasting. After the ritual, similarly appropriate music may well be played and this may even be live and popular (a sing-song at the vicar or pagan priestess' house). However, during the ritual there will tend to be differences since the Christian ceremony will only punctuate the service with hymns, anthems, etc., whereas the pagan equivalent may well have background music throughout the proceedings. It may be used quite specifically at times for raising energy, achieving altered states of consciousness, focusing the mind and dancing to. The variety of music will probably be greater in the pagan event and will certainly not consist of singing hymns to organ accompaniment. The music will share one important attribute with its Christian equivalent. At its best it will raise the soul of the listener or performer to communicate more directly with whichever deity it seeks and gain spiritual nourishment from this.

There are further broad issues that might be mentioned concerning pagans' use of music. Cultural diversity should be considered when discussing the music. Only one reply brought any attention to this mentioning that "Africans would not always relate to European music, etc". Certainly, the vast majority of pagans encountered at conferences, moots and other meetings conform to the description of mainly white and middle class and although in conversation some have described themselves as "working class", no one used the term "upper class". When one informant's name suggested a possible cultural difference (Asian), the music suggested was firmly from the Western tradition. Because of the lack of replies from non-white-British pagans, presumably because of their relative scarcity, it was not possible to discuss their choice of music.

Twenty-three replies provided musical information that it was thought worthwhile to follow up and the people were contacted asking for further clarification, especially concerning their choice of music outside of pagan rituals. Nine replies were received indicating that the wide range of music listened to outside of ceremonies was mainly not used during such events: "I don't use classical music in Wicca, though I listen to some myself." I wanted to discover whether pagans and witches in their ceremonies might use Western music that was intended by the composer to conjure up specific images. I contacted twenty respondents who had previously expressed an interest in my work and had some knowledge of classical music. I sent them a cassette tape of music that I informed them they could keep and they were asked to comment upon the music without knowing the exact nature of the experiment. Further to this I also hoped to discover whether an item that had no pagan associations whatsoever, but used modal harmony throughout, would be thought appropriate for pagan ritual. I limited this experiment to ten extracts of classical music (with one exception) since I had concentrated on such music in the previous essay. The exception was arranged by myself for classical guitar to eliminate the words and it had a classical 'feel' to it. Each item was approximately three minutes in duration and the questions asked of the respondents were:

1. Do you know the name or composer of this piece?
2. Would you use this piece before, during or after a ritual?
3. If during then what types of ritual would it be suitable for?
4. What images does it conjure up for you?
5. Kindly add any additional comments.

The pieces were chosen because I believed they represented concepts which are important to pagans, namely nature, the seasons, religious ritual, etc., and I further hoped that most of the works would not be previously known to the listeners since knowledge of the title would immediately produce images that the music alone may not have provided. The example that had no connection with paganism was the *Fantasia on a Theme by Thomas Tallis* by Vaughan Williams. This was included because of its use of modal harmony throughout. I wanted to discover whether pagans would choose this work even though it has no direct connection to paganism. The works chosen were:

- *Songe d'une nuit du Sabbat* from *Symphonie Fantastique*
  Berlioz
- *Dawn, The Four Sea Interludes* from *Peter Grimmes*
  Britten
- *A Song of Summer*
  Delius
- Opening Prelude to *Akhnaten*
  Glass
- *Koyaanisqatsi*
  Glass
- *Winter Blessing* from *Riven Inside* (arr. for classical guitar)
  Hillyer & Shaw
- *Venus, The Bringer of Peace* from *The Planets*
  Holst
- *The Helios Overture*
  Nielson
- *Fantasia on a theme by Thomas Tallis*
  Vaughan Williams
- *The Magic Fire Music* from *The Valkyrie*
  Wagner

The results were as follows:

Songe d'une nuit du Sabbat from *Symphonie Fantastique*.

According to his own programme notes, this popular movement from Berlioz's *Symphonie Fantastique* represents a witches' sabbath in the sense of an orgiastic, frenzied gathering. It was only recognised by two of the respondents and none felt it suitable for use during a ritual; indeed five people felt the work unsuitable for any part of their meetings. Three felt that it might be used before or after a ritual when a "wild or dark" atmosphere was desired but it was generally found to be unsuitable.

Dawn, The Four Sea Interludes from *Peter Grimmes*

Only one of the respondents recognised this orchestral interlude from Britten's opera about relationships in an English fishing community. As its title implies, it is intended to conjure up pictures of a calm sea at dawn. It was a popular choice for before and during a ritual with several mentions of pathworking being suitable, but no one suggested its use after a ritual and five would not use it at all. Images of the sea were mentioned and even dawn by one respondent who did not know the work. It was felt to produce an "ethereal" feeling of the "otherworld".

A Song of Summer

This gentle orchestral music by the early twentieth century British composer Delius was also only recognised by one person but it was felt by half of the respondents to be appropriate for use during a ceremony and specifically for pathworking. Four people felt it unsuitable for any use and described it as "bland". It produced images of "nature", "summer", "the seasons" and "pastoral scenes" that were felt by two respondents to be useful for relaxation purposes before a ritual.

Opening Prelude to *Akhnaten*

The opera *Akhnaten* by the contemporary American composer Philip Glass takes as its theme scenes from the life of the pharaoh of the title and the music uses a number of minimalist techniques. The opening uses the string section of the orchestra in an ascending repetitive arpeggio figure. Two respondents recognised the composer but nobody knew the work. Opinion was split equally since five felt the music suitable for use during a ritual and the same number refused to use it at all. It was felt appropriate by the former for invocation and one reply associated the music with Epona, a goddess associated with horses.

Koyaanisqatsi

I used the opening music to the film of the same name again with music by Glass. The word comes from the Native American Hopi Indian tribe and can be translated as implying the world is out of balance and in turmoil. It is repeatedly chanted by bass voices with continuous organ arpeggio accompaniment in a resonant environment. Two respondents recognised the music and seven indicated that they would use it during a ritual especially at Samhain or at "dark times". No one felt it suitable for listening to after a ceremony and three people did not like it at all. The prevailing images were those of the "earth", "underground" and monks chanting. The latter is very understandable if the film has not been seen - it starts with Hopi wall paintings in a cave.

Winter Blessing from Riven Inside

I arranged this piece for classical guitar since the original has words that might lead the listener towards the images they presented. The piece is gentle and somewhat sad. Of all the works on the list this item received the fewest total rejections – only two – and it was a popular choice by half the group for during and after a ritual. Beltane and summer was mentioned and three respondents felt it was suitable for handfasting to. Further images of "hillsides" and "woods" were suggested and several people emphasised how much they liked it.

Venus, The Bringer of Peace from The Planets

This orchestral piece was recognised by six respondents and was one of the best known works from the list. Five people felt it suitable for use during ritual during spring, autumn or Eostar and images of "mists" and "streams" were mentioned. It received four complete rejections but most agreed on its atmosphere of "peace" and "beauty" that may, of course, been conditioned into the listeners' minds through knowledge of the title.

The Helios Overture

The Helios Overture by the twentieth century Danish composer Carl Nielson represents the sun rising by using a full symphony orchestra with harmony that is reminiscent of the better known Sibelius. It was not recognised by anyone but six people felt it suitable for use in ritual, notably at esbats and invocations. One reply felt it signified "adoration of the Sun and Greek temples" which is quite remarkable considering he did not recognise the piece. Four replies would not use it and its "floating" sounds were not thought at all suitable for after a ritual.

Fantasia on a theme by Thomas Tallis

I chose this work because it does not have any intrinsic connection with paganism or witchcraft and could more easily be placed within a Christian tradition. Thomas Tallis was famous during the Tudor period for his religious works and Vaughan Williams, the son of an Anglican clergyman, composed many works on Christian themes and edited the *English Hymnal*. However, the work, for string orchestra, is strongly based on modal harmony that is popular with pagans in Celtic music and I wanted to explore whether the music would be acceptable for pagan use. Seven people recognised it - the highest number for any of the items - and five felt it would be suitable for use during rituals of evocation and pathworking. It was also a popular choice for being used to set a solemn atmosphere before a ritual and only two respondents would not use it. Images of "castles" and "the sea at night" were put forward.

The Magic Fire Music from The Valkyrie

The Magic Fire Music is not well known but it is typical of the style of Wagner with a large orchestra and bold harmony. It is meant to conjure up in the listener images of fire since this is its task in the opera. None of the respondents recognised the music and nine felt they would not use it in any part of their meetings. It was referred to as "film music" and the general feeling was summed up by one reply that stated "it did nothing for me".

Only nineteen per cent of the replies recognised the music and twenty-one per cent could name the composer. It was particularly interesting to read comments about the music by individuals who were not aware of the purpose of the music. There were occasional quite specific comments that were appropriate including one mentioned above and another describing *A Song of Summer* as "a summer meadow". However, although most people agreed most of the time with the overall 'feel' of the music, it cannot be claimed that there was a strong consensus of opinion about the specific images produced. The intangible nature of music when combined with people's personal tastes through environment and upbringing almost guarantees that different interpretations will be given to music. There was some agreement concerning the use of music before, during and after rituals. *The Magic Fire Music* by Wagner was particularly unpopular for any use whatsoever. *The Winter Blessing* by Hillyer and Shaw was overall the most popular for use in all three categories and it was the only piece that was thought of as suitable after ritual by half the respondents. Its simple melody and harmony accords well with the lack of flamboyance that many pagans and witches would appear to favour in their ceremonies. The work and therefore the words were not known to any of them, but one mentioned trees, hillsides and nature which was appropriate to the words ("a bare-armed tree..."). However, Beltane and summer were also chosen as suitable times of the year to play the music that is in opposition to the title. There was little disagreement with the suitability of *Koyaanisqatsi* for use at Samhain and several respondents spoke of its "dark power". The equation with monks chanting was understandable and this was not condemned as having Christian connotations. Indeed, it has been found in conversations with witches and pagans that Christian plainsong is often used for its soothing effect in rituals. Any Christian aspects of *The Fantasia on a Theme by Thomas Tallis* were also disregarded since the work was also popular for use before and during ceremonies. This acceptance not only provides evidence of pagans' willingness to appreciate concepts from other religions but also supports the argument that some music has the power to move people whatever their belief system.

I feel that this survey was useful for several reasons. Although dramatic claims of certain musical works having a profound effect on all the respondents cannot be made, it would seem that some of the works succeeded in their composers' aims to represent visual images in musical terms. The more contemplative examples seemed to be chosen more for use during ritual which is a contradiction of the stereotype activity suggested in the *Songe d'une nuit du Sabbat* from *Symphonie Fantastique*. This representation of a witches' sabbath was the only work not to be chosen by anyone as being suitable music for accompanying a ritual. Generally the music was not thought suitable for post ritual activity when socialising is more in order. This was to be expected since none of the pieces fitted the criteria of being "fun and lively". It is clear that the replies were mainly thought out seriously and that the respondents take the choice of music in their ceremonies seriously as an important aspect of their belief system. The actual music that witches prefer, in contrast to the music that is traditionally associated with them (*Night on a bare mountain, Songe d'une nuit du Sabbat,* etc.), is more contemplative, in tune with the cycles of nature and the ritual being celebrated. Its use as an accompaniment to dance, such an important factor in the sensational accounts of witches' sabbaths, is no more important than in any other situation where people are dancing.

This essay set out to explore the use of music in contemporary paganism and witchcraft. The results of the questionnaires provided good evidence that the ritual's leader or the high priest/ess usually chose the music but it had to be compatible with the event and the people present. Live and recorded music was selected according to the availability of suitable performers or the demands of the location, for instance, being overheard by neighbours or outdoor use. It was found that music is mainly believed to be an important aspect of ritual and in different respects it is welcome before and after. Recorded music was mainly used before ritual to set the mood of the event and after it was a part of the social activity. However, during ritual a number of effects were mentioned including its capability to induce altered states of consciousness - anything from mild relaxation to full trance - as well as its power to bind people together.

I divided the music chosen into categories that provided several examples for further discussion. These were classical, folk, New Age, rock and pop, and those that did not easily fit into any of the others. Each of the first three were popular in providing mood enhancement music and a focus for the ritual celebrated; lending support to the authenticity of a tradition; or for personal reasons. Rock and pop music was not used during rituals very often since it was felt to be too distracting, which was also true of other music that had words. Jazz hardly featured at all, which might be caused by its intellectual feel that some might find alien to the sensitivities of pagan worship. The concluding survey allowed pagans to hear music that is traditionally associated with witchcraft or paganism and pass comments about it. They were mainly unaware of the music and therefore chose music as suitable for ritual by its quality and not by title or words - all the pieces were instrumental for this reason. The works selected displayed similar trends to those referred to in the questionnaires. The most popular music was that which might enhance the overall activity of a ritual and allow the participants to enter into the spirit of the event more deeply, probably through music's intangible ability to induce altered states of consciousness. The music favoured in this chapter bore no resemblance to the music that typically accompanies witches' activities in stereotyped traditions.

There is an important issue as to whether an actual tradition of pagan music exists or whether personal taste is the overall contributory factor. Of course, subjectivity enters into every choice one makes, whether it is believed to be objective or otherwise. However, there would appear to be characteristics of music that are generally shared by pagans that are reflected in their personal tastes. Discordant music is unpopular in most categories (classical, folk, etc.) and words are only acceptable when they resonate with pagan concepts. A certain amount of 'conditioning' is encountered with pseudo-Celtic and traditional music, for instance medieval, being popular to lend support to the concept that the religion has a deep-rooted historical lineage. Exotic music from other countries, such as pseudo-Egyptian and Native American, is also favoured, bringing with it mysterious undertones of spirit contact from other realms. The general age range of pagans being beyond their teens may explain the lack of pop commercial music that is encountered. Additionally, one likes to believe that it is a conscientious decision by practitioners of a nature-based religion not to promote the negativity of blatant commerciality.

References

Abel, A. M. 1955: *Talks with Great Composers*. London: Psychic Book Club.

Adler, M. 1997: *Drawing down the Moon*. New York: Arkana.

Aldcroft Jackson, N. 1994: *The Cauldron*, 71, Spring Equinox.

Alder, V. S. 1968: *The Finding of the Third Eye*. London: Rider and Company.

Altom, K. and Braud, W. G. 1976: 'Clairvoyant and telepathic impressions of musical targets', in *Research in Parapsychology*, ed. J. D. Morris, W. G. Roll and R. L. Morris 1975: 171-174. Metuchen, N. J.: Scarecrow Press.

Annals of Psychic Science 1906: London.

Associated Board of the Royal Schools of Music 1958: 'Rudiments and Theory of Music'. London.

Avant, L. 1965: 'Vision in the Ganzfeld', in *Psychological Bulletin*, 64: 245-258.

Ayensu, E. S. and Whitfield, P.1982: *The Rhythms of Life*. London: BCA.

Baines, A. 1992: *The Oxford Companion to Musical Instruments*. Oxford: OUP.

Bardens, D. 1987: *Psychic Animals*. London: R. Hale Ltd.

Baroja, J. C. 1970: 'Basque Witchcraft', in *Man Myth and Magic*, Vol. I. London: Purnell.

Barrett, D. 1996: *Sects, 'Cults' & Alternative Religions*. London: Cassell.

Barton, E. A.: 'Add Music to your Rituals', in *The Lamp of Thoth*. Leeds: The Sorcerer's Apprentice.

Bem, D. J. and Honorton, C. 1994: 'Does psi exist? Replicable evidence for an anomalous process of information transfer', in *Psychological Bulletin*, 115, 1: 4-18.

Berger, A. S. and J. 1991: *The Encyclopaedia of Parapsychology and Psychical Research*. New York: Paragon.

Bertini, M., Lewis, H. and Witkin, H. 1964: 'Some preliminary observations with an experimental procedure for the study of hypnagogic and related phenomena' in *Archivo di Psicologia Neurologia e Psychiatria*, 6: 493-534.

Bessy, M. 1963: *Magic and the Supernatural*. London: Spring Books.

Beth, R. 1990: *Hedgewitch: A Guide to Solitary Witchcraft*. London: Hale.

Bible: The Authorised King James' Version.

Bierman, D. J. 1995: 'The Amsterdam Ganzfeld Series III & IV: Target Clip Emotionality, Effect Sizes & Openness', in *Proceedings of the 38th Parapsychology Convention*.

—— 1997: 'Emotion and Intuition I, II, III, IV, V: Unravelling Variables Contributing to the Presentiment Effect', in *Proceedings of the 40th Parapsychology Convention*.

Bierman, D. J. and Houtkooper, J. 1981: 'The potential observer effect and the mystery of irreproducibility', in *European Journal of Parapsychology*, 3: 345-372.

Blackmore, S. 1987: 'A report of a visit to Carl Sargent's laboratory', in *Journal of the Society for Psychical Research*, 54, (808): 186-198.

—— 1993. *Dying to live*. London: Grafton.

Blake, A. 1997: *The Land Without Music*. Manchester University Press.

Blavatsky, H. P. 1875: 'A word with the singing medium, Mr Jesse Sheppard', in *Boston Spiritual Scientist*, 2, July 8th.

Bord, J. and C. 1990: *Atlas of Magical Britain*. London: Sidgwick & Jackson.

—— 1992: *Modern Mysteries of the World*. London: BCA.

Bostridge, I. 1997: *Witchcraft and its Transformations c.1650-c.1750*. Oxford Clarendon Press.

Bowman, M. 2000: 'Cardiac Celts: Images of the Celts in Paganism', in G. Harvey and C. Hardman, *Pagan Pathways*. London: Thorsons.

Boyes, G. 1993: *The Imagined Village*. Manchester University Press.

Boyling, N. 1968: *Dido and Aeneas*, cited in sleeve notes. Hamburg: Archiv SAPM 198424.

Bozzano, E. 1923: *Phenomenes Psychiques au Moment de la Mort*. Paris.

Brandon, R. 1984: *The Spiritualists*. Prometheus.

—— 1994: *The Life and Many Deaths of Harry Houdini*. London: Mandarin.

Branscombe, P. 1993: 'The Music' by Erik Smith, in *Mozart: Die Zauberflöte*. Cambridge Opera Handbook: CUP.

Braud, W.G. 1975: 'Psi-conducive states', in *Journal of Communication*, 25: 142-152.

Braud, W. G., Wood, R. and Braud, L. W. 1975: 'Free-response GESP performance during an experimental hypnagogic state induced by visual and acoustic ganzfeld techniques: A replication and extension', in *Journal of the American Society for Psychical Research*, 69: 105-114.

Braude, S. E. 1979: *ESP and Psychokinesis*. Philadelphia: Temple University Press.

Brewer's Dictionary of Phrase & Fable 2000: Revised Adrian Room. London Cassell and Company.

Brice, D. 1967: *The Folk Carol of England*. London: Herbert Jenkins.

Briggs, R. 1996: *Witches and Neighbours*. London: HarperCollins.

Britten, E. H. 1870: *The History of Modern American Spiritualism*. New York.

—— 1883: *Nineteenth Century Miracles*. William Britten: Manchester and London.

—— 1900: *Autobiography of E. H. Britten*, ed. Margaret Withinson: Manchester.

Broad, C. D. 1953: *Religion, Philosophy and Psychical Research*. New York: Harcourt, Brace.

Brookesmith, P. 1984: *Incredible Phenomena*. London: BCA.

281

Brooks, J. A. 1990: *Britain's Haunted Heritage*. Norwich: Jarrold Publications.

Broughton, R. 1991: *Parapsychology*. London: Rider.

Brown, A. 2000: *Inside The Wicker Man*. London: Sidgwick and Jackson.

Brown, R. 1971: *Unfinished Symphonies*. London: Souvenir Press.

—— 1974: *Immortals at my elbow*. London: Bachman and Turner.

—— 1977: *Music from Beyond*. Leigh on Sea, Essex: Basil Ramsay.

——1986: *Look Beyond Today*. New York and London: Bantam Press.

Buckland, R. 1999: *Complete Book of Witchcraft*. St. Paul, MN: Llewellyn.

Budd, F. E. 1989: 'English Literature and the Occult', in *A Survey of the Occult*, ed. J. Franklyn. Scotland: Tynron Press.

Burns, R., *The Rigs of Barley*, in *The Poetical Works of Robert Burns*. London: Frederick Warne and Company.

—— *Tam O' Shanter* from *The Poetical Works of Robert Burns*. London: Frederick Warne and Company.

Butler, C. 1636: *The Principles of Musik*. London: John Haviland.

Byron, Lord. 1970: *Manfred* in *Byron's Poetical Works*, ed. F. Page, corrected by J. Jump. 3rd edition Oxford: OUP.

Campbell Holms, A. 1925: *The Facts of Psychic Science and Philosophy*. Keegan Paul.

Carrington, B. and Thresher, M. *The Ghost Book*: St Albans, Herts.

Chan, M. 1979: John Hilton's Manuscript British Library Add. MS 11608. *Music and Letters*, LX: 440-449.

—— 1980: 'The Witch of Endor and Seventeenth-Century Propaganda', in *Musica Disciplina*, ed. Armen Carapetyan, XXXIV: 205-214. American Institute of Musicology: Hänssler-Verlag.

Charlton, D. 1983: 'King Arthur: a Dramatick Opera', in *Music and Letters*, LXIV: 183-192.

Cholij, I. and Price, C. A. 1986: 'Purcell's Bass Sorceress', in *Musical Times*, CXXVII: 615-18.

Clark, S. 1999: *Thinking with Demons*. Oxford: OUP.

Clarke, D. 1995: 'Experience and Other Reasons Given for Belief and Disbelief in Paranormal and Religious Phenomena', in *Journal of the Society for Psychical Research*, 60, (841): 371-384.

Cohn, N. 1957: *The pursuit of the Millenium*. London: Oxford University Press.

Coleman, M. H. 1988: *The Ghosts of the Trianon*. Northamptonshire: Aquarian Press.

Collins, H. M. and Pinch, T. J. 1979: 'The construction of the paranormal', in *Sociological Review Monograph*, 27. Stoke on Trent: Brooks.

Cornell, A. D. 1984: 'Research Report of the Cambridge University Society for Psychical Research', in *Journal of the Society for Psychical Research*, 52, (797).

Critchley, M. and Henson, R. A. 1977: *Music and the Brain*. London: Heinemann.

Crowley, A., *Magick in Theory and Practice* (New York: Castle, 1969).

Crowley, A. 1989: *The Confessions of Aleister Crowley*, ed. J. Symonds and K. Grant London: Arcana Penguin.

Crowley, V. 1996: *Wicca*. London: Thorsons.

Crowther, P. 1981: *Lid off the Cauldron*. London: Muller.

Curnow, L. 1925: 'The Physical Phenomena of Spiritualism', in *Two Worlds Publishing Company*.

Dalton, K. 1994: 'A report on informal ganzfeld trials and a comparison of receiver/ sender sex pairing', in *Proceedings of the 37th Annual Convention of the Parapsychological Association*, August 7-10: Amsterdam.

Dalton, K. 1997: 'Exploring the Links: Creativity and Psi in the Ganzfeld', in *Proceedings of the 40th Annual Convention of the Parapsychological Association*, August 7-10: Brighton.

David Smith, J. 1992: 'The Auditory Hallucinations of Schizophrenia', in *Auditory Imagery*, ed. D. Reisberg. New Jersey: Erlbaum.

Dean, W. 1970: *Handel and the Opera Seria*. Oxford: OUP.

Dearn, G. S. 1977: 'The Renaissance of the Celtic Harp', in *Quest* 30.

Dekker, T., Rowley and Ford 1949: *The Witch of Edmonton*, ed. E. Rhys. London: Benn Ltd.

Delanoy, D. 1987: 'The Reporting of Methodology in ESP Experiments', in *Parapsychology Review*, 18, no. 4.

Dening, J. 1996: *Secret History. The Truth about Richard III and the Princes*. Suffolk: Plantagenet Publishing.

Dent, E. 1965: *Foundations of English Opera*. New York: Da Capo.

—— *Opera*. Middlesex: Penguin Books.

Dingwall, E. J. and Price, H. 1922: *Revelations of a Spirit Medium*. London.

Downes, W. 1992: *The Haunted Colchester Area*. Clacton on Sea, Essex.

—— 1993: *The Ghosts of Borley*. Clacton on Sea. Essex.

Drury, N. and Tillett, G. 1978: *The Occult Source Book*.London: Routledge & Kegan Paul.

Edmunds, I. G. 1978: *The Man who talked with Ghosts*. Nashville: Thomas Nelson.

Edwards, S. 1966: *Spiritualism a critical survey*. Aquarian Press.

Eliot, T. S. 1963: *Collected Poems 1909-1962*. London: Faber and Faber.

Encyclopedia Britannica 1951: Volume 16.

Enigmas Magazine. 1994: Issue November/ December. Letters to the editor.

Evans, C. 1973: 'Parapsychology - what the questionnaire revealed', in *New Scientist*, 25 January..

Evans, H. 1984: *Visions, pparitions and Alien Visitors*. London: BCA.

Eysenck, H. J. and Sargent, C. 1982: *Explaining the Unexplained*. London: Weidenfeld and Nicolson.

Farrar, J. and S. 1984: *A Witches' Bible*. Washington: Phoenix.

Farrar, J. and S. 1990: *Spells and how they work*. London: Hale.

Fiske, R. 1980: *New Grove Dictionary of Music and Musicians*, ed. S. Sadie. Volume I. London: Macmillan.

Flaherty, G. 1992: *Shamanism and the 18th Century*. Oxford: Princeton.

Folklore, Myths and Legends of Britain 1973: London: Reader's Digest.

Forman, J. 1985: *Haunted East Anglia*. Norwich: Jarrold and Sons Ltd.

Fortune, D. 1989: *The Sea Priestess*. Wellingborough: Aquarian.

—— *Moon Magic* 1995: London: SIL Trading Ltd.

Fortune, N. 1959: *King Arthur*. Sleeve notes. Decca Record Company.

Foucault, M. 1993: *Madness and Civilization*. London: Routledge.

Frazer, J. 1994: *The Golden Bough*. London: Chancellor.

Gal, H. 1979: *Schumann's Orchestral Music*. BBC Publications.

Gale, J. 1997: 'The Magic of Folk Rock', in *Talking Stick*, xxv, Autumn: 38-40.

Gardner, G. 1982: *The Meaning of Witchcraft*. New York: Magickal Childe.

Gardner, G. 1999: (Using the pseudonym of 'Scire'.) *High Magic's Aid*. Thame: I-H-O Books.

Gardner, G. 1999: *Witchcraft Today*. Thame: I-H-O Books.

Gardner, K. 1997: *Sounding the Inner Landscape*. Shaftesbury: Element.

Gauld, A. 1968: *The Founders of Psychical Research*. London: Routledge and Kegan Paul.

Gauld, A. 1982: *Mediumship and Survival*. London: Heinemann.

Gauld, A. 1992: *A History of Hypnotism*. Cambridge: Cambridge University Press.

George, R. 1948: 'An ESP experiment with music', in *Parapsychology Bulletin*, 11: 2-3.

Ghiselin, B. 1952: *The Creative Process*. New York: The New American Library.

Godwin, J. 1987: *Music, Mysticism and Magic*. London: Arkana.

Godwin, J. 1987: *Harmonies of Heaven and Earth*. London: Thames and Hudson.

Goethe, J. W. 1967: *Faust. Part One*, transl. P. Wayne. Middlesex: Penguin.

Goldie, M., 1992: 'The earliest notice of Purcell's *Dido and Aeneas*', in *Early Music*, XX no. 3, August: 392-400.

Goldman, J.1996: *Healing Sounds*. Shaftesbury: Element.

Gordon, S. 1992: *The Paranormal*. London: Headline.

Gosselin, C. 1998: 'Esoteric Music', in *Broom Cupboard* 2, issue 3, February: 5-6.

Gouk, P. 2000: *Musical Healing in Cultural Contexts*. Aldershot: Ashgate.

Grahame, K. 1997: *The Wind in the Willows*. London: Folio Society.

Grattan-Guinness, I. 1982: ed. *Psychical Research*. Northamptonshire: Aquarian Press.

—— 1983: 'Coincidences as Spontaneous Psychical Phenomena', in *Journal of the Society for Psychical Research*, 52, (793): 59-71.

Graves, R. 1999: *The White Goddess*. London: Faber.

Green, M. 1970: 'Music for the Elements', in *Quest*, 4 (December): 23.

Green, M. 1991: *A Witch Alone*. Shaftesbury: Element.

Greenwood, S. 2000: *Magic, Witchcraft and the Otherworld*. Oxford: Berg.

Gregory, R. 1987: ed. *The Oxford Companion to the Mind*. Oxford: OUP.

Grimassi, R. 2000: *Encyclopedia of wicca & witchcraft*. Llewellyn: USA.

Guiley, R. E. 1994: *Ghosts and Spirits*. Middlesex: Guinness Publications Ltd.

Guinness Book of Records 1972: ed. McWhirter, N. and McWhirter, R. Middlesex: Guinness Superlatives Limited.

Gurney, E., Myers, F. and Podmore, F. 1886: *Phantasms of the Living*, I. London: Society for Psychical Research.

Habel, M. 1976: 'Psi and varying auditory stimuli in the ganzfeld', in eds. J. D. Morris, W. G. Roll and R. L. Morris *Research in Parapsychology* 1975: 181-184.Metuchen, N. J.: Scarecrow Press.

Haining, P. 1972: *The Anatomy of Witchcraft*. London: Souvenir Press.

—— 1974: *Ghosts*. London: Sidgwick & Jackson Ltd.

Hallam, J. 1975: *Ghosts of London*. London: Wolfe Publishing Ltd.

Halpern, S. 1979: 'Talking sound sense', in *Alpha*. no. 4, September/October. Fleet: Pendulum Publishing.

Haraldsson, E. 1985: 'Representative surveys of psychic phenomena: Iceland, Great Britain, Sweden, USA and Gallup's Multinational Survey', in *Journal of the Society for Psychical Research*, 53, (801): 145-158.

—— 1991: 'Apparitions of the Dead: Analysis of a New Collection of 357 Reports', in *Research in Parapsychology*. Metuchen, N. J.: Scarecrow Press Inc.

Harding, R. E. M. 1967: *The Anatomy of Inspiration*. London: Frank Cass & Co.Ltd.

Hardy, R. & Shaffer, A. 2000: *The Wicker Man*. London: Pan Books.

Harper, C. G. 1994: *Haunted Houses*. London: Studio Editions.

Harries, J. 1974: *The Ghost Hunter's Road Book*. London: Letts & Co.

Harrison, J. 1912: *Themis*. Cambridge: CUP.

Hart's Rules. 1983: Oxford: OUP.

Hartnoll, P. 1966: *Shakespeare in Music*. London: Macmillan.

Harvey, G. 1997: *Listening People, Speaking Earth - Contemporary Paganism* London: Hurst and Company.

Harvey, G. and Hardman, C. 2000: *Pagan Pathways*. London: Thorsons.

Henson, R. A. 1977: *The Language of Music in Music and the Brain*. London: Heinemann.

Herrick, R. 1648: 'The Hag' from *Hesperides: Or, The Works Both Humane & Divine of Robert Herrick Esq. London: Printed for John Williams & Francis Eglesfield 1648.*

Heselton, P. 2000: *Wiccan Roots*. Berks: Capall Bann.

Heywood, R. 1971: 'Notes on Rosemary Brown', in *Journal of the Society for Psychical Research*. 46, (750): 213-217.

Heywood, T. 1882: *The Wise Woman of Hogsdon*, ed. A. Wilson Verity. London: Vizetelly and Company.

Hippisley Coxe, A. D. 1975: *Haunted Britain*. London: Pan Books Ltd.

Holman, P. and Thompson, R. 2001: 'Purcell', in the *New Grove Dictionary of Music and Musicians*, vol. 20, ed. S. Sadie. London: Macmillan Publications Ltd.

Holzer, H., 1974: *The Encyclopedia of Witchcraft and Demonology*. London: Phoebus Publishing Company.

Honorton, C. 1976 a.: 'Length of isolation and degree of arousal as probable factors influencing information retrieval in the ganzfeld', in (eds.) J. D. Morris, W. G. Roll and R. L. Morris *Research in Parapsychology* 1975: 184-186. Metuchen, New Jersey.

—— 1976 b.: *Maimonides Division of Parapsychology and Psychophysics Annual Report*: 1974-1975. Brooklyn, N.Y.: Maimonides Medical Centre.

—— 1977: 'Psi and Internal Attention States', in (ed.) B. B. Wolman *Handbook of Parapsychology*. 435-468. Jefferson, N. C. and London: McFarland & Co. Inc.

—— 1985: 'Meta-analysis of Psi Ganzfeld Research: A Response to Hyman', in *Journal of Parapsychology*, 49: 79-84.

—— et al. 1980: 'Computer psi games: merging of humanistic and laboratory traditions in parapsychology', in *Parapsychology Review*, 11, 2, March/April.

—— et al. 1990: 'Psi communication in the ganzfeld', in *Journal of Parapsychology*, 54: 99-139.

—— Davidson, R. and Bindler, P. 1972: 'Shifts in subjective state associated with feedback-augmented EEG alpha', in *Psychophysiology*, 9: 269-270.

—— Drucker, S. and Hermon, H. 1973: 'Shifts in subjective state and ESP under conditions of partial sensory deprivation', in *Journal of the American Society for Psychical Research*, 67: 191-197.

—— and Harper, S. 1974: 'Psi-mediated imagery and ideation in an experimental procedure for regulating perceptual input', in *Journal of the American Society for Psychical Research*, 68: 156-168.

Hope, M. 1987: *Practical Celtic Magic*. Northampton: Aquarian Press.

Hopkins, A. 1984: *The Concertgoer's Companion*, vol. I. London: Westbridge Books.

Horden, P. 2000: 'Musical Solutions: Past and Present in Music Therapy', in *Music as Medicine. The History of Music Therapy since Antiquity*, ed. Horden, P. Brookfield. USA: Ashgate.

Horder, M. 1981: 'In Her Own Write: A Note On Rosemary Brown', in *Journal of the Society for Psychical Research*, 51, (788): 105-106.

Houdini, H. 1924: *A Magician among the Spirits*. New York.

Howard, K. 2000: 'Shamanism, Music, and the Soul Train', in *Music as Medicine. The History of Music Therapy since Antiquity*, ed. Horden, P. Brookfield. USA: Ashgate.

Hughes, P. 1952: *Witchcraft*. London: Longmans.

Hugin the Bard 2000: *A Bard's Book of Pagan Songs*. St Paul, MN: Llewellyn.

Hutton, R. 1999: 'Modern Pagan Witchcraft', in *The Athlone History of Witchcraft and Magic in Europe* vol. 6, ed. B. Ankarloo and S. Clark. London: The Athlone Press.

Hutton, R. 2000: *The Triumph of the Moon*. Oxford: OUP.

Huxley, A. 1963: *The Doors of Perception and Heaven and Hell*. New York: Harper & Row.

Hyman, R. 1985: 'The Ganzfeld Psi Experiment: A Critical Appraisal', in *Journal of Parapsychology*, 49: 3-43.

——and Honorton, C. 1986: 'A Joint Communique: The Psi Ganzfeld Controversy', in *Journal of Parapsychology*, 50: 351-364.

Indigenous Religious Musics, 2000: ed. K. Ralls-MacLeod and G. Harvey. Aldershot: Ashgate.

Inglis, B. 1985: *The Paranormal*. London: Guild Publishing.

Into the Unknown 1971: New York: Reader's Digest.

Jacobs, A. 1969: 'Some recent trends in opera', in *Twentieth Century Music*, ed. R. Myers. London: Calder and Boyars.

Jahn, R. G., Dunne, B. J. and Nelson, R. D. 1987: 'Engineering Anomalies Research', in *Journal of Scientific Exploration*, 1: 21-50.

Jaynes, J. 1993: *The Origin of Consciousness in the Breakdown of the Bicameral Mind*. London: Penguin Books.

Johnson, K. 1998: *Witchcraft and the Shamanic Journey*. St Paul, MN: Llewellyn.

Johnson, M. 1995: 'Inkubus Sukkubus', in *Pagan Dawn* no. 117, Samhain.

Jones, P. and Pennick, N. 1995: *A History of Pagan Europe*. London: Routledge.

Jones, R. Elfyn 1985: 'Ritual, Myth and Drama', in *Michael Tippett O. M. a Celebration*, ed. G. Lewis. Tunbridge Wells: Baton Press Ltd.

Jordan, M. 2000: *Witches an encyclopedia of paganism and magic*. London: Cathie Kyle.

Keil, H. 1965: 'A GESP test with favourite musical targets', in *Journal of Parapsychology*, 29: 35-44.

Kemp, A. and Sertori, J. 1999: *Practical Paganism*. London: Hale.

Kemp, I. 1984: *Tippett. The Composer and his Music*. London: Eulenberg Books.

Kenner, J. 1973: *Talking to Chopin*. Scanorama. March.

King, F. 1987: *The Magical World of Aleister Crowley*. London: Arrow Books.

—— 1997: *Magic*. London: Thames & Hudson.

Klimo, J. 1987: *Channeling. Investigation on receiving information from paranormal sources*. Los Angeles: Tarcher.

Kobbé, G. 1987: *Kobbé's Complete Opera Book*. London: The Bodley Head.

Kors, A. C. and Peters, E. 2001: *Witchcraft in Europe 400-1700*. Philadelphia: University of Pennsylvania Press.

Kreitler, H. and Kreitler, S. 1972: 'Does extrasensory perception affect psychological Experiments'? *Journal of Parapsychology*, 36: 1-45.

Le Mée, K. 1994: *Chant*. London: Rider.

Legg, R. 1969: *A guide to Dorset Ghosts*. Dorset Publishing Company.

Lehner, E. and Lehner, J. 1971: *Picture Book of Devils, Demons and Witchcraft*. New York: Dover Publications Incorporated.

Leland, C. G. 1974: *Aradia: The Gospel of the Witches*. CW Daniel Company.

Lewsey 1997: *Who's who and What's what in Wagner*. Aldershot: Ashgate.

Luhrmann, T. 1989: *Persuasions of the Witch's Craft*. Oxford: Blackwell Ltd.

Macfarlane, A. 1999: *Witchcraft in Tudor and Stuart England*. London: Routledge.

MacKenzie, A. 1971: *Apparitions and Ghosts*. London: Arthur Barker Limited.

—— 1982: *Hauntings and Apparitions*. London: Heinemann.

MacKinnon, N. 1994: *The British Folk Scene*. Oxford: OUP.

Magliocco, S. and Tannen, H. 1998: 'Introduction', in *The Journal of the Folklore Studies Association of Canada*, 20, 1: 7-17.

Magliocco, S. and Tannen, H. 1998: ''The Real Old-Time Religion'. Towards an Aesthetics of Neo-Pagan Song', in *The Journal of the Folklore Studies Association of Canada*. 20, 1: 175-201.

Man, Myth and Magic 1970: 'Drum'. 2. London: Purnell.

—— 1970: 'The Davenports'. 2. London: Purnell.

—— 1971: 'Night'. 5. London: Purnell.

Mann, W. 1977: *The Operas of Mozart*. London: Cassell.

Maple, E. 1967: *The Realm of Ghosts*. London: Pan Books Ltd.

Marks, D. and Kamman, R. 1980: *The Psychology of the Psychic*. New York: Prometheus Books.

Matthews, R. 1993: *Haunted Edinburgh*. Andover, Hants: Pitkin.

Mauskopf, S. H. 1982: *Psychical Research*, ed. I. Grattan-Guinness. Wellingborough, Northamptonshire: The Aquarian Press.

Mavromatis, A. 1987: *Hypnagogia: The unique state of consciousness between wakefulness and sleep*. London: Routledge and Kegan Paul.

Maxwell-Stuart, P. G. 2001: *Witchcraft in Europe and the New World, 1400-1800* Basingstoke: Palgrave.

McBeath, M. K. 1985: 'Psi and Sexuality', in *Journal of the Society for Psychical Research*, 53, (800): 65-77.

McCoy, E. 1996: *The Sabbats*. St Paul, MN: Llewellyn.

McEwan, G. J. 1989: *Haunted Churches of England*. London: Robert Hale.

McHarg, J. F. 1982: 'The Paranormal and the Recognition of Personal Distress', in *Journal of the Society for Psychical Research*, 51, (790): 201-209.

Mead, R. 1994: *Weekend Haunts*. London: Impact Books Ltd.

Mendez, R. 2001: 'Rock's *Sympathy for the Devil*', in *The Cauldron*. no. 99, February.

Metternich, Princess 1921: *The days that are no more*. London.

Michell, J. and R. J. M. Rickard 1983: *Phenomena*. London: BCA.

Middleton, T. 1994: *The Witch* ed. T. Schafer. London: A & C Black.

Millar, D. 1981: 'Music in the Circle', in *The Cauldron*. no. 22, Beltane.

Milton, J. 1988/ 89: 'A possible 'directive' role of the agent in the ganzfeld', in *European Journal of Parapsychology*, 7, (2-4): 193-214.

—— 1997: 'An Empirical Comparison of the Sensitivity of Direct Hits and ums of Ranks as Outcome Measures for Ganzfeld Studies', in *Proceedings of the Parapsychology Association 40th Annual Convention*, August 7-10, Brighton.

—— and Wiseman, R. 1997: 'Ganzfeld at the crossroads: A meta-analysis of the new generation of studies', in *Proceedings of the Parapsychology Association 40th Annual Convention*, August 7-10, Brighton.

Mitchell, J. V. 1996: *Ghosts of an ancient city*. York: St Peter's School.

Morgan, K. and Morris, R. L. 1992: 'An exploratory investigation into the possible application of anomalous effects on computer systems'. Paper presented at the Sixth International Conference on Systems, Informatics and Cybernetics. Baden-Baden.

Morris, R. L. 1987: 'Spontaneous synchronistic events as seen through a simple communication model', in *Proceedings of Parapsychology Conference in Berkeley, California*. eds. Shapin, B. and Coly, L. New York: Parapsychology Foundation Incorporation.

—— 1998: *Koestler Parapsychology Unit Information Sheet*. University of Edinburgh.

Murray, M. A. 1921: *The Witch-Cult in Western Europe*. Oxford: OUP.

—— 1962: *The God of the Witches*. Hedingham: Daimon Press.

—— 1963: *The Divine King in England*. Oxford University Press Archive, 881053.

Myers, F. W. H. 1903: *Human Personality and its survival of bodily death*. London.

New Grove Dictionary of Music and Musicians 2001: ed. S. Sadie. London: Macmillan Press Ltd.

—— 2001: 'Richard Wagner' articles cited by B. Millington, J. Deathridge and others, vol. 26, 970C-971. London: Macmillan Press Ltd.

New Grove Dictionary of Opera *1992: ed. S. Sadie. London: Macmillan Press Ltd.*

Newman. E. 1972: *Wagner Nights*. London: Putnam and Company.

Nicholas, M. 1994: *Psychics and Mystics*. London: Hamlyn.

Oates, T. 1679: *The Witch of Endor*. London.

Oppenheim, J. 1985: *The Other World*. Cambridge: CUP.

Opera News, New York, Metropolitan Opera Guild, February 17, 1973 and February 28, 1976.

Ornstein, R. E. 1971: 'The techniques of meditation and their implications for modern psychology', in C. Naranjo and R. E. Ornstein, *On the Psychology of Meditation*. New York: Viking Press.

Osis, K. 1983: 'Apparitions Old and New', in *Case studies in Parapsychology*, ed. K. Ramakrishna Rao. N. Carolina and London: McFarland and Company Inc.

Out of this World 1989: London: McDonald and Company.

Owen, A. R. G. 1964: *Can we explain the poltergeist?* New York: Garrett.

Owen, I. R. 1976: *Conjuring up Philip*. New York: Harper and Row.

P. Tessa. 1973: 'Wagner – The Musical Magician', in *Quest*. no. 16, December.

Pagan Dawn 1979: Samhain, London.

Pagan Federation 1996: *Witchcraft Information Pack*. London.

—— 2000: *Information Pack*. London.

—— 2001: What *is Paganism?* London.

Palmer, J. and Aued, I. 1975: 'An ESP test with psychometric objects and the ganzfeld: Negative findings', in eds. J. D. Morris, W. G. Roll and R. L. Morris *Research in Parapsychology*, 1974: 50-53. Metuchen, N. J.: Scarecrow Press.

Palmstierna, E. 1937: *Horizons of Immortality*. Constable.

Panati, C. 1975: *Supersenses*. London: Jonathan Cape.

Parker, A. 1975: 'Some findings relevant to the change in state hypothesis', in eds. J. D. Morris, W. G. Roll and R. L. Morris. *Research in Parapsychology*, 1974: 40-42. Metuchen, N. J.: Scarecrow Press.

—— 1975: 'A pilot study of the influence of experimenter expectancy on ESP scores', in eds. J. D. Morris, W. G. Roll and R. L. Morris. *Research in Parapsychology*. Metuchen, N. J.: Scarecrow Press.

Parker, D. & J. 1992: *The Power of Magic*. London: Beazley.

Parrinder, G. 1958: *Witchcraft*. Middlesex: Penguin Books.

Parrott, I. 1966: *The Music of an 'Adventure'*. London: Regency Press.

—— 1978: *The Music of Rosemary Brown*. London: Regency Press.

Paul, P. 1985: *Some unseen power*. London: Robert Hale.

Payne, J. K. 1995: *A Ghosthunter's Guide to Essex*. Romford: Ian Henry Publications.

Persinger, M. 1989: 'Psi phenomena and temporal lobe activity', in *Research in parapsychology*. 1988. Metuchen, N. J.: Scarecrow Press.

Picknett, L. 1990: *The Encyclopaedia of the Paranormal*. London: Guild Publishing.

Pitcairn, R. 1833: *Criminal Trials in Scotland from A.D. M.CCCC.LXXXVIII to A.D. M.DC.XXIV. I. Part 2*. Edinburgh: Tait.

—— 1833: *Criminal Trials in Scotland from A.D. M.CCCC.LXXXVIII to A.D. M.DC.XXIV. III*. Edinburgh: Tait.

Plank, S. E. 1990: 'And now about the Cauldron Sing: Music and the Supernatural on the Restoration Stage', in *Early Music*, XVIII, August: 392-407.

Playfair, G. L. 1985: *The Haunted Pub Guide*. London: Harrap.

—— and Hill, S. 1978: *The Cycles of Heaven*. London: Souvenir Press.

Poole, K. B. 1995: *Britain's Haunted Heritage*. Leicester: Magna Books.

Price, C. 1986: *Dido and Aeneas an Opera*. Norton Critical Scores. London: W. W. Norton & Company.

Price, H. 1940: *The Most Haunted House in England*. London.

—— 1993: *Poltergeist*. London: Bracken Books.

Prince, W. F. 1963: *Noted witnesses for psychic occurrences*. University Books: New York.

Purkiss, D. 1996: *The Witch in History*. London: Routledge.

Purser, J. 1992: *Scotland's Music*. Edinburgh: Mainstream Publishing Company.

Puttick, B. 1994: *Ghosts of Hertfordshire*. Newbury, Berkshire: Countryside Books.

Radford, K. 1989: *Fireburn*. London: Guild.

Radin, D. I. 1997: *The Conscious Universe*. San Francisco: HarperEdge.

Radin, D. I. and Nelson, R. D. 1989: 'Evidence for consciousness-related anomalies in random physical systems', in *Foundations of Physics*, 19.

Radin, D. I., McAlpine, S. and Cunningham, S. 1994: 'Geomagnetism and Psi in the Ganzfeld', in *Journal of the Society for Psychical Resarch*, 59, (834): 352-363.

Radin, D. I. and Rebman, J. M. 1996: 'Are Phantoms Fact or Fantasy? A Preliminary Investigation of Apparitions Evoked in the Laboratory', in *Journal of the Society for Psychical Research*, 61, (843): 65-87.

Ralls-MacLeod, K. 2000: *Music and the Celtic Otherworld*. Edinburgh: Polygon.

Randi, J. 1995: *The Supernatural A-Z*. London: Headline.

Rhine, J. B. 1934: 'Extra Sensory Perception', in *Journal of Boston Society for Psychical Research*.

Rhine, J. B. and Pratt, J. G. 1948: *Parapsychology*. Oxford: Blackwell.

Rhine, L. E. 1961: *Hidden Channels of the Mind*. New York: Wm. Sloane Assocn.

Robbins, R. H. 1965: *The Encyclopedia of Witchcraft and Demonology*. London: Peter Nevill Limited.

Rogo, D. S. 1970: *NAD*. New York: University Books.

Rogo, D. S. 1972: *NAD 2*. New Jersey: University Books Incorporated.

Rogo, D. S. 1976: 'An exploration of some parameters of psi in ganzfeld', in eds. J. D. Morris, W. G. Roll and R. L. Morris. *Research in Parapsychology*, 1975:174-179. Metuchen, N. J.: Scarecrow Press.

Roney-Dougal, S. M. 1986: 'Subliminal and PSI Perception', in *Journal of the Society for Psychical Research*, 53, (805): 405-434.

—— 1991: *Where Science & Magic Meet*. Shaftesbury: Element.

Roney-Dougal, S. M. and Vogl, G. 1993: 'Some Speculations on the Effect of Geomagnetism on the Pineal Gland', in *Journal of the Society for Psychical Research*, **59**, (830): 1-15.

Rooley, A. 1983: 'New light on John Dowland's songs of darkness', in *Early Music* January: 6-21.

Roper, L. 2002: *Oedipus & the Devil*. London: Routledge.

Rosenthal, H. and Warrack, J. 1979: *The Concise Oxford Dictionary of Opera*. 2nd Edition. Oxford: OUP.

Rouget, G. 1985: *Music and Trance*. Chicago: University of Chicago Press.

St Aubyn, A. and Hanbury, Z. 1996: *Ghostly Encounters*. London: Robson Books.

Salim, V. 1983: *Ghost Hunter's Guide to Sheffield*. Sheaf Publishing Ltd.

Samson, J. 2001: 'Romanticism', in *New Grove Dictionary of Music and Musicians*, vol. 21. Macmillan Publications Ltd.

Sargent, C. 1980: *Exploring Psi in the Ganzfeld*. New York: Parapsychology Foundation.

—— 1987: 'Sceptical fairytales from Bristol', in *Journal of the Society for Psychical Research*, July 54, (808): 208-218.

Scarre, G. and Callow, J. 2001: *Witchcraft and Magic in Sixteenth- and Seventeenth-Century Europe*. Hants: Palgrave.

Schlitz, M. J. and Honorton, C. 1992: 'Ganzfeld Psi Performance within an Artistically Gifted Population', in *Journal of the American Society for Psychical Research*, April 86, no.2.

Schmeidler, G. 1946: *Journal of Experimental Psychology*, 36: 271-276.

—— 1987: 'Psychokinesis: Recent Studies', in *Advances in Parapsychological Research* ed. S. Krippner. Jefferson, N. C. and London: McFarland and Company.

Schmeidler, G. and McConnell, R. A. 1958: *ESP and personality patterns*. London: OUP.

Schoen, M. 1927: *The Effects of Music*. London: Kegan Paul.

Scott, C. 1935: *An outline of Modern Occultism*. London: Routledge.

Scot, R. 1972: *The Discoverie of Witchcraft*. New York: Dover.

Sharpe, E. J. 1970: 'Music', in *Man, Myth and Magic*, vol. 5. London: Purnell.

Sharpe, J. 1996: *Instruments of Darkness. Witchcraft in England 1550-1750*. London: Penguin.

Sheldrake, R. and Smart, P. 1997: 'A Survey in North-West England', in *Journal of the Society for Psychical Research*, 61, (847): 353-364.

Shepard, J. 1870: 'How I became a Musical Medium', *in Medium and Daybreak Journal*. May 6th. London.

Shepard, L. A. 1984: *Encyclopaedia of Occultism and Parapsychology*. Detroit: Gale Research Company.

Shulman, R. 1938: 'An experiment in ESP with sounds as stimuli', in *Journal of Parapsychology*, 2: 322-325.

Sidgwick, E. 1911: *Proceedings of the Society for Psychical Research*, 25: 353-362.

Sidgwick, H. 1894: *Census of Hallucinations*. Society for Psychical Research: London.

Simos, M. a.k.a. Starhawk 1997: *The Pagan Book of Living and Dying*. New York: HarperCollins.

Simpson, J. and Roud, S. 2000: *A Dictionary of English Folklore*. Oxford: OUP.

Skelton, R. 1988: *The practice of witchcraft today*. London: Hale.

Sloboda, J. A. 1994: *The Musical Mind*. Oxford: Clarendon Press.

Smith, M., Tremmel, L. and Honorton, C. 1976: 'A comparison of psi and weak sensory influences on ganzfeld mentation', in eds. J. D. Morris, W. G. Roll and R. L. Morris, *Research in Parapsychology*, 1975: 191-194. Metuchen, N. J.: Scarecrow Press.

Smyth, F. and Stemman, R. 1981: *Mysteries of the Afterlife*. London: BCA.

Smythies, J. R. 1967: Editor *Science and ESP*. London: Routledge & Kegan Paul.

Society for Psychical Research. 1882-3: 'Objects of the Society', in *Proceedings of the Society for Psychical Research*, 1: 3-6.

Spenser, E., *Amoretti and Epithalamion*, 1594: v.19, 342, *Selected Shorter Poems*, ed. D. Brooks-Davies. London: Longman, 1995.

Spencer, J. and A. 1992: *The Encyclopaedia of Ghosts and Spirits*. London: BCA.

Stanford, R. G. 1984: 'Ganzfeld - ESP Research: A Survey and Critical Analysis', in *Advances in Parapsychological Research*. 4. ed. S. Krippner. Jefferson, N. C. and London: McFarland and Company.

—— 1986: 'Toward understanding the role of noise in ganzfeld-ESP research', in *Parapsychology Review*, March-April, 17 (2): 5-8.

—— 1987: 'Ganzfeld and hypnotic-induction procedures in ESP research: Toward understanding their success', in *Advances in Parapsychological Research*, 5. ed. S. Krippner. Jefferson, N. C. and London: McFarland and Company.

Stanford. R. G. and Mayer, B. 1974: 'Relaxation as a psi-conducive state: A replication and exploration of parameters', *in Journal of the American Society for Psychical Research*, 68: 182-191.

Stanford, R. G. and Neylon, A. 1975: 'Experiential factors related to free-response clairvoyance performance in a sensory uniformity setting (ganzfeld)', in eds. J. D. Morris, W. G. Roll and R. L. Morris, *Research in Parapsychology*, 1974: 89-93. Metuchen, N. J.: Scarecrow Press.

Stevens, D. 1980: *Musicology - A Practical Guide*. London: Macdonald.

Stevenson, I. 1975, 1977, 1980, 1983: *Cases of the Reincarnation Type*, I-IV. Charlottesville: University Press of Virginia.

Stewart, R. J. 1988: *Where is Saint George?* London: Blandford Press.

Stokes, D. M. 1987: 'Theoretical Parapsychology', in *Advances in Parapsychological Research*, 5 ed. S. Krippner. Jefferson, N. C. and London: McFarland & Co.

Storr, A. 1992: *Music and the Mind*. London: Harper/ Collins.

Stow, J. *A Survey of London*. 1598: 2nd edn., 1602. Stroud: A. Sutton, 1994.

Sturge-Whiting, J. R.: *The Mystery of Versailles*. London: Rider and Company.

Sturzaker, J.: 'Jazz'. Unspecified article in Museum of Witchcraft, Boscastle.

Summer, L. and J. 1996: *Music. The New Age Elixir*. New York: Prometheus.

Summers, M. 1965: *Witchcraft and Black Magic*. London: Arrow Books.

Suster, G. 1986: *John Dee*. Crucible.

Sutcliffe, S. J. 2003: *Children of the New Age*. London: Routledge.

Sylvestre, R. E. 1901: *Gambols with Ghosts*. Mind reading Spiritualistic effects. Catalogue no.16 no. 152.

Symonds, J. 1970a: *Man Myth and Magic*. 3. London: Purnell.

—— 1970b: *Man Myth and Magic*. 1. London: Purnell.

Tabori, P. and Underwood, P. 1973: *The Ghosts of Borley*. Newton Abbot: David and Charles.

Tame, D. 1984: *The Secret Power of Music*. Northamptonshire: Turnstone Press Ltd.

Tart, C. T. 1969: *Altered staes of consciousness*. New York: J. Wiley & Sons, Inc.

Terry, J. 1976: 'Comparison of stimulus duration in sensory and psi conditions', in eds. J. D. Morris, W. G. Roll and R. L. Morris. *Research in Parapsychology*, 1975: 179-181. Metuchen, N. J.: Scarecrow Press.

Terry, J. and Honorton, C. 1976: 'Psi information retrieval in the ganzfeld: Two confirmatory studies', in *Journal of the American Society for Psychical Research*, 70: 207-217.

Terry, J., Tremmel, L., Kelly, M., Harper, S. and Barker, P. 1976: 'Psi information rate in guessing and receiver optimization', in eds. J. D. Morris, W. G. Roll and R. L. Morris. *Research in Parapsychology*, 1975: 194-198. Metuchen, N. J.

Thomas, K. 1971: *Religion and the decline of magic*. London: Weidenfeld & Nicolson.

Tickill, A. 1993: 'Rattles and Drums in Northern European Traditions', in *Gippeswic*. 6. 14-16.

Till, N. 1992: *Mozart and the Enlightenment*. London: Faber.

Tilmouth, M. 1986: 'Dramatic Music (Locke)', in *Musica Britannica*, LI. London: Stainer and Bell.

Tindall, G. 1967: *A Handbook on Witches*. London: Panther.

Tippett, M. 1959: *Moving into Aquarius*. London: Routledge and Kegan Paul.

Trevor-Roper, H. R. 1984: *The European Witch–Craze of the C16th and C17th* Middlesex: Peregrine.

Truzzi, M. 1987: 'Introduction' to *Advances in Parapsychological Research*. 5. ed. S. Krippner. Jefferson, N. C. and London: McFarland and Company.

Tuitéan, P. and Daniels, E. 1999: *Pocket guide to wicca*. California: Crossing Press.

Tweedale, C. 1940: *News from the Next World*. London: Werner Laurier.

Tyrrell, G. N. M. 1954: *The Personality of Man*. Middlesex: Penguin Books.

Underwood, P. 1971: *Gazeteer of British Ghosts*. London: Souvenir Press.

—— 1983: *Ghosts of Cornwall*. Bossiney Books.

—— 1984: *This Haunted Isle*. London: Harrap.

—— 1988: *The Ghost Hunter's Guide*. London: Javelin.

—— 1993a: *Ghosts and how to see them*. London: BCA.

—— 1993b: *The Ghost Hunter's Almanac*. Kent: Eric Dobby Publishing.

—— 1996: *Ghosts and haunted places*. London: Piatkus.

Valiente, D. 1973: *An ABC of Witchcraft, Past and Present*. London: Robert Hale.

—— 1978: *Witchcraft for Tomorrow*. London: Robert Hale.

—— 1989: *The Rebirth of Witchcraft*. Washington: Phoenix Publishing.

Vasilescu, E. and Vasilescu, E. 1996: 'The Mechanism of Telepathy', in *Journal of the Society for Psychical Research*, 61, (845): 211-220.

Vernon, P. E. 1970: *Creativity*. Middlesex: Penguin Books.

von Reuter, F. 1928: *Psychic experiences of a Musician*. London: Simpkin.

—— 1931: *A Musician talks with unseen friends*. London: Rider and Co.

Walther, E. 1986: 'Telepathy: A testable Hypothesis', in *Journal of the Society for Psychical Research*, 53, (802): 201-209.

Watson, A. and Drury, N. 1987: *Healing Music*. Bridport: Prism Press.

Watson, L. 1998: 'The biology of being: A natural history of consciousness', in *The Spirit of Science*, ed. D. Lorimer. Edinburgh: Floris Books.

Webber Lloyd, J. 1984: *Travels with my 'cello*. London.

Werkhoven, H. N. 1998: *The International Guide to New Age Music*. New York: Billboard Books.

West, D. J. 1954: *Psychical Research Today*. London: Duckworth & Co. Ltd.

—— 1995: 'Note on a recent psychic survey', in *Journal of the Society for Psychical Research*, 60, (838): 168-171.

Wheatley, D. 1960: *The Satanist*. London: Arrow Books.

—— 1973: *The Devil and all his works*. London: Arrow.

White, R. A. 1964: 'A Comparison of Old and New Methods of Response to Targets in ESP Experiments', in *Journal of the American Society for Psychical Research*.

—— 1987: 'A Select Bibliography of Books on Parapsychology, 1982-85', in *Advances in Parapsychological Research*. 5. Ed. S. Krippner. Jefferson, N. C. and London: McFarland and Company.

Whittall, A. 1982: *The Music of Britten & Tippett*. Cambridge: CUP.

Wilkinson, H. P. and Gauld, A. 1993: 'Geomagneticism and Anomalous Experiences, 1868-1980', in *Proceedings of the Society for Psychical Research*, 57, (217): 275-310.

Willin, M. J. 1999: *Paramusicology*. Ph. D. thesis. University of Sheffield Library.

Willin, M. J. 2004: *Music in Pagan and Witchcraft Ritual and Culture*. Ph. D. thesis. University of Bristol Library.

Wilson, C. 1994a: *The Supernatural*. London: Magpie Books.

—— 1994b: London: Magpie Books.

—— and Holroyd, S. 1981 *Mysteries of the Mind*. London: BCA.

Wilson, I. 1995: *In search of Ghosts*. London: Headline Book Publishing.

Wiseman, R. and Morris, R. L. 1995: *Guidelines for testing psychic claimants*. University of Hertfordshire Press.

Wisniewski, Prince A. 1894: *The Journal of Light*. April 28th London.

Wood, B. and Pinnock, A. 1992: 'Unscarr'd by turning times'?: the dating of Purcell's *Dido and Aeneas*, *Early Music*, XX no. 3, August: 372-390.

Wybold, R. 1995: 'The Pagan Music Scene', in *Quest*, 101, March.

York, M. 1995: *The Emerging Network: A Sociology of the New Age and Neo-Pagan Movements*. Lanham, Maryland: Rowan and Littlefield.

References to Web Sites

www.Amazon.com   Reference to Philip Chapman

www.dcdwithin.com   Reference to Dead Can Dance

http:www.gardenofbadthings.co./medwyn.htm   Reference to Medwyn Goodall

http://www.mikeoldfield.org)   Reference to Mike Oldfield

ravenrec@panix.com   Reference to Gabrielle Roth

http://www.holistic.ie/cosmic_sounds/artists.htm)   Reference to Phil Thornton

http://www.shifting.f2s.com/alleyne-johnson/pevc.html

Reference to Ed. Alleyne –Johnson

http://www.isis-crystals.com/acatalog/iSiS_Crystals_Online_C_137.html

Reference to Rusty Crutcher

http://www.maka.net/songbook/circle.htm#circle8   Reference to chants

http://www.rit.edu/~elnppr/faqs/obfaq.html   Reference to Oingo Boingo

www.putumayo.com   Reference to *Putumayo*

www.music.webcity.com.au/browse.cgi?keywords=%5ER&Stype=Artist-15k-

Reference to Rabbit Sungaru

http://www.prana.cz/a_hudba.html   Reference to Prana

http://www.jtwinc.com/clannad/celb.htm.   Brennan, M. (1995). A Celtic lebration

Index

303